Ambrose's Patriarchs

Ambrose's Patriarchs

Ethics for the Common Man

MARCIA L. COLISH

UNIVERSITY OF NOTRE DAME PRESS

NOTRE DAME, INDIANA

Copyright © 2005 Marcia L. Colish
Published by the University of Notre Dame Press
Notre Dame, Indiana 46556
www.undpress.nd.edu
All Rights Reserved

Manufactured in the United States of America

Library of Congress Cataloging-in-Publication Data

Colish, Marcia L.
Ambrose's patriarchs : ethics for the common man / Marcia L. Colish.
p.   cm.
Includes bibliographical references and index.
ISBN 0-268-02364-6 (alk. paper)
ISBN 0-268-02365-4 (pbk. : alk. paper)
1. Ambrose, Saint, Bishop of Milan, d. 397—Ethics.   2. Christian ethics.
3. Patriarchs (Bible)   I. Title.
BR65.A316C64   2005
241'.0414—dc22

2005004933

CONTENTS

ACKNOWLEDGMENTS

I began the research on which this book is based as I was completing my many years of teaching at Oberlin College, and I finished it after I had moved to Connecticut to take up, in retirement, a position as Visiting Fellow in the History Department at Yale University. I have received an extremely warm welcome there not only from my home department but also from the Religious Studies Department and from the Medieval Studies Program. Colleagues in all these fields have provided supportive settings in which I have been invited to deliver short papers drawn from some of the material in this book. Other institutions that have provided venues in which I have presented parts of this material include the University of San Francisco, the Medieval Institute at Western Michigan University, and the Faculty of Letters at the University of Porto, which hosted the XI Congress of Medieval Philosophy in 2002. I am grateful to all of the audiences involved for their attention and their helpful comments.

I would also like to thank the staffs of the interlibrary loan departments at both the Oberlin College Library and the Sterling Memorial Library at Yale University, without whose assistance the research for this book would have been, literally, impossible. The help of the faculty support staff of Yale's Information Technology Department, particularly that of David Snyder, was invaluable in resolving problems relating to the word processing of the text. My research in Lyon and Montpellier was facilitated enormously by the aid of Annette Molho and Blanche Sousi. Finally, but in no sense in the last place, I would like to express my gratitude to a number of colleagues whose erudition saved me many steps that my research would otherwise have had to take, providing me with important information and pointing me toward essential references. The book that follows would have been less complete and less accurate had I not been the beneficiary of their learning. In alphabetical order, they are Martin Claussen, Adela Collins, Bentley Layton, Ramsay MacMullen, Dale Martin, John Matthews, and Celia Schultz. None of them, of course, is responsible for the views expressed in the book or any flaws it may contain.

M. L. C.

Among the works of Ambrose of Milan, the four treatises he dedicated to the Old Testament patriarchs have received comparatively little scholarly attention, and what attention they have been given has generally been quite one-dimensional. Commentators interested in the content of these works, and not just in their literary form, have approached them from a variety of monocular perspectives. One group of scholars has focused exclusively on *Quellenforschung*, whether concerned with classical literature and philology or with Ambrose's Jewish and Christian predecessors. Some scholars within this group want to document his fidelity to his sources, whether as their transmitter or as an unoriginal plagiarist. Others, by placing these works under the heading of the Hellenization of post-biblical Christian thought, want to show that Ambrose distanced himself from his biblical and exegetical sources, whether they regard that development as good, bad, or indifferent. On the other hand, historians of patristic biblical exegesis have focused on Ambrose's treatment of the patriarchs, in comparison with that of his predecessors and contemporaries, and on his interpretation of the parts of the book of Genesis where their stories are found, in the context of larger patristic debates on the relationship between the Old and New Testaments. For their part, historians of the fourth-century Milanese liturgy have brought to light two other and interrelated aspects of these treatises—the role they played in the ritual life of the Milanese Christian community, and the specific members of that community to which they were addressed—topics generally ignored by scholars who display the other kinds of interests just noted.

This question of audience is, in fact, central to an understanding of the argument of each of the patriarch treatises and to that of the four treatises considered as a group. The question of audience also explains why Ambrose chose to convey his message by reflecting on the lives of Abraham, Isaac, Jacob, and Joseph, and in the particular medium he selected. On one level, the patriarch treatises can be classified as hortatory ethical works. Apologists and patristic authors frequently wrote in this vein. When they did so, they typically targeted the perceived ethical needs of particular subsets of Christians: matrons, widows, consecrated virgins, monks, or priests. Ambrose too contributed to the edification of three such groups, producing works aimed specifically at priests in *De officiis*, at widows in *De uiduis*, and at consecrated virgins most notably in *De uirginibus* and *De uirginitate*. However, it was not specialized audiences such as these, with their distinctive ethical needs, who were his addressees in the sermons on which he based the patriarch treatises; rather, his hearers were average lay Christians, adult converts to Christianity from Roman paganism. In particular, his audience consisted of those catechumens in the Milanese Christian community whom he was preparing, each Lent, for their baptism on the following Easter Sunday. During any given Easter season in late-fourth-century Milan, this audience was likely to contain a diverse mix of lay people with no special vocation except the call to become full-fledged members of the church.

With this audience of average lay people in mind, it becomes much clearer why Ambrose chose the lives of Abraham, Isaac, Jacob, and Joseph as vehicles for their moral instruction. For Ambrose wrote a number of other treatises dealing with Old Testament personages—Noah, Cain and Abel, Job, David, Elijah, Tobias, and Naboth—from whose lives he also extracted moral messages. But he did not use these personages as the focus of the pre-baptismal catechesis to which he applied the lives of the patriarchs. For example, Ambrose also used the patriarchs, along with a host of other biblical and extra-biblical worthies, as moral examples in his *De officiis*. But he treated them rather differently there. Unlike his handling of their lives in the patriarch treatises, in the *De officiis* he does not present sustained biographies of the biblical figures he cites. Nor does he show any interest in reading their *uitae* typologically. His citations illustrate individual virtues rather than offering models of fully lived lives. Ambrose's choice of examples in his works on virginity and widowhood are also suggestive by way of comparison with the patriarch treatises. In his virginity treatises, his examples are typically the virgin martyrs of the early church, primarily female but with an occasional male witness. In *De uiduis,* Ambrose's examples are all women, from both the Old and the New Testaments, who were widows or who Ambrose thinks were widows. Their examples range from a retired life of prayer and fasting, in the case of Hannah, to an activist political career as warrior and judge, in the case of Deborah, suggesting that Ambrose envisioned a wide range of public and private roles in the church for widows. In an analogous way, his presentation of the Old Testament patriarchs as models of sanctity whom the average lay Christian can and should emulate reflects his felt need to develop an ethics for the common man, one that, in his estimation, is practical, relevant, and attainable. Among patristic authors, Ambrose was the first to do so.[1]

What that resultant ethics for the common man turns out to be needs to be uncovered. Equally important is the underlying conception of human nature on which this ethics rests. This too is an aspect of Ambrose's patriarch treatises that has generally been ignored or misinterpreted by previous commentators. For, to the extent that they have extrapolated an Ambrosian anthropology and ethics from these works, earlier scholars have depicted him as a radical Platonist, an ascetic with a dualistic view of human nature. On a closer reading, however, it can be seen that this interpretation fails to take account not only of Ambrose's audience in these works but also of his appeal to other philosophical traditions, notably Aristotelianism and Stoicism, and his highly nuanced understanding of the ways in which the anthropology and ethics of these schools harmonize with biblical anthropology and ethics. In addition, both classical literature and Roman law enter the equation when Ambrose adjudicates to what extent and in what particulars the classical legacy concurs with Christianity.

---

1. There is a Latin dialogue offering an ethics for the layperson, the *Consultationes Zacchaei et Apollonii,* whose anonymous author wrote in the mid-390s at the earliest, thus most likely postdating Ambrose's patriarch treatises. However, its goal and strategy are quite different. The text has two books. In the first, Zacchaeus catechizes the catechumen Apollonius on the theological contents of the Christian faith and Apollonius is then baptized. In the second, the dialogue moves from theory to practice as Zacchaeus lays out two different ethical programs: one, for the *mediocres,* involves the proper use of marriage and property and advocates moderation; the other, for the *clarissimi,* advocates extremely ascetic and eremitic monasticism. While the author seeks biblical warrants for asceticism, he offers no Old Testament examples of virtue for the *mediocres.* Although this same work treats both forms of praxis and the author argues that Christians of both sorts will be saved by faith and love and by practicing the virtues of their respective callings, he clearly finds the lifestyle of the *clarissimi* more praiseworthy. On this work, see Claussen, "Pagan Rebellion and Christian Apologetics." I am indebted to Prof. Claussen for bringing this reference to my attention.

In the book that follows, after two chapters that explore, respectively, the historiographical issues touched on in this Introduction and the form, literary strategy, and exegetical methods Ambrose draws on in the patriarch treatises, we will devote a chapter to the anthropology that these treatises collectively yield—one that developed, in Ambrose's thought, over the course of their composition. Then, in the next four chapters, we will consider how Ambrose illustrates this anthropology in the moral biographies of the protagonists of each of the patriarch treatises. The resultant findings, presented in the Conclusion, will enable us to summarize Ambrose's ethics for the common man in these works and to indicate how that ethics modifies and enlarges previous views of Ambrose the ethicist more generally.

CHAPTER 1

Assessments of Ambrose

One of the most striking features about the scholarship on Ambrose of Milan to date has been its narrowness of focus. Like the proverbial blind men and the elephant, each subset of commentators has examined one aspect or another of Ambrose's career and his *oeuvre*, reading the part for the whole. The result is a notable lack of consensus on what is important about Ambrose or even on what he was truly like as a person, a thinker, and a bishop. Leaving aside the purely philological analyses of his writings by classicists interested only in his Latinity, his rhetorical style, his vocabulary, and his recourse to the *auctores*,[1] a remarkably diverse number of Ambroses can be found in the existing literature.[2] Thus we have Ambrose the ecclesiastical statesman, Ambrose the pastor, Ambrose the Trinitarian theologian, Ambrose the practical ethicist, Ambrose the pure and simple fideist, Ambrose the synthesizer of classicism and Christianity. We have Ambrose as unphilosophical or as deeply indebted to philosophy, Ambrose as essentially unoriginal, Ambrose as critiquing and departing from his sources, Ambrose as an outstanding rhetorician, Ambrose as a disorganized writer. And we have Ambrose the exegete with a shallow grasp of the Bible, Ambrose the exegete who made a fundamental contribution to Latin

---

1. A good overview is provided by Lazzati, *Il valore letterario della esegesi ambrosiano*, 7 n. 3. See also Otten, "Caritas and the Ascent Motif"; Oberhelman, *Rhetoric and Homiletics*, 24–25, 35, 51, 52, 59, 125–26, with extensive bibliography; Cramer, *Baptism and Change*, 70–71; McLynn, *Ambrose of Milan*, 238, 239.

2. Good recent, if partial, overviews are provided by Markschies, *Ambrosius von Mailand und die Trinitätstheologie*, 1–6; Sanders, *"Fons vitae Christus,"* 7–14.

biblical interpretation, an Ambrose whose understanding of the morphology of current neo-Arian and paleo-Arian groups was hazy, and an Ambrose who cleverly lumped these groups together for tactical reasons. For some, Ambrose is systematic; for others, he is unsystematic.

One way of dealing with these dichotomies, as Ramsay MacMullen suggests, is simply to accept them all as simultaneously accurate. As he puts it, "Confronting the need to survive, great political leaders rise above consistency."[3] But most scholars writing on Ambrose have looked for, and have found, a less complicated and less opportunistic Ambrose.

Easily the earliest and most longstanding historiographical debate that has affected the interpretation of Ambrose's patriarch treatises is a confessionally motivated one that began in the age of the Protestant Reformation, that was revived in the nineteenth century by Adolf von Harnack, and that survives to this day as the debate over "Hellenization" in Ambrose and in the early church more generally. As a code word, Hellenization stands for two aspects of the classical tradition. One is the use of the forms, language, and substance of Greek philosophy. The other, also formulated under another set of code words as "arcane discipline," refers to the practice of biblical allegoresis, viewed as a subterfuge for incorporating elements from the pagan mystery cults of late antiquity into Christianity.[4] Among those authors who have deplored Hellenization as a falling away from *scriptura sola* fideism, some place Ambrose on the side of biblicism, claiming that he expressly rejected classicism in its favor; others accuse him of muddying its pure stream, especially by labeling the rites of Christian initiation as "mysteries" and by introducing allegoresis into Latin biblical exegesis. On the other hand, historians of the Milanese liturgy have pointed out that Ambrose, like other early co-religionists, distinguished quite clearly between Christian rites and those of the pagan mystery cults, and that his mystagogical exegesis is simply the explanation he gave, to the newly baptized, of the meaning of the sacraments they had just received, noting that they were prefigured in the Old Testament and perfected in the New.[5] Historians of

---

3. MacMullen, *Christianizing the Roman Empire,* 77, and more specifically with respect to pagan practices, 74–77.

4. Excellent overviews are provided by Jacob, *"Arkandisziplin," Allegorese, Mystagogie,* 45–117; Lutz-Bachmann, "Hellenisierung des Christentums?"; Rowe, "Adolf von Harnack and the Concept of Hellenization."

5. The fullest and most recent study is Satterlee, *Ambrose of Milan's Method.* See also Labriolle, *The Life and Times of St. Ambrose,* 243; Rand, *Founders of the Middle Ages,* 9–10; Medeiros,

exegesis have observed that the term "mystery" is itself biblical and that the many figures of speech and parables that abound in the biblical text made allegorical exegesis look perfectly legitimate and scriptural in the eyes of Ambrose.[6]

As for the influence of Greek philosophy on Ambrose, critics of the Protestants who attack Ambrose for succumbing to its charms do so largely from a pragmatic perspective. One recent formulation invokes the language of sociology of religion: the clothing of Christian doctrine in Greek philosophical language during the patristic period, we are told, should best be understood as enculturation, a process the church has had to undergo repeatedly over time in order to make its teachings comprehensible to people living in diverse cultural and historical settings.[7] Another approach links pragmatism with a distinctly Catholic theological principle. From this viewpoint, Ambrose adopted philosophical terms and concepts not only because, as a polemicist, he needed to use language with as much clarity and precision as he could muster, but also because he espoused the principle of Scripture-and-tradition as the locus of theological authority. His Christian precursors and contemporaries, who embodied ecclesiastical tradition, had done likewise.[8]

Most of the scholars who have addressed the uses of philosophy in Ambrose's patriarch treatises have taken a rather different tack. One whole group is interested in tracking down Ambrose's references to Greek philosophy, from

---

"The *De Mysteriis* and *De Sacramentis*"; Parodi, *La catechesi di sant'Ambrogio*, 86–89, 121–26, 142–43; Petit, "Sur les catéchèses post-baptismales de saint Ambroise"; Kelly, *Early Christian Creeds*, 32, 35, 49, 62, 87, 100, 168–71; Yarnold, "Baptism and the Pagan Mysteries in the Fourth Century"; Riley, *Christian Initiation*, 2, 17, 38–44, 220; Schmitz, *Gottesdienst im altchristlichen Mailand*, 214–29; C. Mohrmann, "Observations sur le *De Sacramentis* et le *De Mysteriis*"; Jackson, "Ambrose of Milan as Mystagogue," 96–103; Mazza, *Mystagogy*, x–xi, 2–13; Colpe, "Mysterienkulte und Liturgie," 207–17; Cramer, *Baptism and Change*, 47, 53–54, 56–59, 66, 100; Studer, "Ambrogio di Milano teologo mistagogico." The effort to understand patristic mystagogy under the heading of the ancient literary topos of *obscuritas* seems misplaced; cf. Jacob, "The Reception of the Origenist Tradition," in *Hebrew Bible/Old Testament*, 1:692, citing Fuhrmann, "Obscuritas."

6. The fullest discussion is in Francesconi, *Storia e simbolo*. See also Maldon, "St. Ambrose as an Interpreter of Holy Scripture"; Labriolle, *The Life and Times of St. Ambrose*, 152, 164; Pizzolato, *La dottrina esegetica di Sant'Ambrogio*, 10–11, 40, 52, 62–87, 140, 239, 316; Nauroy, "L'Écriture dans la pastorale," 393–400; Jackson, "Ambrose of Milan as Mystagogue"; Jacob, "*Arkandisziplin*," *Allegorese, Mystagogie*, 45–117; Satterlee, *Ambrose of Milan's Method*, 2–4, 124–44, 185–205, 220–36.

7. Lutz-Bachmann, "Hellenisierung des Christentums?"

8. Markschies, *Ambrosius von Mailand und die Trinitätstheologie*, 215–16.

whatever school, in order to argue for his dependence on these sources or even to highlight his perceived lack of intellectual originality.[9] Taking a more positive look at Ambrose's dependence on Greek philosophy, another group appraises that same phenomenon favorably, seeing in Ambrose a transmitter who kept treasured classical ideas alive and available in the Latin Middle Ages.[10] There is a particular subset of scholars in this last-mentioned group whose members emphasize Ambrose's appeals to Plotinus and who seek to date the *De Isaac* and *De Jacob* to 386, or at most to 384–87, the small window of opportunity when Augustine was in Milan, in order to make Ambrose the source of Augustine's Neoplatonism.[11] But other scholars challenge this claim. For some, more important sources of Augustine's Neoplatonism were the "books of the Platonists" that he read and the oral teaching he acquired within a circle

9. Hagendahl, *Latin Fathers and the Classics*, 115: "As is well known, Ambrose's writings are not very original: they are largely compilations, being derived from Greek authorities." This notion of Ambrose as a plagiarist with respect to Christian as well as classical sources goes back to Jerome. See Nauroy, "Jérôme, lecteur et censeur de l'exégèse d'Ambroise," and, most recently, Layton, "Plagiarism and Lay Patronage of Ascetic Scholarship."

10. The single most influential scholar here is Pierre Courcelle; see "Plotin et saint Ambroise"; idem, "Nouvelle aspects du platonisme chez saint Ambroise"; idem, "Anti-Christian Arguments and Christian Platonism," 165–66; idem, "Tradition platonicienne et traditions chrétiennes du corps-prison"; idem, *Recherches sur les Confessions de Saint Augustin*, 16, 106–17, 122, 124–38; idem, "Ambroise de Milan, 'professeur de philosophie'"; idem, *Recherches sur Saint Ambroise*, 16; idem, *Connais-toi toi-même de Socrate à Saint Bernard*, 1:122–23, 125. Courcelle has been seconded by Taormina, "Sant'Ambrogio e Plotino"; Hadot, "Platon et Plotin dans trois sermons"; Solignac, "Nouveaux parallèles entre saint Ambroise et Plotin"; Moreschini, intro. to his trans. of Ambrose, *De Isaac uel anima*, 9–13; Palla, intro. to his trans. of Ambrose, *De Iacob et uita beata*, 220–21; Lenox-Conyngham, "Sin in St. Ambrose"; Moorhead, *Ambrose*, 172–73; Drecoll, "Neuplatonismus und Christentum." To the extent that Stoic ideas appear in the patriarch treatises, the above-mentioned scholars think that Ambrose appropriated them by way of Plotinus or other intermediaries. Scholars who emphasize Stoic influences in these works include Thamin, *Saint Ambroise et la morale chrétienne*, 313–14, 326, 328; Nauroy, "La méthode de la composition et la structure du *De Iacob*," 120–21; Hill, "Classical and Christian Tradition," 81–87, 89–90, 148, 150–76; Vasey, *The Social Ideas in the Works of St. Ambrose*, 47; Spanneut, "Le Stoïcisme dans l'histoire de la patience chrétienne," 108–9, 111; Colish, *The Stoic Tradition*, 2:48–58; Moorhead, *Ambrose*, 178. There are also scholars who see Ambrose as more eclectic in his use of philosophy; see Bardy, "L'Entrée de la philosophie"; Szydzik, "*Ad imaginem dei*," 11; Iacoangeli, "'Humanitas' classica e 'sapientia' cristiana," 132–42; M. Zelzer, "Ambrosius von Mailand"; eadem, "Symmachus, Ambrosius, Hieronymus," 149–57.

11. This notion was first put forth by Courcelle, "Plotin et saint Ambroise," 46–56; idem, *Recherches sur les Confessions de Saint Augustin*, 124–38; idem, *Late Latin Authors and Their Greek Sources*, 137 n. 48; followed by Hadot, "Platon et Plotin dans trois sermons"; Solignac, "Nouveaux parallèles entre saint Ambroise et Plotin"; Moreschini, intro. to his trans. of *De Isa.*, 9; Markus, *The End of Ancient Christianity*, 49; Testard, "Saint Ambroise de Milan," 375.

of Neoplatonic dévotés in Milan.[12] Alternatively, it has been argued that this alleged Milanese circle never actually existed, or that even if it did, its influence on Augustine would have been irrelevant,[13] given the fact that Augustine's interest in the Neoplatonic tradition and his use of it were quite different from those of both Ambrose and his Milanese contemporaries.

The approaches of the scholars just discussed are all versions of *Quellenforschung*. Their goal has been to locate Ambrose's philosophical sources and to determine whether he appropriated them directly or indirectly. The methodology used for this purpose is presenting textual data in parallel columns in the effort to document similarities between Ambrose and his sources by the careful comparison of selected texts, typically detached from their literary contexts and their roles in the arguments of Ambrose's works. The preponderance of one source or another as Ambrose's authority is assessed quantitatively, in terms of the length and number of his citations and the closeness of the textual parallels subjected to analysis.

But there is also a quite different approach to the investigation of Ambrose's positive use of classical philosophy, one that invokes a more qualitative and contextualized methodology. Whichever schools of philosophy they emphasize among Ambrose's sources, scholars in this group maintain that, far from merely taking over ideas, motifs, and terminology from Greek philosophy whole hog, Ambrose used these materials independently, ringing his own changes on them and combining them with Christian ethical ideas when he deemed them compatible.[14] As to why Ambrose would have seen the classical and Christian traditions as compatible in the first place, these scholars have

12. Literature on this position is provided by Wiesner, intro. to his ed. and trans. of Ambrose, *De bono mortis*, 19–30. See, more recently, Solignac, "Il circolo neoplatonico milanese," 43–50, 54–56.

13. Madec, "Le milieu milanais"; idem, "Le 'platonisme' des pères"; Drecoll, "Neuplatonismus und Christentum," 121.

14. See, for example, Courcelle, "L'humanisme chrétien de saint Ambroise"; Dassmann, *Die Frömmigkeit des Kirchenvaters Ambrosius*, 41–44; Piccolo, "Per lo studio della spiritualità ambrosiana"; Wiesner, intro. to his ed. and trans. of Ambrose, *De bono mortis*, 19–30, 46–62; Nauroy, "La méthode de la composition et la structure du *De Iacob*," 125–28; idem, "La structure du *De Isaac*"; Madec, *Saint Ambroise et la philosophie*, 55–71, 94, 97, 116, 121, 122–23, 168, 174–75, 238–44, 340–42, 344–47; Spanneut, "Le Stoïcisme dans l'histoire de la patience chrétienne"; Colish, *The Stoic Tradition*, 2:56–57; Testard, "Saint Ambroise de Milan"; M. Zelzer, "Ambrosius von Mailand"; eadem, "Symmachus, Ambrosius, Hieronymus," 149–57; Markshies, *Ambrosius von Mailand und die Trinitätstheologie*, 1–6.

pointed to two principal phenomena. One is the fact that ethical parallels actually existed between these two traditions, commonalities associated with Roman conventions and social expectations no less than with Greek philosophy.[15] The other is the fluidity, at this time, of Christian ethics itself. This situation has been well described by Wayne A. Meeks:

> Christian moralizing begins in history, begins in the midst of Israel and in the midst of a Hellenized and Romanized world of manifold native cultures; it is not even possible to say precisely when and where it begins to be distinctively Christian, and difficult to know, in the whirl of syncretism, what distinguishes it. There has not ever been a purely Christian morality unalloyed with the experiences and traditions of others.[16]

If these observations are correct, one would have to say that, rather than synthesizing a full-fledged Christian ethics with the ethics of Greece and Rome, seen as distinct and independent systems of thought, Ambrose proceeded by combining, selectively, elements from both traditions when he felt that they were mutually supportive. In so doing, he was helping to create and to develop a vision of Christian ethics itself, a vision capable of drawing on the resources of non-Christian culture.

In contrast with this line of interpretation, another group of commentators accents what its members see as sharp and irreconcilable conflicts between Greco-Roman ethics and an ethics drawn exclusively from the Bible. In their estimation, Ambrose saw the Bible as the only legitimate and authoritative source of ethical teaching. While acknowledging the references to classical philosophy that Ambrose undeniably makes, they argue that he makes these references either in a purely formal or thematic way, divesting them of any pagan content,[17] or more drastically, that he brings philosophy forward only for the purpose of demonstrating its basic inadequacy and incommensurability with biblical ethics.[18] This entire interpretative tradition reflects the durability of Harnack's general position.

---

15. Swain, "Biography and the Biographic in the Literature of the Roman Empire," 9 nn. 16–17.

16. Meeks, *The Origins of Christian Morality*, 216.

17. Markshies, *Ambrosius von Mailand und die Trinitätstheologie*, 79–83.

18. Szydzik, "*Ad imaginem dei*," 17–18; idem, "Die geistigen Ursprünge der Imago-Dei-Lehre," 163–76; Dassmann, *Die Frömmigkeit des Kirchenvaters Ambrosius*, 181–84; Madec, *Saint*

A less extreme approach is one that seeks, rather, to understand Ambrose's ethics in the patriarch treatises in the light of previous Hellenistic Jewish and Christian sources. The figures who receive the most attention here, whether as exegetes, as indirect sources of Greek philosophy, or both, are Philo and Origen. Commenting on Ambrose's use of Philo, we find both straightforward *Quellenforscher*[19] and authors who also note Ambrose's departures from Philo, whether by Christianizing him or by downplaying his contemplative focus in preference for an ethical one.[20] In a parallel manner, we find scholars assessing Ambrose's use of Origen purely as *Quellenforscher*[21] as well as considering his departures from Origen, particularly his less mystical and more literal, ethical, and pastoral reading of the biblical text.[22] Some scholars are interested in

Ambroise et la philosophie, 177–79; idem, "L'Homme intérieure selon saint Ambroise," 296–306; idem, *"Verus philosophus et amator dei"*; Pizzolato, *La dottrina esegetica di Sant' Ambrogio*, 30; Iacoangeli, "Anima ed eternità nel *De Isaac*"; Lenox-Conyngham, "Ambrose and Philosophy"; M. E. Mohrmann, "Wisdom and the Moral Life"; Sanders, *"Fons vitae Christi,"* passim.

19. Ihm, "Philon und Ambrosius"; Palanque, *Saint Ambroise et l'empire romain*, 509; Daniélou, "Abraham dans la tradition chrétienne," 70–71, 82; Harrington, "Joseph in the Testament of Joseph, Pseudo-Philo, and Philo," 127–30; Lucchesi, *L'Usage de Philon*, 42–49, 54, 55, 57, 60, 62, 64, 66, 82, 84, 86, 118; Berton, "Abraham dans le *De officiis*," 312–13; Hollander, "The Portrayal of Joseph."

20. Stenger, "Das Frömmigkeitsbild des hl. Ambrosius," 4–65; De Vivo, "Nota ad Ambrogio, *De Abraham* I 2, 4," in *Ambrosius Episcopus*, 2:235, 237–40; Savon, *Saint Ambroise devant l'exégèse de Philon*, 1:13, 14, 85, 141–95, 234, 240, 350–76; Nikiprowetzky, "Saint Ambroise et Philon"; Gori, intro. to his trans. of Ambrose, *De Abr.*, 15–19; Piredda, "La tipologia sacerdotale del patriarca Giuseppe"; Bonato, "Il ruolo universale del sacerdozio di Cristo"; Niehoff, *The Figure of Joseph in Post-Biblical Jewish Literature*, 54–83; Runia, *Philo in Early Christian Literature*, 292–96, 301–8, 347; Van der Lof, "The 'Prophet' Abraham," 17–18, 26–27; Jacob, "The Reception of the Origenist Tradition," in *Hebrew Bible/Old Testament*, 1:683–84. The only commentator on Ambrose's use of Philo who considers Philo's influence ambiguous is Feldman, "Josephus' Portrait of Joseph."

21. Baus, "Das Nachwirkung des Origenes"; Palla, "Temi del *Commento* origeniano al *Cantico dei Cantici*"; Iacoangeli, "Anima ed eternità nel *De Isaac*," 108–11; Clark, "The Uses of the Song of Songs"; De Lubac, *Medieval Exegesis*, 1:142, 154–55.

22. Stenger, "Das Frömmigkeitsbild des hl. Ambrosius," 65–66, 98–109; Daniélou, "L'Unité des deux testaments"; Jacob, "The Reception of the Origenist Tradition," in *Hebrew Bible/Old Testament*, 1:683–84; Savon, "Ambroise lecteur d'Origène," 232–34. Markschies, "Ambrosius und Origenes," distinguishes between exegetical method, which he thinks Ambrose derived from Origen, and their common agreement on the relationship between the Old and New Testaments, and Ambrose's exegetical focus, which he sees as far more ethically and historically oriented than that of Origen. As Clark, *Reading Renunciation*, 170–71, has well put it, in contrast to authors such as Ambrose, Origen viewed the literal or historical sense of Scripture as "problematic, unprofitable, and even nonsensical." I thank Dale Martin for bringing this last reference to my attention.

comparing Ambrose's straightforward appropriations of both Philo and Origen,[23] while others focus on his rethinking of these two predecessors.[24] Finally, and confusingly so, in the work of a single scholar, Goulven Madec, we find an alternative approach to the influence of Philo and Origen on Ambrose. On the one hand, Madec sees a stage heavy with Plotinian influence in Ambrose's earlier works, followed by a stage in which he appeals principally to Philo and Origen. But on the other hand, Madec also maintains that Ambrose was attached to Philo early on and that he then moved later to Plotinus.[25]

As this historiographical survey indicates, there is no consensus on any of the issues pertaining to Ambrose's sources or his use of them in the patriarch treatises. At the same time, the existing literature is surprisingly silent on the question of how Ambrose used the book of Genesis in constructing the *uitae* of the patriarchs. Silence reigns, equally, on Ambrose's use of Roman law in these works and on his substantive references to both Greek and Latin authors whose writings were staples in the school tradition.

It is hoped, in the analysis of the patriarch treatises that follows, that fresh light can be shed on these matters, yielding new insights into them and possibly resolving some of the debates discussed in this chapter. But first we need to consider the nature of the patriarch treatises themselves, their form and strategy of argument viewed in the light of the specific audience for which Ambrose composed them.

23. Völker, "Das Abraham-Bild bei Philo, Origenes, und Ambrosius"; Daniélou, "La typologie d'Isaac"; Szydzik, "Die geistigen Ursprünge der Imago-Dei-Lehre," 15–16; Dörrie, "Das fünffach gestufte Mysterium"; Argal Echarri, "Isaac y Rebeca," 150–51; Sagot, "La triple sagesse dans le *De Isaac*"; eadem, "Le 'Cantique des Cantiques' dans le 'De Isaac.'"

24. Kellner, *Der heilige Ambrosius,* 183–86; Dassmann, *Die Frömmigkeit des Kirchenvaters Ambrosius,* 50–56, 58, 61–74, 101–2; Hadot, "Explication du 'De Isaac' d'Ambroise"; Madec, "L'Homme intérieure selon saint Ambroise," 291–306; idem, *Saint Ambroise et la philosophie,* 107–8, 111, 121; Savon, *Saint Ambroise devant l'exégèse de Philon,* 1:78–81; idem, "Ambroise lecteur d'Origène," 232–34; Gryson, "La médiation d'Aaron d'après saint Ambroise"; idem, "Les Lévites, figure du sacerdoce véritable"; Nauroy, "L'Écriture dans la pastorale"; Testard, "Saint Ambroise de Milan."

25. Madec, *Saint Ambroise et la philosophie,* 66, 116, 121, 168, 242, 243; but contrariwise, 52–53.

CHAPTER 2

Why the Patriarchs?

Jean-Rémy Palanque launches his brief discussion of Ambrose's patriarch treatises with the remark that they seem to have been "mal compris."[1] Noting that the four treatises do not resemble each other either in literary form or in emphasis—*De Abraham* and *De Joseph* being largely exegetical, and *De Isaac* and *De Jacob* being more ethical than exegetical[2]—Palanque himself does little to clarify why Ambrose wrote them. On the other hand, Raymond Thamin thinks that these works can best be understood as Ambrose's *parua moralia,* a modest corpus that merely reinforces the ethics of his *De officiis,* his *magnum opus* on that subject, albeit with a far more ascetic tone.[3] As to why Ambrose chose to convey his moral teachings through the lives of the patriarchs, some scholars have suggested that he was merely following in Philo's footsteps,[4] or taking the advice of previous Christian writers,[5] or that he seized on these personages because the Old Testament offers more to work with, by way of moral examples, than the New Testament.[6] Other scholars have noted that more is at issue than ethical instruction in these works: Ambrose also wants to show how

---

1. Palanque, *Saint Ambroise et l'empire romain,* 443. This, although he notes, 509, that the treatises were based on sermons Ambrose delivered to the *competentes.*
2. Ibid., 440–45.
3. Thamin, *Saint Ambroise et la morale chrétienne,* 324–43. He is seconded by Dudden, *The Life and Times of St. Ambrose,* 2:502–3, and by Hill, "Classical and Christian Tradition," 6, 36, 40, 148, 150–207.
4. Thamin, *Saint Ambroise et la morale chrétienne,* 324.
5. Humphries, *Communities of the Blessed,* 211–13.
6. Badura, *Die leitenden Grundsätze der Morallehre des hl. Ambrosius,* 19–20.

the patriarchs' lives forecast the Christian revelation to come.[7] Remarkably, none of these scholars considers the question of the audience for which the patriarch treatises were composed and the role of that audience in shaping Ambrose's approach to both their form and content.

This omission is surprising. For, in his introduction to the first critical edition of the patriarch treatises published in 1897, Karl Schenkl makes two important points that are central to attaining the understanding of these works whose absence Palanque laments. First, Schenkl observes that Ambrose produced these treatises in the order in which the book of Genesis reports the patriarchs' lives. They form a corpus, and were understood as such. They are found together in a number of the earliest manuscripts that preserve them, and Cassiodorus presents them as a group in his *Institutes*.[8] This point is an important one. It indicates that these treatises will remain opaque unless we consider the ways in which they are interrelated. The second major observation that Schenkl makes has to do with the specific audience for which the patriarch treatises were written. Ambrose, he notes, produced them first as sermons delivered to catechumens, only later redrafting them as treatises.[9]

Catechumens, yes; but there is more to the story than that. A fuller light is shed on this audience when we recognize the way in which converts were prepared for reception into the church of Milan in Ambrose's time. The procedure we are about to describe is site-specific to Milan, for different local churches followed their own distinct initiation practices in the fourth century. How candidates were received in Milan is a subject that Ambrose himself illuminates. He left detailed descriptions of the process in his *De mysteriis* and *De sacramentis*, on the basis of which modern scholars have been able to reconstruct it clearly.[10]

---

7. Dudden, *The Life and Times of St. Ambrose*, 2:522–37; Lazzati, *Il valore letterario della esegesi ambrosiana*, 72–74.

8. Schenkl, intro. to his ed. of Ambrose, *Opera*, CSEL, 32:1, iii–v. Cf. Cassiodorus, *Institutes* 1.1.5, 1.5.4, 1.6.6, in *An Introduction to Divine and Human Readings*, trans. Jones. Also noted by Lucchesi, "Note sur un lieu de Cassiodore"; Hill, "Classical and Christian Tradition," 148, 150. Palanque, *Saint Ambroise et l'empire romain*, 443, also notes this fact but regards it as irrelevant.

9. Schenkl, intro. to his ed. of Ambrose, *Opera*, CSEL, 32:1, ii.

10. Ambrose, *The Mysteries. The Sacraments*, trans. Deferrari. The issue of the authenticity of the *De sacramentis*, which evoked debate in the past, has been resolved in favor of Ambrose's authorship by C. Mohrmann, "Observations sur le *De Sacramentis* et le *De Mysteriis*," in *Ambrosius Episcopus*, 1:112–14. The best and fullest account of the initiation of those to be baptized in Ambrose's Milan is Parodi, *La catechesi di sant'Ambrogio*, xxi–xxvi, 35–37, 55–89, 98–189. See also

To begin with, Milanese catechumens were divided into two groups. Some were *aspirantes,* sympathetic to the Christian message and open to learning more about it. They were signed by the bishop with the sign of the cross and attended church services, absorbing the basic tenets of the faith by listening to Bible readings and sermons. They might remain in this status for as long as they felt was needed. The second group of catechumens, the *competentes,* were those who felt ready to make a commitment. They indicated their desire to receive baptism on the coming Easter by enrolling their names with the bishop on the Feast of the Epiphany, but no later than the first Sunday of Lent. During Lent they received a special course of instruction twice daily from the bishop in the form of sermons that he prepared for this express purpose. In the early weeks of Lent, the bishop placed his catechetical emphasis on ethics. This, precisely, was the context in which Ambrose made use of the lives of the patriarchs as sermon material. During Holy Week, the bishop's emphasis shifted to dogma. The centerpiece of this week's activity was the *traditio symboli*. The bishop went over the propositions of the creed, explaining them carefully; the *competentes* committed them to memory in preparation for their public recitation of the creed. Here it is worth highlighting two elements of fourth-century church practice in Milan. First, the creed was not recited as part of the mass at this time. It was not included in the liturgy of the mass until the reign of bishop Peter (784–805), under Carolingian influence.[11] In any case, all catechumens, whether *aspirantes* or *competentes*, were dismissed from the mass following the Scripture readings and sermon. They were not present to witness the canon of the mass, the recitation of the Lord's Prayer, or the communion service. And second, the creed that was handed over to the *competentes* during the final week of Lent was not the Nicene Creed, despite the

---

Riley, *Christian Initiation,* 17, 27–28, 33–35, 48–50, 58, 63–64, 84, 86–89, 108, 140–50, 153–54, 193–94, 205–7, 225–27, 242–61, 300–301, 305–12, 353–63, 388–96, 413–15, 438–45, 454; Schmitz, *Gottesdienst im altchristlichen Mailand,* 3–6, 8–15, 27–34, 35–229; Finn, *Early Christian Baptism and the Catechumenate,* 58–61; idem, *From Death to Life,* 222–30. Also of interest are Labriolle, *The Life and Times of St. Ambrose,* 41–65, 243; Medeiros, "The *De Mysteriis* and *De Sacramentis,*" 1–44; Cataneo, "Storia del rito ambrosiano," in *Storia di Milano,* 3:768, 829–31; Petit, "Sur le catéchèse post-baptismale de saint Ambroise"; Mitchell, "Ambrosian Baptismal Rites"; Yarnold, "The Ceremonies of Initiation"; Monachino, *S. Ambrogio e la cura pastorale,* 57–103; Jacob, "The Reception of the Origenist Tradition," in *Hebrew Bible/Old Testament,* 1:692–93; Navoni, "Notizia sulla liturgia ambrosiana," 231; Savon, *Ambroise de Milan,* 47 n. 29; Satterlee, *Ambrose of Milan's Method,* 145–205.

11. Cataneo, "Storia del rito ambrosiano," in *Storia di Milano,* 3:789; Monachino, *S. Ambrogio e la cura pastorale,* 103.

contemporary debates centering on it. Rather, it was an early version of what later became known as the Apostles' Creed, with a wording, in Milan, that differed slightly from the form of the creed used in Rome.[12] Given the comparatively untechnical language of this creed, the bishop at this point had, and seized on, the opportunity to hammer his version of Christology and Trinitarian theology into the minds of his *competentes*, along with the other doctrines in the creed, making sure that they grasped and held firmly the correct teaching in an age when alternative positions on these matters were rife. For this final week of pre-baptismal catechesis, in order to emphasize the imminence of their reception of that sacrament, the bishop moved the site of his instruction of the *competentes* from the cathedral to its adjacent baptistry.

Following their baptism on Easter morning—a rite that, in Milan, included the foot-washing of the candidates—and their return to the main church to celebrate the mass of Easter Sunday, to pray the Lord's Prayer in public for the first time, and to receive their first communion, the neophytes were reassembled, again in the baptistry, for a course of post-baptismal instruction from the bishop. This final stage in their initiation took place during the week after Easter. In this phase of his catechesis, the bishop's emphasis was on the spiritual meaning of the sacraments of baptism and the Eucharist, the meaning of the Lord's Prayer and how one should pray, and on how one should read the Bible. This is the instruction of neophytes that has been termed a "mystagogical" catechesis. Ambrose's operative assumption was that, since the newly baptized had just experienced the grace of the sacraments and the gifts of the Holy Spirit, they would be able to understand, in a more profound way, the theology involved in the topics on which he spoke during Easter Week. They were now deemed capable of grasping the meaning of the liturgy and the prayer life of the church, which they would henceforth be actively practicing. The biblical passages on which the bishop commented in the sermons he delivered during this post-paschal educational process were chosen because they were texts yielding more than a merely literal significance. He thereby gave the neophytes a model of how they ought to approach the sacred text as well as deeper insights into the ritual praxis that would now be incumbent upon them.

---

12. Parodi, *La catechesi di sant'Ambrogio,* 59, with the Milanese text given at 117–18 and the Roman text at 116–17. Kelly, *Early Christian Creeds,* 172–73, also gives both the Roman and the Milanese versions of the creed and, in general, argues for the similarities in text and praxis between these two centers rather than their differences; see 32, 171, 173–81, 205–11, 255–56, 323, 370.

On the eighth day after Easter, their initiation complete, the neophytes joined the rest of the congregation at mass, no longer wearing their white baptismal robes or grouped together in a special section of the nave, and participated in the offertory for the first time. They were now regarded as fully integrated into the congregation, not set apart in any way from their fellow Christians.

It is certainly the case that, in any given Easter season, Milanese baptizands were likely to come from any and every walk of life. At the same time, a consideration of the initiation process just described as well as internal evidence found within the patriarch treatises provide a clearer sense of the demographic profile of the audience for which these treatises were originally composed. They were lay people, adult converts from Roman paganism. They engaged in a range of economic activities and professions. They were both male and female, some unmarried but mostly married, with children and household slaves. Many of them were male heads of households, legally in charge of their dependents, men who played varied roles in civic as well as domestic and economic life. Given the twice-daily sermons they attended during the Lent prior to their baptism and during the Easter Week following it, the *competentes* were likely to have been relatively wealthy, able to spare the necessary time from their private and public pursuits.

Judging from the language and contents of the patriarch treatises, the *competentes* were well educated. Ambrose freely refers to philosophical doctrines without explaining them on the assumption that the *competentes* will recognize his references. He also quotes or alludes to classical authors who were the basic stock of the school tradition without giving their names. Sometimes he cites his quotations of and references to classical literature and philosophy in the untranslated Greek. Ambrose also makes repeated use of concepts and terminology drawn from Roman law. Of course, we have no way of knowing how much he may have edited these texts in turning them from sermons into treatises. But the treatises, at least, reveal certain expectations on his part, expectations that he shared with other North Italian bishops at the time.[13] Like them, he assumes that his *competentes* are comparatively well off, that they are persons with domestic and public responsibilities, that they are literate in Greek as well as Latin, familiar with the literary classics in both languages, and familiar as well with Roman law and classical ethics.

---

13. Lizzi, "Ambrose's Contemporaries and the Christianization of Northern Italy," 166–73; followed by Salzman, *The Making of a Christian Aristocracy*, 82, 200–219.

Given *competentes* with these traits, why did Ambrose choose to catechize them by means of sermons on Abraham, Isaac, Jacob, and Joseph? These were not the only Old Testament worthies he used as the basis of ethical teaching. Aside from citing a host of biblical figures as examples in his *De officiis* and other works, Ambrose devoted ethical treatises, sometimes arising as sermons, to a range of other Old Testament personages, from Cain and Abel to Noah, from Tobias to Elijah, Naboth, Job, and David.[14] Important as these figures were, however, they lacked a critical attribute possessed uniquely by the four patriarchs. Ambrose was well aware of the fact that the *competentes* identified themselves as members of, and participants in, the Roman historical tradition. But now they were about to be incorporated into an older and much more venerable historical community: the covenanted people of God whose history began with Abraham. They were to become Israelites, with a new fatherland. In the peroration at the end of *De Isaac*, Ambrose adjures his *competentes* in the following terms: "Let us flee to our real, true fatherland. There is our fatherland and there is our Father, by whom we have been created, and there is the city of Jerusalem, which is the mother of all men" (Fugiamus ergo in patriam uerissimam. Illic patria nobis et illic pater, a quo creati sumus, ubi est Hierusalem ciuitas, quae est mater omnium).[15] He adds, "We therefore are souls, if we wish to be Hebrews of those who are companions of Jacob, that is, imitators of him" (Nos igitur animae sumus, si uolumus esse Hebraei de iis qui sunt socii Iacob, id est imitatores eius).[16]

But how was it that the *competentes* had learned to identify themselves with the Roman historical tradition in the first place? The answer to this question was obvious to Ambrose, since he himself had received the same kind of classical education that he presupposed in them. Romans learned who they were, and how to behave, by studying history and rhetoric. For their part, the historians and rhetors taught and argued by holding up, as examples to imitate or avoid, well-known figures from the Roman past. Imitation and the use of

---

14. Noted by Moorhead, *Ambrose*, 73.

15. Ambrose, *De Isaac uel anima* 8.78, ed. Schenkl, trans. Moreschini; trans. McHugh in Ambrose, *Seven Exegetical Works*, 63.

16. Ambrose, *De Isa.* 8.79; McHugh trans., 65. Hahn, *Das wahre Gesetz*, 33–43, and Cataneo, *La religione a Milano*, 42–45, maintain, unconvincingly, that Ambrose was here appealing, by means of the patriarchs, to the Jewish population of Milan. Likewise, Fitzgerald, "Ambrose at the Well," 80–81, 88, thinks that this work was aimed at a diversified audience including Jews and other non-Christians as well as unbaptized Christians.

exempla uirtutis were fundamental features of classical literature and classical education alike.[17] In turning Milanese Roman citizens into Israelites, therefore, it made sense to Ambrose to use exactly the same technique, substituting the patriarchs as the new *maiores.* Any estimate of his debts to the classical tradition must include his appropriation of this pedagogical strategy as useful, and doubly so, since the *competentes* would easily be able to recognize and relate to his tactic of holding up Old Testament worthies as examples of virtue. Moreover, side by side with this classical practice, New Testament authors themselves advert to the same Old Testament worthies as examples. Ambrose thus had a doubly powerful and incontestably authoritative warrant for doing likewise.[18]

In addition to citing the patriarchs as *exempla uirtutis,* Ambrose is quite overt in explaining why he does so. The patriarchs, he observes, are real historical individuals, whose lives are composed of events that actually took place in a specific time and place. At the beginning of *De Abraham,* Ambrose explains why historical examples of the sort he proposes to offer are superior, as a means of moral education, to works such as Plato's *Republic* and Xenophon's *Cyropaedeia.*[19] Plato's *Republic* describes a fabulous never-never land, not the real world; it has no basis in fact. Xenophon's mirror of princes is a collection of abstract ethical principles. Now the abstract analysis of virtue is fine in its own way, but in motivating people to act, examples drawn from the lives of real people are more efficacious. Discourse and reasoning may convince us intellectually, Ambrose observes, echoing Seneca, but examples of virtue show us reason in action and inspire us to act as well.[20] Moreover, each Old Testament

17. On this point see Russell, "*De imitatione*"; Moos, *Geschichte als Topik,* 1–13, 22–112; Swain, "Biography and the Biographic in the Literature of the Roman Empire," 14, 22, 32–36; Cribiore, *Gymnastics of the Mind,* 132. On the general tendency of patristic writers to appropriate classical rhetoric, subsuming it to their own needs, with a heavy use of figural representation and narrative involving biography, see Heim, "Les figures du prince idéal au IVe siècle," 277–83, 289–91, 293–301; Cameron, *Christianity and the Rhetoric of Empire,* 23, 50, 92–93.

18. This double warrant is noted by Welter, *L'Exemplum dans la littérature,* 13; Malherbe, *Moral Exhortation,* 11 and passim. Scholars who do not note the New Testament parallels include Kellner, *Der heilige Ambrosius,* 40, 57–65, 73–74; Wilken, "The Christianizing of Abraham"; Madec, *Saint Ambroise et la philosophie,* 183–86, 240–41; Jackson, "Ambrose of Milan as Mystagogue"; Mazza, *Mystagogy,* 14–44; M. E. Mohrmann, "Wisdom and the Moral Life," 166–71; Finn, *From Death to Life,* 28; Satterlee, *Ambrose of Milan's Method,* passim.

19. Ambrose, *De Abraham* 1.1.2, ed. and trans. Gori.

20. Ambrose, *De Iacob et uita beata* 1.1.1–1.2.7, ed. Schenkl, trans. Palla. Also noted by Moos, *Geschichte als Topik,* 82–84. Cf. Seneca, *Ep.* 6.5: "longum iter est per praecepta, breue et efficax per exempla."

patriarch has his own personal assortment of virtues. Hence, their examples take us from the abstract to the concrete, from the general to the specific. As Ambrose notes in *De Joseph,* examples "are more precise and penetrate the mind more easily the more they have been defined and delimited" (expressiora sunt eoque facilius mentem penetrant quo magis circumscripta ac determinata sunt).[21]

As to why the four patriarchs serve this purpose better than other Old Testament worthies who may also convey moral lessons, Ambrose offers a number of reasons beyond the obvious and all-important fact that the patriarchs were the first bearers of the covenant. They illustrate several classical ethical convictions that Ambrose shares: the idea that virtue can be taught,[22] the view that we have a natural attraction to virtue,[23] and the notion that the path of virtue is a gradual one. As he puts it, "And so I have said from the start that a human mind, which was not perfect from the beginning, was formed and progresses through gradual increments" (Et quia a principio dixi mentem hic formare hominis, quae a principio <non> perfecta fuerat, sed per incrementa a gradus quosdam proficit).[24] Ambrose calls attention to the point that not all the patriarchs started out as morally perfect individuals. But if they had vices, they remedied them: "they were not unaware of their faults, but corrected them" (nec uitia nescisse, sed emendasse).[25]

While some protagonists of the patriarch treatises had to undergo a more extensive moral education than others, they all eventually emerge as saints. They therefore serve as good models for converts whose task is to reject pagan error and vice and to acquire Christian virtue. Although each patriarch has his own salient virtues, they all share one virtue both with each other and with the post-biblical saints: they labor for the salvation of their brethren. "For this is the recompense and the life of the saints, that they have also brought about the redemption of others" (haec enim est merces et uita sanctorum, quod alios redemerunt).[26] To be sure, the patriarchs "excelled in merit, and in the order and conduct of life" (uitae et merito et ordine praecesserunt).[27] Therefore, it

---

21. Ambrose, *De Ioseph* 1.1, ed. Schenkl, trans. Palla; my trans.
22. Ambrose, *De Iac.* 1.1.1, 1.3.9.
23. Ambrose, *De Abr.* 2.1.1, 2.6.26; Ambrose, *De Iac.* 1.1.1, 1.3.9.
24. Ambrose, *De Abr.* 2.6.26; my trans. The emendation is the editor's.
25. Ambrose, *De Ios.* 1.4; McHugh trans., 190.
26. Ibid. 12.71; McHugh trans., 231. See also Ambrose, *De Abr.* 1.6.48, 2.8.60, 2.11.93.
27. Ambrose, *De Abr.* 2.9.64; my trans.

behooves us to "follow in their shining footsteps along a kind of path of blame-lessness opened up to us by their virtues" (*eorum uirtute reseratum enitentibus uestigiis persequamur*).[28] In so doing, each of the *competentes* will be able to become a "fellow-citizen of the saints" (*ciuis sanctorum*).[29]

While not without its difficulties, the learning process leading the *competentes* to that happy destination is far from impossible. For in addition to show-ing how they themselves learned to be virtuous in their own time and place, the patriarchs provide models for the Milanese converts of Ambrose's day that are accessible as well as relevant. Like most of his *competentes,* they were mar-ried men, rulers of households, concerned with providing for their families, raising their children, governing servants, administering property, getting along with their neighbors, and acting in the public sphere. Thus they constitute outstanding and pertinent guides for contemporary Christians who need to know how to live in this world yet not be of it. Moreover, the patriarchs reflect the fact that some features of the *competentes'* Greco-Roman tradition will con-tinue to serve them well as they become full-fledged Christians. For the patri-archs possess all the virtues of the philosophers, and more.[30] This observation on Ambrose's part suggests that, even as the *competentes* are to be naturalized as new Israelites by imitating the patriarchs, so the patriarchs are to be recast as classical philosophers teaching by example. Finally, important as the patriarchs are as guides to virtue, Ambrose notes that they have another message to con-vey as well, "for the deeds of the patriarchs are types of future events" (*Gesta igitur patriarcharum futurorum mysteria sunt*).[31]

This last point indicates the fact that, with other Christian exegetes, Am-brose subscribes to the commonplace view that earlier biblical events fore-shadow later ones and that the patriarchs are "types" of Christ. While this notion was scarcely controversial, there is another issue connected to Old Tes-tament exegesis that was hotly debated in his time and on which Ambrose makes a pointed and unwavering statement in the patriarch treatises. Some contemporary Christians maintained that the New Testament had superseded the Old Testament completely, or that the only meaningful way to read the Old Testament was as an allegory of truths dimly present that had been brought

28. Ambrose, *De Ios.* 1.1; McHugh trans., 189.
29. Ambrose, *De Isa.* 6.54, citing Eph 2:19; my trans. See also Ambrose, *De Isa.* 8.79.
30. Ambrose, *De Abr.* 2.10.70.
31. Ambrose, *De Ios.* 14.85; my trans.

fully to light by the Christian revelation. Associating this supersessionist position with heretics such as the Manichees, the Gnostics, and the Marcionites, Ambrose staunchly opposes such an outlook.[32] He wants to make his own position crystal clear to his *competentes*. In his view, the Holy Spirit informed equally the authors of both testaments. Historically and morally, the Old Testament thus remains a thoroughly valid and authoritative text. Therefore, the ethical examples of the patriarchs, lived out in real time, should be appropriated literally and not just allegorically. There is a good deal of biblical intertextuality in the patriarch treatises, and Ambrose validates his own exegetical position not only by drawing on other books of the Old Testament besides Genesis but by citing New Testament texts as well. While some of these New Testament passages serve the needs of typology, he includes many of them simply because they reinforce the ethical messages that he finds in the patriarch's lives.[33]

Two additional points need to be made about Ambrose's treatment of the Bible in the patriarch treatises. First, it is agreed by all students of his exegesis that Ambrose used the Septuagint as his biblical source for the Old Testament. An excellent Hellenist, he found this Greek translation of the Old Testament more consistently useful than the assorted versions of the *Vetus Latina,* which he also consulted. His own quotations from Genesis in the patriarch treatises do not match any of the known versions of the *Vetus Latina.* Jerome's Latin Vulgate text was not available to him. The Latin form of the passages Ambrose cites are his own personal translations of the Greek Septuagint text.[34] Second, and this fact will emerge more clearly in later chapters, what Ambrose reports

---

32. The single most important study of this theme is Hahn, *Das wahre Gesetz*. See also Newton, *The Old Testament Saints Not to Be Excluded;* Labriolle, *The Life and Times of St. Ambrose,* 164; Daniélou, "L'Unité des deux testaments dans l'oeuvre d'Origène"; Pelikan, *The Christian Tradition,* 1:15–27; Pizzolato, *La dottrina esegetica di Sant'Ambrogio,* 10–11, 40, 52, 62–87, 140, 239, 316; Francesconi, *Storia e simbolo;* Nauroy, "L'Écriture dans la pastorale," 371–85; Mazza, *Mystagogy,* 14–44; Meeks, *The Origins of Christian Morality,* 207–10; Satterlee, *Ambrose of Milan's Method,* 222–23, 227–28, 245–46. Figueroa, *The Church and the Synagogue in St. Ambrose,* stands alone in regarding Ambrose, unconvincingly, as a supersessionist.

33. Clark, *Reading Renunciation,* 122–28, 154, and passim, discusses the ways in which patristic authors used intertextuality not only for typological purposes but also to extract their own preferred interpretations from biblical texts, although here only in aid of the promotion of asceticism; for Ambrose, her focus is on his treatises for widows and consecrated virgins, not on the patriarch treatises.

34. Nauroy, "L'Écriture dans la pastorale," 389–91, with a good summary of the literature on this point.

the book of Genesis as saying sometimes departs from modern editions of that text, based as they are on the Hebrew Bible rather than on the Septuagint. Sometimes these discrepancies are the result of Ambrose's following of his predecessors, such as Philo and Origen, who likewise used the Septuagint. But we will also encounter passages in the patriarch treatises where Ambrose departs from both his primary and his secondary sources,[35] saying something different, whether by altering or by omitting material present in the biblical text. In some contexts this practice is a tactic for circumventing exegetical embarrassments. But elsewhere the biblical material that Ambrose distorts or omits would actually have strengthened the argument he is trying to make.

Before proceeding to the theory of human nature developed by Ambrose in the patriarch treatises, it will be useful to offer some observations on the literary form of these treatises, their dates, and their interrelationships. There is no single formal model for the patriarch treatises. Two of them, *De Abraham* and *De Jacob*, contain two books, while *De Isaac* and *De Joseph* are single books. In *De Abraham*, the first book recounts events in the patriarch's life on which Ambrose makes ethical comments, taking the story up through Isaac's marriage to Rebecca and Abraham's death more or less in chronological order. The second book revisits many of the same events, this time viewing Abraham more abstractly as "mind," while adding some new elements to his story.

The two books of *De Jacob* are organized quite differently. The first book outlines a theory of human nature and an analysis of the passions; the second opens with an account of how Jacob's virtues manifest the theory presented in the first book. Then an abrupt transition occurs in which Ambrose introduces an account of the martyrdom of the Maccabees taken from 1–2 and 4 Maccabees, prefaced by observations on the martyrdom of their priest, Eleazar, which Ambrose uncharacteristically opens by speaking in the first person singular. This martyrdom section does not appear at first glance to be smoothly integrated into the argument found in the rest of *De Jacob* or into the arguments of the patriarch treatises in general. Ambrose otherwise focuses on martyrs as *exempla uirtutis* primarily in his treatises dedicated to consecrated virgins, not only because he can draw on a wealth of early Christian female martyr saints for their edification but also because he participates in the general post-Constantinian tendency among Christian writers to assimilate

---

35. Noted by Jacob, "The Reception of the Origenist Tradition," in *Hebrew Bible/Old Testament,* 1:692–93.

martyrdom to the monastic calling as such.[36] It has been argued that, in the case of patriarch treatises with two books, the first book treats the protagonist historically and was intended for the *competentes* during Lent, while the second treats the protagonist typologically and was intended for the post-baptismal mystagogical instruction of neophytes.[37] This argument scarcely makes sense of either *De Abraham* or *De Jacob*.

The patriarch treatises presented in a single book are as different in structure from each other as both are from the two-book treatises. It is true that there are formal similarities between *De Isaac* and *De Joseph*. In each case Ambrose features the protagonist's role both as a moral example and as a typological reference to Christ within the selfsame book, indicating that he regarded instruction in typological exegesis as appropriate for *competentes* before their baptism. However, while he recounts Joseph's life and virtues in chronological order, in *De Isaac* he does something quite different. Possibly on account of the paucity of detail on Isaac's life in the Genesis account, in this treatise Ambrose focuses on Rebecca, Isaac's wife. His theme is the moral instruction that Rebecca undergoes, making her worthy of her marriage to Isaac and preparing her to assume her role as a matriarch in the covenanted people of God. In constructing her educational process, Ambrose makes use of two templates: the precepts of the Delphic Oracle and the Song of Songs.

At the beginning of *De Joseph*, Ambrose indicates to his audience that he has already discussed with them the lives of Abraham, Isaac, and Jacob, underlining their paramount virtues, before turning to those of Joseph.[38] This observation indicates that this was the order in which he composed these respective works. But when in Ambrose's career did he write the patriarch treatises, or the sermons on which he based them? This question has aroused considerable scholarly debate, and it has to be said that no consensus is in sight. The most exhaustive general survey of this issue, one that analyzes the opinions of scholars from the Maurist editors of Ambrose up through the mid-1970s, is provided by Maria Grazia Mara.[39] As she notes, the dates offered for *De Abraham*

---

36. Malone, *The Monk and the Martyr;* Dassmann, "Ambrosius und die Märtyrer," 61–65, 67–68; Gori, intro. to his trans. of Ambrose, *Verginità e vedovanza,* 1:51–52; Markus, *The End of Ancient Christianity,* 71; Mirri, *Il monachismo femminile secondo sant'Ambrogio di Milano,* 65–88; Freyburger, "De l'*amicitia* païenne aux vertus chrétiennes."

37. Parodi, *La catechesi di sant'Ambrogio,* 145; Nauroy, "L'Écriture dans la pastorale," 374–75.

38. Ambrose, *De Ios.* 1.1–2.

39. Mara, "Ambrose of Milan, Ambrosiaster, and Nicetas," in *Patrology,* 4:156–59.

range from 382/83 to ca. 387 to 388; those for *De Isaac* range from 387 to 388 to 391; for *De Jacob*, from 386 to 387 to 388; and for *De Joseph* from 387 to 388 to 389/90. Scholars writing more recently than Mara perpetuate the disagreements she charts. Maurice Testard dates *De Abraham* to 382/83, *De Isaac* to 386, *De Jacob* to 386, and *De Joseph* to 388. A major concern driving Testard's analysis is that he wants Augustine to have heard *De Isaac* and *De Jacob* while he was in Milan. He joins the followers of Pierre Courcelle in seeking to make Ambrose the source of Augustine's Neoplatonism.[40] Neither Courcelle nor any of these followers, including Testard, appears to be aware of the fact that the audience for these works, as sermons, were the *competentes* during the first weeks of the Lent before their baptism. Augustine was a member of this audience only in the Lent of 387, a date not considered by this group of scholars. Offering her own specifications for the chronology of Ambrose's works in her survey of views from 1974 to 1997, Michaela Zelzer comments only on *De Isaac* among the patriarch treatises, dating it to 389/90.[41] In the same year as Zelzer, Boniface Ramsay asserts that *De Abraham* was written anywhere in the 380s, *De Isaac* in 387/91, *De Jacob* in 386/87, and *De Joseph* in 387 or 388.[42] Most recently, John Moorhead gives the dates of *De Abraham* as ca. 382 or the years following, *De Isaac* as 387/91, *De Jacob* as 386/87, and *De Joseph* as ca. 388, while Allan Fitzgerald offers the relatively unpopular date of 395/96 for *De Isaac*.[43]

As we have noted above and in the previous chapter, those scholars who stress the year 386 in dating the patriarch treatises, particularly *De Isaac* and *De Jacob*, do so because of the philosophical influence on Augustine that they want to ascribe to Ambrose. This notion, as we have seen, is problematic both on account of the precise, and short, duration of Augustine's status as one of

---

40. Testard, "Saint Ambroise de Milan," 375. The single most influential scholar here is Pierre Courcelle; see "Plotin et saint Ambroise"; idem, "Nouvelle aspects du platonisme chez saint Ambroise"; idem, "Anti-Christian Arguments and Christian Platonism," 165–66; idem, "Tradition platonicienne et traditions chrétiennes du corps-prison"; idem, *Recherches sur les Confessions de Saint Augustin*, 16, 106–17, 122, 124–38; idem, "Ambroise de Milan, 'professeur de philosophie'"; idem, *Recherches sur Saint Ambroise*, 16; idem, *Connais-toi toi-même de Socrate à Saint Bernard*, 1:122–23, 125. Courcelle has been seconded by Taormina, "Sant'Ambrogio e Plotino"; Hadot, "Platon et Plotin dans trois sermons"; Solignac, "Nouveaux parallèles entre saint Ambroise et Plotin"; Moreschini, intro. to his trans. of Ambrose, *De Isaac uel anima*, 9–13; Palla, intro. to his trans. of Ambrose, *De Iacob et uita beata*, 220–21; Lenox-Conyngham, "Sin in St. Ambrose"; Moorhead, *Ambrose*, 172–73; Drecoll, "Neuplatonismus und Christentum."

41. M. Zelzer, "Zur Chronologie der Werke des Ambrosius," 92.

42. Ramsay, *Ambrose*, 57–58.

43. Moorhead, *Ambrose*, 219–20; Fitzgerald, "Ambrose at the Well," 79.

the *competentes* of the 387 Easter season as well as with respect to his more general access to philosophy and the kind of draw it held for him.

There is also another reason why 386 has appealed to some scholars as the date for the *De Jacob*. Concentrating not on the work's philosophical content but on the reference Ambrose makes in it to the martyrdom of the Maccabees, they seek to account for this peculiarity in terms of the Milanese basilica crisis of 386.[44] In one of the most dramatic episodes of his career, Ambrose rejected the attempt of the imperial court, resident in Milan and neo-Arian in belief, to take over the Portian basilica for its celebration of Lent and Easter and for the initiation of its own baptizands. A standoff resulted in which, seeking to force Ambrose to capitulate, the emperor ordered troops to surround Ambrose's basilica on the Monday of Holy Week 386. Within its walls, Ambrose kept up the spirits of his congregation with prayers, sermons, and round-the-clock hymn singing until the imperial troops and the emperor gave way the following day. The emperor had sought to pave the way for his seizure of the Portian basilica by issuing an edict the previous January guaranteeing freedom of public worship to neo-Arians and orthodox alike, disobedience of which counted as sedition, a capital crime.

To those Milanese Christians who had lived through the events of 386 or who held them in recent memory, the theme of martyrdom, starting with the ordeal of Eleazar, might well have seemed relevant, however unrelated it might be to the life of the patriarch Jacob. For by involving his congregation in his own act of civil disobedience, Ambrose was putting their necks on the block no less than his own. In the end, Ambrose and the orthodox faith were the victors. But that outcome, in 386 and the years following, was not likely to have been a foregone conclusion. While some scholars have warned against trying to correlate the dating of Ambrose's works with specific historical events,[45] it seems plausible to think that in the years immediately after 386 Ambrose might have thought it important to impress upon his *competentes*, by referring to the Maccabees in *De Jacob*, that baptism was a serious commitment that might well bring with it the price tag of martyrdom.[46] If so, however, he could not

---

44. See, most recently, Colish, "Why the Portiana?" To the scholars opting for 386 discussed there may be added Brown, *Power and Persuasion in Late Antiquity*, 111.

45. Moorhead, *Ambrose*, 6. But cf., on general principles, Williams, *Ambrose of Milan*, 10.

46. A good review of the literature on this point is provided by Palla in the intro. to his trans. of Ambrose, *De Iac.*, 215–16. See, more recently, Nauroy, "Les frères Maccabés dans l'exégèse d'Ambroise"; idem, "Du combat de la piété à la confession du sang"; Moorhead, *Ambrose*, 135–37.

have preached that message to them in 386, for the basilica crisis came to a head during Holy Week, at which point his message to the *competentes* had already moved from ethics to the *traditio symboli,* a fact not taken into account by scholars who want to date *De Jacob* to 386.[47] If one wants to correlate the dating of *De Jacob* with the basilica crisis of 386, then the earliest possible date for that work would have to have been the early weeks of Lent in 387.

The dating of *De Joseph* has also evoked the interest of scholars interested in linking it with the Milanese basilica crisis of 386. The passage in this treatise to which they point is the one in which Joseph, in prison, correctly interprets the dreams of two eunuchs, servants of the Pharaoh, his chief butler and chief baker. In the case of the butler, Joseph tells him that he will return to the Pharaoh's favor and regain his office; in the case of the baker, he tells him that he has lost the Pharaoh's favor permanently and that he will lose his life as well.[48] Now one of the ministers of the emperor Valentinian II, sent to Ambrose to request his attendance at an imperial consistory as a means of settling the basilica crisis in 386, was the eunuch Calligonus. Ambrose refused the invitation. In 388, Calligonus fell from the favor of Valentinian II's successor, Maximus, and was put to death. Several scholars read the pertinent passage of *De Joseph* as an allusion to Calligonus and his fate but nonetheless date the treatise to 386.[49] It is perfectly conceivable that Ambrose was indeed making a reference to Calligonus in *De Joseph.* But if such is the case, the earliest possible date for the work would have to have been the Lent of 389, not 386, since Calligonus did not fall from imperial favor until late in the year 388.

In sum, as to what is known and what can reasonably be inferred about the dating of the patriarch treatises, the following may be said: First, whenever they were first delivered as sermons, we have no way of knowing how much time elapsed between their initial oral delivery and the dates when Ambrose completed their redaction as treatises. In the case of passages in these works

---

Moorhead, 137, also sees in this section of *De Jacob* an annexation, for Christianity, of Horace's "dulce et decorum est pro patria mori" (*Carm.* 3.2.13).

47. This notion was first put forth by Courcelle, "Plotin et saint Ambroise," 46–56; idem, *Recherches sur les Confessions de Saint Augustin,* 124–38; idem, *Late Latin Authors and Their Greek Sources,* 137 n. 48; followed by Hadot, "Platon et Plotin dans trois sermons"; Solignac, "Nouveaux parallèles entre saint Ambroise et Plotin"; Moreschini, intro. to his trans. of *De Isa.,* 9; Markus, *The End of Ancient Christianity,* 49; Testard, "Saint Ambroise de Milan," 375.

48. Ambrose, *De Ios.* 6.29–34.

49. Palanque, *Saint Ambroise et l'empire romain,* 522; Palla, intro. to his trans. of Ambrose, *De Ios.,* 337, 339; McLynn, *Ambrose of Milan,* 296–97; Moorhead, *Ambrose,* 155.

that can be connected with events in 386 or 388, it is impossible to know whether the passages in question formed part of the original sermons or whether they were added to sermons already in use for the moral instruction of the *competentes*. It is clear that *De Abraham* was composed first and that *De Joseph* was composed last. We find it acceptable to regard the Maccabees section of *De Jacob* as a response to possible imperial persecution of orthodox Christians, and the fate of the Pharoah's baker as an allusion to the unfortunate Calligonus. If these views are correct, it follows that the earliest possible date of *De Jacob* in its present form is the beginning of Lent in 387; whereas the *terminus post quem* of *De Joseph* in its present form is the beginning of Lent in 389, the paschal season after Calligonus' fall. It has not been proved with certitude, by the methods used by any previous scholars, whether *De Isaac* precedes or postdates the composition of *De Jacob*.

But this does not exhaust our options in considering where, in the sequence of the four patriarch treatises, we should position *De Isaac*, and what follows may offer an answer to the debated matter of its date relative to that of *De Jacob*. Despite the divergence of their organization, form, and literary strategy, the patriarch treatises constitute a coherent series, as Cassiodorus recognized long ago. They are designed to inculcate Christian virtue gradually into the minds of Ambrose's *competentes* as well as to teach them the proper relations between the Old Testament and the New Testament. While they treat many common themes and often draw on common arguments and images, these works are best understood as a group. As such, they fall into two subgroups. *De Abraham* and *De Isaac* are about conversion, the abandonment of pagan error and vice, and the cultivation of correct Christian doctrine and virtue. *De Abraham* does this in Abraham's own case. *De Isaac* is about the conversion of Rebecca, dividing the framework that Ambrose takes from the Delphic Oracle's precepts and the Song of Songs into four stages to describe Rebecca's progress to the status of model wife and matriarch. While the protagonists of the treatises in this first subgroup both undergo moral enlightenment, Abraham's learning curve is steeper and more difficult, and it involves a wider range of issues than is the case with Rebecca. Given the developmental model of moral education embedded in the patriarch treatises,[50] this suggests that *De Isaac* follows *De Abraham* and precedes *De Jacob*.

---

50. Dassmann, *Die Frömmigkeit des Kirchenvaters Ambrosius*, 6. Cf. Palanque, *Saint Ambroise et l'empire romain*, 442, who does not see any connection between *De Jacob* and the other patriarch treatises.

For their part, making up the second subgroup of treatises, *De Jacob* and *De Joseph* both present personages deemed to have possessed moral excellence from their youth. They do not need to undergo an ethical learning process. Both of these patriarchs have to deal with major trials and tribulations, enduring injustice at the hands of others. Both meet the challenges they face and the tests they confront with flying colors. Both are modeled on the Stoic sage, possessing equanimity come what may. Both manifest public as well as private virtues. As between them, there is a progression as we move from *De Jacob* to *De Joseph*. Both patriarchs exemplify the virtue of fraternal forgiveness and reconciliation. But Joseph adds prudent statesmanship to his catalogue of virtues.

Since the protagonists of all four patriarch treatises are saints in Ambrose's eyes, and since an attribute of the saints is that they intercede for and redeem others, this quality can be found in all of them, with the circle of those whom they affect widening as we move from Abraham to Joseph. Abraham tries to intercede with God on behalf of the residents of Sodom and Gomorrah, if unsuccessfully; while Abraham's intentions are generous, God has other plans. In the end, Abraham's intercession is limited to the rescue of his nephew Lot and Lot's daughters. For his part, Isaac saves Rebecca, winning her over to virtuous service to the covenant. And in the persona of the Bride of the Song of Songs, Rebecca, following her union with her Bridegroom, urges him to leave their nuptial chamber in order to save other would-be converts who, unlike his wife, still need his help. Jacob saves his wives, Leah and Rachel, from the idolatry and polytheism of their father, Laban. He also redeems his estranged brother, Esau, from fratricidal hatred. As for Joseph, in his capacity as the Pharaoh's chief minister, his sage policy with regard to Egypt's agrarian resources enables him to save his own family in Canaan from starvation when they come to buy grain in Egypt. At the same time, he also saves the people of other nations who come to Egypt to buy grain.

These considerations make it reasonable to think that the patriarch treatises, conceived as a sequence of stages in the moral education of incipient Christians, were indeed composed in the order in which the book of Genesis tells their protagonists' stories. Just as we can track development from the protagonist as convert to the protagonist as perfected sage, and from a narrower to a wider horizon in the protagonists' service to others, so the actual view of human nature that undergirds the ethics of the patriarch treatises develops as we move through the sequence. To that anthropology we now turn.

Human Nature in the Patriarch Treatises

CHAPTER 3

As we saw at the end of the last chapter, Ambrose's patriarch treatises form, and were early seen as forming, a series, treating their protagonists in chronological order, with *De Abraham* and *De Isaac* addressing the theme of conversion while *De Jacob* and *De Joseph* depict sages whose constancy enables them to triumph over the vicissitudes they face. All of Ambrose's patriarchs possess the classical cardinal virtues of prudence, temperance, courage, and justice as well as a variety of other virtues. Each plays a role in the redemption of others. Jacob and Joseph add the virtue of fraternal reconciliation and display Stoic equanimity with particular prominence. Joseph adds to his array of moral excellences the virtues of the statesman. The fact that Joseph comes last in the series is a happy accident, for Ambrose's conception of virtue in these treatises is relentlessly civic. Christian and classical ethics join hands in the patriarch treatises; even as Ambrose adjures his *competentes* to become new Israelites, so he presents the patriarchs as sages manifesting philosophical as well as biblical virtues.

Underlying and supporting these ethical portraits is a theory of human nature that likewise draws on both the Bible and Greek philosophy. The principal schools of philosophy to which Ambrose appeals are Aristotelianism and Stoicism, although he subjects the anthropology and psychology of both schools to his own modifications. Furthermore, Ambrose's anthropology develops as he moves from *De Abraham* to *De Isaac* and *De Jacob*. This claim runs counter to the views of the vast majority of commentators on Ambrose's anthropology, who see him as an unreconstructed Platonist, an advocate of extreme asceticism in the light of a dualistic view of human nature in which the soul is our true identity and the body is the source of our moral problems.[1] Now it is true, as many of these scholars have noted, that Ambrose alludes specifically to a number of Platonic and Neoplatonic motifs and doctrines. Also, he repeatedly urges his *competentes* to detach themselves from their carnal senses. He states, in *De Abraham*, that our vices stem from these same carnal senses.[2] Yet, as we will see, it is precisely this last point that Ambrose modifies profoundly in *De Isaac* and *De Jacob*, thereby giving a decidedly non-Platonic coloration to his advice regarding detachment and to his use of Platonic and Neoplatonic imagery.

As for the philosophical positions he substitutes, the classical doctrines on which Ambrose calls are diverse, and he does not place them all on a level playing field. Some philosophical positions he accepts just as they are, and weaves them seamlessly and without attribution or comment into the fabric of his own argument. Some philosophical positions he finds correct and fully compatible with biblical ethics and anthropology. In such cases, he buttresses them with scriptural passages that document and reinforce the parallels. At times, in dealing with doctrines he finds compatible with Christianity, he adverts to an apologetic and patristic commonplace, which derived, in turn, from Hellenistic Jewish apology and which claims that the Greek philosophers acquired

---

1. Courcelle, "Plotin et saint Ambroise"; idem, "Nouvelle aspects de platonisme chez saint Ambroise"; idem, "L'humanisme chrétien de saint Ambroise"; idem, "Anti-Christian Arguments and Christian Platonism," 165–66; idem, *Recherches sur les Confessions de Saint Augustin*, 106–17, 122, 124–38; idem, *Late Latin Writers and Their Greek Sources*, 137–38; idem, "Ambroise de Milan, 'professeur de philosophie'"; idem, *Recherches sur saint Ambroise*, 16; idem, *Connais-toi toi-même de Socrate à saint Bernard*, 1:122–23, 125; idem, "Saint Ambroise devant le précepte delphique," 185–86. See also Thamin, *Saint Ambroise et la morale chrétienne*, 324; Wilbrand, "Ambrosius und Plato"; Taormina, "Sant'Ambrogio e Plotino"; Hadot, "Platon et Plotin dans trois sermons"; Solignac, "Nouvelles parallèles entre saint Ambroise et Plotin"; Seibel, *Fleisch und Geist beim heiligen Ambrosius*, 15–50, 97–99, 119–22, 129–45, 194–97; Dörrie, "Das fünffach gestufte Mysterium," 83–92; Dassmann, *Die Frömmigkeit des Kirchenvaters Ambrosius*, 17; Loiselle, "'Nature' de l'homme," 1–4, 12, 24–25, 31, 35–37, 44–46, 48–49, 77–78, 90, 117–20, 127, 143, 168, who also denies (8) that Ambrose's anthropology ever changed or developed; Brown, *The Body and Society*, 348–49; Markus, *The End of Ancient Christianity*, 34–38, 49; Clark, *Reading Renunciation*, 89; Moorhead, *Ambrose*, 172–73; Tolomio, "'Corpus carcer' nell'Alto Medioevo," 5–6, 10–11, 13. Although Hill, "Classical and Christian Tradition," generally portrays Ambrose as a Stoic, she sees him as teaching a Platonic body-soul dualism (153), and a doctrine of extreme asceticism (5, 14, 16, 70, 266). An alternative approach, emphasizing Ambrose's biblical anthropology to the exclusion of all else, is found in Szydzik, *"Ad imaginem dei"*; idem, "Die geistigen Ursprünge der Imago-Dei-Lehre"; his strategy is to consider primarily Ambrose's *Hexaemeron* and *De paradiso*, ignoring the patriarch treatises.

2. Ambrose, *De Abr.* 2.6.28, ed. and trans. Gori.

their teachings from the Old Testament.[3] Sometimes Ambrose thinks that, while philosophy is accurate so far as it goes, it fails to go the distance and needs correction or amplification in the light of Holy Scripture or of his own personal insights. Finally, at some points he thinks that philosophy must be rejected because it is just plain wrong. In the patriarch treatises, this last category of references is the smallest. The other positions are far more typical, with Aristotelianism and Stoicism weighing in alongside Platonism and conditioning strongly the way Ambrose actually appropriates the Platonic and Neoplatonic material to which he refers.

In *De Abraham*, despite his Platonic-sounding remark on the body with its physical senses as the source of human vice, Ambrose comes down vigorously in favor of a hylomorphic understanding of human nature. Rather than speaking primarily of body and soul, he speaks of the rational and irrational aspects of the human constitution.[4] Both are integral to our nature, as are soul and body. Ambrose compares their interconnection to two children born of the same parents, and to husbands and wives, bound intimately even if in hierarchical relationships.[5] He observes that "the whole human person is saved, in body and soul, not just one part" (Iam enim non ex parte, sed totus homo saluatur in corpora, saluatur in anima).[6] Here he yokes the anthropology of Aristotle to that of the Bible. Such being the case, the goal of ethics is not to teach us to live as if we had no bodies. In extirpating our vices, here held to stem

---

3. Ibid. 1.2.4, 2.1.5, 2.10.69–70. For the fullest discussion of this commonplace, see Droge, *Homer or Moses?* See also Kellner, *Der heilige Ambrosius,* 31–40; Labriolle, *The Life and Times of St. Ambrose,* viii–ix, 187–88; Huhn, "Bewertung und Gebrauch"; Chadwick, *Early Christian Thought and the Classical Tradition,* 13–17, 32, 43–45; Feldman, "Abraham the Greek Philosopher in Josephus"; Oberti Sobrero, *L'Etica sociale in Ambrogio di Milano,* 92–94; Wiesner, intro. to his ed. and trans. of Ambrose, *De bono mortis,* 47–48; Pelikan, *The Christian Tradition,* 1:33–35; Gager, *Moses in Greco-Roman Paganism,* 38–39, 66–67, 76–79; Madec, *Saint Ambroise et la philosophie,* 53, 60, 94, 177–79; Pizzolato, "La Sacra Scrittura fondamento," in *Ambrosius Episcopus,* 1:414–26; Amir, "Die Begegnung des biblischen und des philosophischen Monotheismus"; Hill, "Classical and Christian Tradition," 178; Moorhead, "The Greeks, Pupils of the Hebrews"; Gori, intro. to his ed. and trans. of Ambrose, *De Abr.,* 21–23; Nauroy, "L'Écriture dans la pastorale," 381–82; M. Zelzer, "Ambrosius von Mailand," 212; Lenox-Conyngham, "Ambrose and Philosophy," 118–20; M. E. Mohrmann, "Wisdom and the Moral Life," 6; Assmann, *Moses the Egyptian,* 4–5, 29–44, 55–56, 149; Runia, "L'exégèse philosophique et l'influence de la pensée philonienne."

4. Ambrose, *De Abr.* 1.4.29, 2.6.28. Gori, intro. to his ed. and trans. of this text, 131, argues for a threefold distinction in Ambrose's view of human nature.

5. Ambrose, *De Abr.* 2.6.28. Noted by Stenger, "Das Frömmigkeitsbild des hl. Ambrosius," 8; Szydzik, "Ad imaginem dei," 44.

6. Ambrose, *De Abr.* 1.4.29; my trans.

from the physical senses, we must recognize that we cannot extirpate the passions leading to them, for the passions occur naturally. Nor is our goal to induce a state of anesthesia. Rather, our goal is to govern our desires, redirecting them to morally worthy ends, a position common to Plato, Aristotle, and the Middle Stoic Panaetius.[7] This constellation of ideas is found in all the patriarch treatises and must be kept in mind in interpreting Ambrose's frequent assertions that virtue requires the flight from physical pleasures. What he really means is that we should acquire the self-discipline we need in order to use well both the rational and the infrarational aspects of our nature.

Ambrose develops the anthropology outlined in *De Abraham* much farther in *De Isaac* and *De Jacob*, also taking it in some decidedly independent directions. In these two treatises his injunctions to flee physical pleasures are rooted even more expressly in a hylomorphic conception of human nature. With Aristotle, Ambrose states that our soul is our form and our body is our matter. The two are integrally united and cannot be separated in this life without destroying the human person whom they constitute.[8] Far from merely reinforcing his position in *De Abraham*, Ambrose then proceeds to take a major step away from it. He now argues that vices as well as virtues can arise in the soul. The only reason why the body is blamed for our sins is that the soul needs the body to carry them out: "Why," he asks rhetorically, "do we accuse the body, as if it were weak? For our physical members are the weapons of injustice and the weapons of justice; . . . the body is the servant of the will" (Quid carnem quasi infirmam accusamus? Membra nostra arma sunt iniustitiae et arma iustitiae; . . . caro autem uoluntatis ministra).[9]

When the soul allows the body to deceive it, the intellectual faculties of imagination and will are involved. Ambrose is a staunch defender of free will, which he sees as essential in the psychogenesis of both vice and virtue. As he observes, "We are not constrained to obedience by necessity, as if we were slaves, but by the judgment of our will, whether we tend toward virtue or are inclined toward vice" (Non enim seruili ad oboedientiam constringimur neces-

---

7. Ibid; more on this point is found in Ambrose, *De Iacob et uita beata* 1.1.1–1.1.4, ed. Schenkl, trans. Palla. Hill, "Classical and Christian Tradition," 154, ascribes this idea to Plato alone. Stenger, "Das Frömmigkeitsbild des hl. Ambrosius," 15–19, notes the point without ascription.

8. Ambrose, *De Isaac uel anima* 2.3, 3.6, ed. Schenkl, trans. Moreschini. Noted by Sanders, "Fons vitae Christus," 179–81.

9. Ambrose, *De Iac.* 1.3.10; my trans. See also ibid. 1.1.1. Noted by Loiselle, "'Nature' de l'homme," 30 n. 20, 79–80, 90–91.

sitate, sed uoluntate arbitra, siue ad uirtutem propendimus siue ad culpam inclinamur).[10] In those instances when we succumb to vice, our exercise of free will is the cause: "We cannot attribute our problem to anything but our own will" (Non est quod cuiquam nostram adscribamus aerumnam nisi nostrae uoluntati).[11] Now the will is a faculty of the soul. Thus, when we fall into sin, according to Ambrose, "the soul . . . is the author of her own evils" (Anima igitur . . . ipsa sibi auctor malorum est).[12] Likewise, our will, responding to reason, can turn us back from sin and error and orient us toward virtue: "Our will, following reason, calls us away" (uoluntas reuocat rationem secuta).[13]

Ambrose shares with the Neoplatonists a privative theory of evil. But for him, privation means lack of virtue, the loss of rational self-control. It is not the moral pendant of a metaphysics of non-being. As he puts it, "Evils, then, arise from goods, for there are no evils but deprivations of goods" (Ex bonis igitur mala orta sunt; non enim sunt mala nisi quae priuanter bonis).[14] In *De Isaac*, Ambrose describes the body as the clothing of the soul, not in the sense that we can freely take it off and put it on, but because, as with the clothing that protects the body, the soul needs to protect its own physical clothing and keep it in good condition.[15] Here as well, Ambrose analogizes the body, no less than the soul, to a field that can yield vice or virtue, depending on how we choose to cultivate it.[16]

In defining the nature of the soul, Ambrose takes sharp exception to all schools of philosophy that regard the soul as composed of matter. Nor does he see the soul as an Aristotelian entelechy. Rather, it is the image of God in us, which an ethical life enables us to recover.[17] In defining the body—and this point is all-important—Ambrose, citing Romans 7:23, agrees with St. Paul that "the body" and "the flesh" are not the same thing. As a created physical entity, a natural phenomenon, the body is ethically neutral. Ambrose invokes the

---

10. Ambrose, *De Iac.* 1.1.1; my trans.

11. Ibid. 1.3.10; my trans.

12. Ambrose, *De Isa.* 7.61; trans. McHugh in Ambrose, *Seven Exegetical Works*, 51.

13. Ambrose, *De Iac.* 1.1.1; McHugh trans., 119.

14. Ambrose, *De Isa.* 7.60; McHugh trans., 50–51. This point has been noted by Hill, "Classical and Christian Tradition," 169.

15. Ambrose, *De Isa.* 2.3, 8.79. Noted by Szydzik, "*Ad imaginem dei*," 50–51.

16. Ambrose, *De Isa.* 3.7, 7.60, 8.68–70. Cf. Ambrose, *De Abr.* 2.6.26, where virtue can be cultivated only in the soul.

17. Ambrose, *De Isa.* 2.4. Noted by Loiselle, "'Nature' de l'homme," 39–41, 49–53, 169; Hill, "Classical and Christian Tradition," 228.

Platonic image of the body as a cage or prison of the soul. But he does not understand this notion in a Platonic sense. For Ambrose, the real prison of our souls is not our bodies but our "flesh," that is, our sinfulness, wherever in the human constitution it may arise: "Where 'flesh' is applied to a human being, a sinner is meant" (ubi autem caro pro homine nuncupatur, peccator exprimitur).[18]

In elaborating the etiology of our moral states, Ambrose's *De Jacob* also goes beyond his *De Abraham* in its discussion of the passions. He continues to assert that right reason must govern the passions, adding that it must do so "according to what is natural or what is advantageous" (aut de naturalibus suscipitur aut de utilibus),[19] a clear echo of Cicero's *honestum* and *utile*. But Ambrose argues here that the passions can be subdivided under three headings, depending on which aspect of the human constitution gives rise to them.[20] Some passions, such as gluttony and wantonness, arise in the body. Some passions, such as pride, avarice, ambition, strife, and envy, arise in the soul. Some passions arise in both the body and the soul. Under this third heading, Ambrose lists the Stoic quartet of pleasure, pain, fear, and desire. But he reformulates this doctrine, placing his own original stamp on it. The Stoics saw all the passions as arising in the mind, deriving from false judgments: pleasure and pain reflect false judgments about what we currently experience; fear and desire reflect false judgments about what we anticipate. In addition to viewing these passions as arising in both mind and body, Ambrose expands their number to seven and analyzes them according to a different principle altogether, the sequence in which they occur. Unreasonable desire leads to pleasure, which leads

18. Ambrose, *De Isa.* 2.3; my trans.; see also ibid., 6.52; Ambrose, *De Iac.* 2.9.28; Ambrose, *De Ioseph* 6.31, ed. Schenkl, trans. Palla; my trans. For the uncritical view that Ambrose is expressing straightforward Platonism here, see Courcelle, "L'Âme en cage"; idem, "Tradition platonicienne et traditions chrétiennes du corps-prison"; idem, "Le corps tombeau"; Loiselle, "'Nature' de l'homme," 32–34, 143; Tolomio, "'Corpus carcer' nell' Alto Medioevo," 5–6, 10–11, 13. On the other hand, a number of scholars have noted the way Ambrose Christianizes this theme in the light of Pauline theology. See Szydzik, "*Ad imaginem dei*," 44; Dassmann, *Die Frömmigkeit des Kirchenvaters Ambrosius*, 41–44, 181–84; Otten, "Caritas and the Ascent Motif"; Madec, "L'Homme intérieur selon saint Ambroise"; Nauroy, "La méthode de la composition et la structure du *De Iacob*"; Palla, intro. to his trans. of Ambrose, *De Iac.*, 218–19; Iacoangeli, "Anima ed eternità nel *De Isaac*," 108–11; Sanders, "*Fons vitae Christus*," 23–25. Christman, "Ambrose of Milan on Ezekiel 1," does the same for Ambrose's *De uirginibus* and *De uirginitate*, where this theme also occurs. Clark, *Reading Renunciation*, 341–43, notes a number of patristic authors who understand "the flesh" in a Pauline sense but does not include Ambrose among them.

19. Ambrose, *De Iac.* 1.1.2; my trans. Noted by Taormina, "Sant'Ambrogio e Plotino," 77–80; Nauroy, "La méthode de la composition et la structure du *De Iacob*," 124.

20. Ambrose, *De Iac.* 1.1.1, 1.2.5.

to joy. Fear leads to pain, which leads to sadness. Along with joy and sadness, Ambrose cites another passion, mental agitation, the common outcome of pleasure and pain. This doctrine of the passions certainly reinterprets and amplifies on Stoic psychology by enlarging the number and widening the range of the passions as well as by reconceptualizing their sources and operative conditions, even as Ambrose smoothly incorporates into his position, as passions of the mind, mental states catalogued in the New Testament as sins. There is a real parallel here with his integration of Aristotelian anthropology with the doctrine that the whole man is saved, in body and soul. In dealing with the passions, Ambrose displays even more independence in the handling of his sources.

It is in the light of the concept of human nature just presented that Ambrose's use of Platonizing imagery and examples needs to be understood. While he alludes to Plotinus' golden chain of virtue in *De Isaac,* he regards the soul's fall from the good as a function of voluntary choice, an act of free will, not an unwilled metaphysical event.[21] When he invokes the myth of the charioteer from Plato's *Phaedrus* in *De Abraham*, he conflates it with the winged chariot of the prophet Ezekiel.[22] In his vision, Ezekiel sees a man, a lion, an ox, and an eagle. Ambrose equates these creatures with Plato's subdivision of the soul: reason, spirit, and passion (λογιστικόν, θυμικόν, ἐπιθυμη-τικόν), respectively, adding a fourth faculty, discernment (διορατικόν), not found in Plato. The four creatures also stand for the four cardinal virtues as defined by Aristotle: wisdom, courage, temperance, and justice. Ambrose joins the Stoics in arguing that the sage possesses all these virtues, which mutually coinhere; and with Aristotle, he gives pride of place to justice because its norm is the public good.[23] With Aristotle, whom he names, and against the Stoics, he adds that along with the cardinal virtues there exist lesser goods, such as the income gained from work in business, commerce, or agriculture, and attributes such as beauty, health, and vigor. These lesser goods are accidental in that a sage may possess them or not. But they are lesser goods on a trajectory that culminates in the supreme good; they are not Stoic preferables or *adiaphora*.[24]

---

21. Ambrose, *De Isa.* 7.61.

22. Ambrose, *De Abr.* 2.8.54. On the Christianizing of this image here and elsewhere, see the references to Dassmann, Otten, Madec, Nauroy, Iacoangeli, and Christman in n. 18 above.

23. Ambrose, *De Abr.* 2.10.68–70. Ambrose's identification of Ezekiel's creatures with the cardinal virtues has been noted by Savon, *Saint Ambroise devant l'exégèse de Philon,* 1:234; Moorhead, *Ambrose,* 178.

24. Ambrose, *De Abr.* 2.10.68–70. Hill, "Classical and Christian Tradition," 156, has noted the Aristotelian derivation of this doctrine.

Ambrose returns to the myth of the charioteer in *De Isaac*, framing it there as well with a biblical chariot, in this case the chariot of Aminadab mentioned in the Song of Songs. The driver remains reason, now piloting eight horses representing the cardinal virtues and their opposing vices. The driver skillfully guides the good horses, bridled and yoked by justice and moderation, charity and faith, winning the race and its prize, Christ.[25] The Platonic image has been Christianized, but with the cardinal virtues intact. And the journey of the soul, as Ambrose envisions it, is not a mystical Plotinian flight from the alone to the Alone. Rather, "its flight is not to depart from earth but to remain on earth, to hold to justice and temperance, to renounce the vices in material things, not their use" (Fuga autem est non terras relinquere, sed esse in terris, iustitiam et sobrietatem tenere, renuntiare uitiis non usibus elementorum).[26] The ethics flowing from the anthropology Ambrose elaborates in the patriarch treatises is thus an ethics of moderation, not one of asceticism.[27]

The theme of moderation also receives reinforcement in the scheme for the moral education of Rebecca that is the subject of *De Isaac*, reminding the reader that the language of the Song of Songs, with which Ambrose combines it in this treatise, is, on its literal level, nuptial. At the beginning of *De Isaac*, Rebecca, as the bride-in-training, is counseled to follow the precepts of the Delphic Oracle: know thyself, nothing in excess, thou art. She must acquire self-knowledge and self-discipline before she can unite with her bridegroom. "Nothing in excess," let it be noted, not moral extremism, is to be the norm of self-discipline for Ambrose's *competentes*. It is also the template through which his frequent appeals to detachment[28] are meant to be appropriated. In the final

25. Ambrose, *De Isa.* 8.65–66. Ambrose also refers to the chariot of Aminadab at *De Abr.* 2.8.54. North, *Sophrosyne*, 365, follows Courcelle and Hadot (as noted in n. 1 above) in giving this passage a purely Platonic reading.

26. Ambrose, *De Isa.* 3.6; McHugh trans., 14. On moderation as a norm elsewhere in the patriarch treatises, see also Ambrose, *De Abr.* 1.4.26, 1.7.59, 2.2.7, 2.6.31, 2.6.34, 2.8.46, 2.10.68, 2.11.82; *De Isa.* 3.5, 7.61, 8.65, 8.79; *De Iac.* 1.2.5-1.3.9, 1.8.37, 2.1.4, 2.4.15, 2.5.21, 2.6.27, 2.10.43; *De Ios.* 2.5.

27. As is noted by Berton, "Abraham dans le *De officiis*," 312–15, 316; Sanders, *"Fons vitae Christus,"* 25–27, 99–102. It may be observed that even in Ambrose's works aimed at people in celibate callings, he does not denigrate marriage and sexuality, which he treats as natural, noting that only those with a special divine calling can transcend nature in this area of life. See Bickel, *Das asketische Ideal*, 21–23, 27, 37; North, *Sophrosyne*, 365, although she does not systematically consider the patriarch treatises; Colish, *The Stoic Tradition*, 2:53–54. This viewpoint has been ignored by those scholars who want to treat Ambrose as a radical Platonist and advocate of extreme asceticism, above all sexual asceticism, as in n. 1 above.

28. Ambrose, *De Isa.* 1.1, 1.2, 2.3, 2.4, 2.5, 2.6, 3.6, 3.7, 3.8, 4.11, 4.13, 4.16, 4.23, 4.25, 4.27, 4.32, 4.34, 5.46, 6.52, 6.54, 7.59, 7.60, 7.61, 8.78, 8.79.

peroration of this work, Ambrose makes it quite clear that Rebecca has not been educated to become an ascetic or a contemplative who departs from life in this world. In an ethical program and in language that combine classical and Christian values, he adjures his *competentes* to take Rebecca as their model:

> Let us not flee either with ships or chariots or horses, . . . but let us flee with the spirit and the eyes and feet that are within. Let us accustom our eyes to see what is bright and clear, to look upon the face of continence and of moderation, and upon all the virtues, in which there is nothing scabrous, nothing obscure or involved. And let each one look upon himself and his own conscience; let him cleanse his inner eye, so that it may contain no dirt. For what is seen ought not to be discordant with him who sees, because God has wished that we be conformed to the image of his Son. Thus the good is known to us and it is not far from any one of us, for "in him we live and move and have our being, for we also are his offspring" (Acts 17:28) as the Apostle asserted that the Gentiles said.

> Nec nauibus fugiamus aut curribus aut equis, . . . sed fugiamus animo et oculis aut pedibus interioribus. Adsuescamus oculos nostros uidere quae dilucida et clara sunt, spectare uultum continentiae et temperentiae omnesque uirtutes, in quibus nihil scabrum, nihil obscurum et tortuosum sit. Et ipsum spectet quis et conscientiam suam: illum oculum mundet, ne quid habeat sordium; quod enim uidetur non debet dissonare ab eo qui uidet, quoniam conformes nos deus imaginis uoluit esse filii sui. Cognitum igitur nobis est illud bonum nec longe est ab unoquoque nostrum; *in ipso enim uiuimus et sumus et mouemur; ipsius enim et genus sumus*, ut apostolus gentiles posuit significare.[29]

Despite Ambrose's emphasis on the self-initiated and self-conducted moral and intellectual labor of introspection and purification that her educational program involves, he does not present Rebecca, once perfected, either as a partner in a *mariage blanc* or as a fully autarchic Stoic sage. She is a bride whose marriage is consummated; and her bridegroom, first as teacher and finally as spouse, is always with her. And, not content with a one-on-one relationship with her husband, once united with him, she encourages him to leave their

---

29. Ibid. 8.79; McHugh trans., 63–64. I have altered his wording slightly.

bridal chamber in order to help others who still need his assistance.[30] Ambrose here reminds his *competentes* of the limits of purely human agency in departing from past error and sin; along with their own strenuous efforts, they will need grace and the sacrament of baptism for which they are preparing.[31] He also reminds them that the calling of the baptized is not only to seek their own salvation but also to assist in the salvation of others.

These general anthropological principles and the ethics of moderation that flow from them play out somewhat differently in the lives of the protagonists of each of Ambrose's patriarch treatises, depending on their particular histories and characters as related in the book of Genesis. Also at work in differentiating his treatment of them is the particular exegetical agenda that he wants to highlight in each case. All four protagonists put their own particular spin on the cardinal virtues that they all possess as well as manifesting other virtues, both classical and Christian. As sages, they are cut from the cloth of a Stoicism and an Aristotelianism that Ambrose has re-elaborated, altered in part, and joined with Christian doctrine. They are not Platonists or Neoplatonists, notwithstanding his recourse to Platonizing concepts and metaphors. The patriarchs, individually and collectively, set an ethical standard for the Christian layperson approaching baptism that is, above all, relevant, attainable, and crafted to suit the needs of the audience of *competentes* to which it is directed. Fittingly, Ambrose launches their Lenten catechesis with Genesis' first convert, Abraham.

---

30. Ibid. 4.11, 4.19, 5.43–46, 7.57, 8.69. Courcelle, "Saint Ambroise devant le précepte delphique," 185–86, has noted Ambrose's reference to the first precept of the Delphic Oracle alone but not to his Christianizing of the advice Rebecca receives concerning all three precepts.

31. Ambrose, *De Isa.* 8.76, 8.79.

CHAPTER 4

Abraham

Although, as the previous chapter has shown, Ambrose's anthropology in the patriarch treatises is not as fully developed in *De Abraham* as it later becomes in *De Isaac* and *De Jacob*, this treatise, which opens the series, sets the tone for the group as a whole. Methodologically, it reveals clearly the freedom with which Ambrose makes use of his sources, whether they are philosophical, exegetical, biblical, literary, or legal. In interpreting the book of Genesis, *De Abraham* requires Ambrose to deal head-on with several knotty exegetical problems. He hopes to address them here so definitively that he will not need to consider similar issues when they arise in the lives of subsequent patriarchs. Ambrose certainly takes the occasion in *De Abraham* to hammer home his position on the inspired nature of the Genesis text and its relation to the New Testament by citing New Testament passages that corroborate the moral message found in Abraham's life and by explaining how personages and events in that *uita* point ahead to later developments in Old Testament history as well as to the Christian revelation to come.

Ambrose is quite explicit in *De Abraham* in specifying what he thinks can be appropriated positively from Greek philosophy in his delineation of Abraham as an ideal moral example. He also details the philosophical doctrines that he thinks Christians should set aside. His references to philosophy are more elaborate in *De Abraham* than in the later patriarch treatises, as are his quotations from Greek and Latin literature. Most of these literary references are decorative or function as *scholia* shedding light on one factual point or another. In only one case does Ambrose treat literature as embodying philosophical wisdom. Roman law also finds a place in *De Abraham*, sometimes reinforcing Ambrose's message and sometimes not. His exegetical predecessors, Philo and Origen, also loom large, although he often modifies their content or emphasis.

As the opening salvo in the catechetical program for his *competentes*,[1] *De Abraham* presents Ambrose with the opportunity, and indeed the need, to indicate expressly why he has chosen the patriarchs as ethical guides for them, and why the patriarchs' lives, lived out in real historical time, surpass works such as Plato's *Republic* and Xenophon's *Cyropaideia* as vehicles of ethical instruction.[2] The *Republic*, Ambrose explains, depicts a fabulous *polis* that has never existed; the *Cyropaideia* is a mirror of princes, a compilation of abstract and disembodied precepts. But examples teach more readily than precepts, he adds, invoking a standard classical argument. Ambrose also finds authoritative warrants for treating Abraham as an example of virtue in New Testament writers and in previous Jewish and Christian authors such as Philo and Origen. But in his explanation of his practice in the text of *De Abraham*, he adheres to the contrast between history and the literary genres represented by the works of Plato and Xenophon mentioned. The witness of Abraham's life in real history, he observes, is unencumbered by fiction, technical jargon, or sophistic arguments. It shows that "a simple faith is greater than the meretricious guile of eloquence" (iste gessit maiorque ambitioso eloquentiae mendacio simplex ueritatis fides).[3] Adverting to the apologetic commonplace that the Greek philosophers, in any case, derived those of their ideas that are correct from the Old

---

1. Noted, with specific reference to *De Abraham*, by Kellner, *Der heilige Ambrosius,* 101; Palanque, *Saint Ambroise et l'empire romain,* 509; Finn, *Early Christian Baptism and the Catechumenate,* 59–61; Jacob, "The Reception of the Origenist Tradition," in *Hebrew Bible/Old Testament,* 1:692–93; Sanders, *"Fons vitae Christus,"* 206.

2. Ambrose, *De Abraham* 1.1.2, ed. and trans. Gori.

3. Ambrose, *De Abr.* 1.2.3, trans. Tomkinson in Ambrose, *On Abraham,* 2. On this point see Russell, "*De imitatione*"; Moos, *Geschichte als Topik,* 1–13, 22–112; Swain, "Biography and the Biographic in the Literature of the Roman Empire," 14, 22, 32–36; Cribiore, *Gymnastics of the Mind,* 132. On the general tendency of patristic writers to appropriate classical rhetoric, subsuming it to their own needs, with a heavy use of figural representation and narrative involving biography, see Heim, "Les figures du prince idéal au IVe siècle," 277–83, 289–91, 293–301; Cameron, *Christianity and the Rhetoric of Empire,* 23, 50, 92–93. This double classical and biblical warrant is noted by Welter, *L'Exemplum dans la littérature,* 13; Malherbe, *Moral Exhortation,* 11 and passim. Scholars who do not note the New Testament parallels include Kellner, *Der heilige Ambrosius,* 40, 57–65, 73–74; Wilken, "The Christianizing of Abraham"; Madec, *Saint Ambroise et la philosophie,* 183–86, 240–41; Jackson, "Ambrose of Milan as Mystagogue"; Mazza, *Mystagogy,* 14–44; M. E. Mohrmann, "Wisdom and the Moral Life," 166–71; Finn, *From Death to Life,* 28; Satterlee, *Ambrose of Milan's Method,* passim.

Testament,[4] he lists under that heading the Stoic view that the sage possesses all things and that he follows right reason and the law of nature, the cardinal virtues as defined by Aristotle, and the advice of the Pythagoreans and the Seven Sages to follow God.

Ambrose also catalogues the philosophical doctrines that he deems incorrect.[5] These include the belief in quintessence, the harmony of the spheres (which he takes Origen to task for holding), the Epicurean pleasure-pain calculus, and the "Pythagorean creed," that is, numerology, astrology, and geomancy.[6] In addition to these straightforward attacks, Ambrose encrypts erroneous philosophy, equated with "Egypt," in the person of Abraham's Egyptian slave-concubine, Hagar: "Philosophical erudition abounded in Egypt" (philosophica eruditio abundauit in Aegypto),[7] he observes, which is one reason, along with the requirements of marital chastity, why Abraham must repudiate Hagar and their son Ishmael. In defining Egypt as false philosophy, Ambrose departs from Philo, who equates Egypt with the attachment to corporeal and external goods and the school disciplines as well as with sophistry.[8] This particular example alerts us to the fact that Ambrose does not always agree with the previous exegetical interpretations of Abraham with which he was conversant. In contrast with the view that Ambrose was a slavish adherent of Philo, or of Philo and Origen, the evidence shows that, while Ambrose makes

---

4. Ambrose, *De Abr.* 1.2.4, 2.2.5, 2.10.69–70. For the fullest discussion of this commonplace, see Droge, *Homer or Moses?* See also Kellner, *Der heilige Ambrosius,* 31–40; Labriolle, *The Life and Times of St. Ambrose,* viii–ix, 187–88; Huhn, "Bewertung und Gebrauch"; Chadwick, *Early Christian Thought and the Classical Tradition,* 13–17, 32, 43–45; Feldman, "Abraham the Greek Philosopher in Josephus"; Oberti Sobrero, *L'Etica sociale in Ambrogio di Milano,* 92–94; Wiesner, intro. to his ed. and trans. of Ambrose, *De bono mortis,* 47–48; Pelikan, *The Christian Tradition,* 1:33–35; Gager, *Moses in Greco-Roman Paganism,* 38–39, 66–67, 76–79; Madec, *Saint Ambroise et la philosophie,* 53, 60, 94, 177–79; Pizzolato, "La Sacra Scrittura fondamento," in *Ambrosius Episcopus,* 1:414–26; Amir, "Die Begegnung des biblischen und des philosophischen Monotheismus"; Hill, "Classical and Christian Tradition," 178; Moorhead, "The Greeks, Pupils of the Hebrews"; Gori, intro. to his ed. and trans. of Ambrose, *De Abr.,* 21–23; Nauroy, "L'Écriture dans la pastorale," 381–82; M. Zelzer, "Ambrosius von Mailand," 212; Lenox-Conyngham, "Ambrose and Philosophy," 118–20; M. E. Mohrmann, "Wisdom and the Moral Life," 6; Assmann, *Moses the Egyptian,* 4–5, 29–44, 55–56, 149; Runia, "L'exégèse philosophique et l'influence de la pensée philonienne." The point about Stoic natural law has been noted by Hill, "Classical and Christian Tradition," 202.

5. Ambrose, *De Abr.* 2.1.3, 2.8.58, 2.11.80.

6. Ibid. 2.11.80.

7. Ibid. 2.10.73; Tomkinson trans., 92; see also ibid. 1.4.22, 1.4.31, 2.6.34. Ambrose's view of "Egypt" in *De Abraham* has been noted by Berton, "Abraham dans le *De officiis,* " 315–16.

8. Philo, *On Abraham* 21.103–22.107, trans. Colson; idem, *Questions and Answers on Genesis* 3.16, 3.19–20, 3.23–25, 3.35, trans. Marcus.

extensive use of these authors, he does not draw on them uncritically, often altering their emphasis so as to accent a historical and ethical message rather than a purely allegorical or contemplative one.[9]

Returning to the issues raised by Ambrose's treatment of Egypt, he seems to be giving philosophy rather low marks in *De Abraham*. However, there are many more philosophical references in this work of which he approves. Thus, although Abraham is a convert, an "athlete of the Lord" (athleta domini),[10] who must struggle and overcome obstacles, Ambrose supports the ancient Stoic principle that there is no middle ground between wisdom and folly,[11] although it conflicts with Abraham's program of gradual moral education. Another Stoic doctrine that is in harmony with Ambrose's theme here and throughout the patriarch treatises is the equanimity of the sage, to which he annexes the principle that the sage alleviates the misfortunes of others.[12] He agrees with the

9. Scholars arguing for Ambrose's slavish adherence to Philo include Ihm, "Philon und Ambrosius"; Thamin, *Saint Ambrose et la morale chrétienne,* 319; Palanque, *Saint Ambroise et l'empire romain,* 509; Daniélou, "Abraham dans la tradition chrétienne," 70–71, 82; Lucchesi, *L'Usage de Philon,* 42–49, 54, 55, 57, 60, 62, 64, 66, 82, 118; Pizzolato, "Una società cristiana alle prese con un testo radicale," 277–93; Berton, "Abraham est-il un modèle?" More typical are the scholars who view Ambrose as modifying or departing from Philo; see Stenger, "Das Frömmigkeitsbild des hl. Ambrosius," 4–65; De Vivo, "Nota ad Ambrogio, *De Abraham* I 2, 4," in *Ambrosius Episcopus,* 2:235–40; Savon, *Saint Ambroise devant l'exégèse de Philon le Juif,* 1:14, 85, 141–95, 234, 240; Nikiprowetzky, "Saint Ambroise et Philon," 193–95; Runia, *Philo in Early Christian Literature,* 292–96, 301–8, 347; Van der Lof, "The 'Prophet' Abraham," 17–18, 26–27; Jacob, "The Reception of the Origenist Tradition," in *Hebrew Bible/Old Testament,* 1:683–84. Scholars seeking to demonstrate Ambrose's dependence on Origen have tended to focus on works other than *De Abraham;* see Baus, "Das Nachwirkung des Origenes"; Palla, "Temi del *Commento* origeniano al *Cantico dei Cantici*"; Iacoangeli, "Anima ed eternità nel *De Isaac,*" 108–11; Clark, "The Uses of the Song of Songs"; De Lubac, *Medieval Exegesis,* 1:142, 154–55. More typically, in reading the first of the patriarch treatises, they emphasize his differences from Origen; see Stenger, "Das Frömmigkeitsbild des hl. Ambrosius," 65–66, 98–109; Chadwick, *Early Christian Thought and the Classical Tradition,* 74–76, 112; Trigg, *Origen,* 179–88; Clark, *Reading Renunciation,* 170–71, although without reference to Ambrose's patriarch treatises. Daniélou, "L'Unité des deux testaments dans l'oeuvre d'Origène," depicts Origen as somewhat inclined to the supersessionism that Ambrose firmly rejects and sees Ambrose as more interested in the literal sense of the Old Testament than either Philo or Origen. Völker, "Das Abraham-Bild bei Philo, Origenes, und Ambrosius," sees Philo and Origen as more interested than Ambrose in portraying Abraham as both a Stoic sage and an ecstatic visionary, while Ambrose emphasizes Abraham's faith and earthly virtues; Passetti, "I temi di Abramo 'peregrinus' e 'adventa,'" agrees with Völker, adding that Philo, Origen, and Ambrose had different concerns, especially with respect to the themes flagged in his paper.

10. Ambrose, *De Abr.* 1.2.6; my trans.

11. Ibid. 2.10.77.

12. Ibid. 1.6.48, 2.8.60, 2.11.93; cf. Ambrose, *De Ioseph* 12.71, ed. Schenkl, trans. Palla.

Stoics that the cardinal virtues of wisdom, temperance, courage, and justice mutually entail each other so that a person who has one of these virtues has them all, but with Aristotle he gives pride of place to justice.[13] Citing unspecified "natural philosophers" (secundum physiologos), he analogizes the soul to a field that we must cultivate,[14] and he states that the sage has four attributes that guide his social interactions. First, he seeks friendly relations with all he encounters. Second, if others decline his friendship, he does not respond with enmity. Third, if others prove hostile to him, he keeps his peace. Finally, if others pursue him, he defends himself as best he can.[15]

Easily the most heavily discussed philosophical passage in *De Abraham*, which, as we have noted in chapter 3, Ambrose reworks in *De Isaac*, is his conflation of the myth of the charioteer in Plato's *Phaedrus* with the vision of the prophet Ezekiel.[16] Here Ambrose rings changes, at the same time, on Ezekiel, Philo, and Plato. For Plato, the chariot is the soul; the driver is reason; and his two winged horses are passion and spirit, capable of moving the chariot in a virtuous direction if reason guides them properly. In Philo's use of the image, the chariot is winged; God is the charioteer; and the chariot represents the world, in an argument set in the context of God's destruction of Sodom and Gomorrah.[17] Ezekiel's chariot is also winged, and his ride in it enables him to see four creatures: an ox, a lion, a man, and an eagle. Ambrose says that Plato's chariot, not its horses, is winged, and, *pace* Philo, that the chariot represents heaven. In Ambrose's account, Ezekiel's visionary creatures stand for Plato's subdivisions of the soul, representing, respectively, passion, spirit, and reason. He adds a fourth faculty, discernment, not found in Plato. For Ambrose, Ezekiel's creatures also signify the cardinal virtues, with the ox as temperance, the lion as courage, the man as wisdom, and the eagle soaring over all as

13. Ambrose, *De Abr.* 2.10.68.

14. Ibid. 2.6.26; my trans.

15. Ibid. 2.8.29.

16. Ibid. 2.8.54; for literature on this passage, which notes the way in which Ambrose Christianizes this theme in the light of Pauline theology, see Szydzik, "*Ad imaginem dei*," 44, 50–51; Dassmann, *Die Frömmigkeit des Kirchenvaters Ambrosius,* 41–44, 181–84; Otten, "Caritas and the Ascent Motif"; Madec, "L'Homme intérieur selon saint Ambroise"; Nauroy, "La méthode de la composition et la structure du *De Iacob*"; Iacoangeli, "Anima ed eternità nel *De Isaac*," 108–11. Christman, "Ambrose of Milan on Ezekiel 1," does the same for Ambrose's *De uirginibus* and *De uirginitate*, where this theme also occurs.

17. Philo, *On the Migration of Abraham* 12.67, trans. Colson and Whitaker; idem, *Questions and Answers on Genesis* 4.51.

justice, the paramount virtue.[18] Ambrose's reasons for giving primacy to justice combine Aristotelian and Roman values. While the other cardinal virtues may be confined to private life, justice pertains as well to public duties. With Aristotle, he adds that, besides these cardinal virtues, there exist lesser and external physical goods, such as the income earned from work in business, commerce, or agriculture, and such attributes as beauty, health, physical well-being, and energy. Ambrose calls these lesser goods accidental, since the sage may possess them, or not. But they are lesser goods on a scale of values that culminates in the highest good, as the Aristotelians teach; they are not Stoic *adiaphora* or preferables. While Ambrose agrees that the happy life includes these physical goods, he adds that the true physical goods are chastity and patience. He places temperance on his list of accidental goods as well as on the roster of the cardinal virtues.

Ambrose's treatment of physical goods as acceptable is largely consistent with the anthropology he develops in *De Abraham*. As we saw in chapter 3, while he holds in this work that vices arise in the body, which is therefore the cause of our moral problems[19]—a position he was shortly to abandon—he regards the human body and soul as intimately and integrally related, joining Aristotelian hylomorphism with a soteriology in which the whole man is saved, in both body and soul.[20] This being the case, the goal of ethics, as manifested in Abraham's life, is to teach us how to use well the physical goods appropriate to persons living the active life in this world. Abraham was no ascetic; and in urging his *competentes* to flee the attractions of their physical senses, Ambrose is adjuring them to embrace moderation as well.[21] Ambrose cautions against aiming at a state in which our passions are extirpated and we can no longer feel their stirrings. He agrees with Plato, Aristotle, and Panaetius that such a condition is unattainable. What we can and should do is govern our desires, reordering them rationally so that they are oriented to morally worthy ends. In this sense, he agrees with Plato that the chariot is the human soul and the driver is reason. But the race in which the driver competes

---

18. Ambrose, *De Abr.* 2.10.68–70.
19. Ibid. 1.2.4; see chapter 3, 33–34.
20. Ibid. 1.4.29, 2.6.28.
21. Ibid. 1.4.26, 1.7.59, 2.2.7, 2.6.31, 2.6.34, 2.8.46, 2.10.68, 2.11.82. Noted by Stenger, "Das Frömmigkeitsbild des hl. Ambrosius," 14–19; Berton, "Abraham dans le *De officiis*," 312–13, 316–17; Sanders, "*Fons vitae Christus*," 25–27, 99–102.

does not leave the body behind. For the goal of moral education is to arm us with the self-discipline we need to use well, and reasonably, both the rational and the infrarational aspects of human nature.

With this in mind, let us turn to the argument of *De Abraham*, which Ambrose presents in two books. At the beginning of Bk. 1, noting that Moses, the putative author of the Pentateuch, "offers him [Abraham] to us as a model worthy of imitation" (Moyses quoque imitandum nobis descripserit),[22] he observes, regarding that first book, that "our treatise concerning him will be moral and simple from the outset" (de quo nobis moralis primo erit tractatus et simplex).[23] Bk. 1 treats Abraham's life from his call to leave his native Chaldea up through his death, satisfied that his son Isaac is suitably married to Rebecca and that the young couple are prepared to take up their assigned duties as bearers of the covenant into the next generation. Bk. 2 retraces some, but not all, of the events discussed in Bk. 1, up through the sacrifice of Isaac, with Abraham now understood figuratively as the human mind, or rationality. His story now illustrates how reason, although weakened by original sin, can be reformed and then how it can learn how to rule the infrarational aspects of human nature, guided by natural law.[24]

While Ambrose thus presents the allegorical exegesis he offers in Bk. 2 as a deepening of the simple ethical message he provides in Bk. 1, the second book has no lack of ethical content. Nor is Bk. 1 devoid of typological exegesis; indeed, there is more of it in the first book than in the second. In his opening words in Bk. 1, Ambrose states that he wants "to consider, in an orderly way, the deeds which the soul of this patriarch underwent" (per ordinem huius quoque patriarchae gesta considerare animum subiit).[25] But the notion of order does not necessarily mean that Ambrose intends to discuss every event in the life of Abraham or that his narrative will invariably follow the chronology of the book of Genesis. Rather, his principle of selectivity is to focus on what he sees as the meaning of Abraham's deeds as they reveal his experience as a convert, the "progress in the ideal form of virtue" (uirtutis formae quendam

22. Ambrose, *De Abr.* 1.1.2; my trans.

23. Ibid. 1.1.1; Tomkinson trans., 1.

24. Ibid. 2.1.1, 2.2.25; a good summary is provided by Gori, intro. to his ed. and trans. of *De Abr.*, 10–15. See also Stenger, "Das Frömmigkeitsbild des hl. Ambrosius," 4, 23–25, 34; Lazzati, *Il valore letterario della esegesi ambrosiano;* Hill, "Classical and Christian Tradition," 202.

25. Ambrose, *De Abr.* 1.1.1; my trans.

processum)[26] that he eventually acquires. The mind of Abraham, Ambrose observes, "did not start out perfect, but progressed through gradual increments" (a principio <non> perfecta fuerat, sed per incrementa et gradus quosdam proficit).[27] Thus, even the initial shortcomings of the patriarch are instructive, no less than the ways in which he rids himself of them.

In *De Joseph*, where Ambrose indicates what he regards as the paramount virtue of each patriarch, the virtue he singles out in Abraham's case is faith, a choice that certainly places him within the Western Christian consensus on Abraham.[28] But farther along in Bk. 1, he notes that, in addition to manifesting "simple faith in the truth" (simplex ueritatis fides), Abraham also displays "prudence, justice, charity, and chastity" (prudentia, iustitia, caritate, castimonia).[29] He passes the tests he has to confront not just "as faithful" but also "as courageous" and "as a just man" (ut fidelis . . . ut fortis . . . ut iustus).[30] These, however, are only some of the additional virtues that Ambrose finds in Abraham, virtues that must be acquired in the course of Abraham's moral instruction as a convert. As we will see shortly, there also are others.

But, Ambrose maintains, Abraham possesses faith from the start. This is not a virtue that he has to learn; it is inborn. Ambrose understands Abraham's faith less as an epistemic state, the assent to particular theological propositions as true, than as complete and unquestioning obedience to God's commands, however novel, bizarre, or apparently self-contradictory they may be and however many hardships they may entail—an obedience that transcends all human loves and commitments. Abraham manifests this faith consistently, from his initial willingness to leave home for a destination as yet undisclosed by God, through his wanderings in foreign and dangerous lands, to its climax in his assent to the sacrifice of Isaac.

---

26. Ibid. 2.1.1; my trans. On Abraham as a convert, see Daniélou, "Abraham dans la tradition chrétienne," 70–71; Berton, "Abraham dans le *De officiis*," 312–13.

27. Ambrose, *De Abr.* 2.6.26; my trans. The emendation is Gori's. The gradual progress of Abraham has been noted by Stenger, "Das Frömmigkeitsbild des hl. Ambrosius," 19–27.

28. Ambrose, *De Ios.* 1.1. On the primacy of Abraham's faith, see Thamin, *Saint Ambroise et la morale chrétienne*, 325; Hahn, *Das wahre Gesetz*, 322–28. On the Western Christian consensus on Abraham, see Daniélou, "Abraham dans la tradition chrétienne," 68–69; Wilken, "The Christianizing of Abraham."

29. Ambrose, *De Abr.* 1.2.3; my trans; see also ibid. 1.2.4, 1.2.6–9, 1.3.21, 1.4.27–29, 1.5.32.

30. Ibid. 1.2.4; my trans. Noting Abraham's justice are Berton, "Abraham dans le *De officiis*," 318–19; Pizzolato, "Una società cristiana alle prese con un testo radicale," 277–93; both emphasize the point that Abraham goes well beyond justice as *suum cuique tribuere*, accepting self-sacrifice and the relief of the sufferings of others.

This basic feature of Abraham's psychology has been interpreted as Philonic,[31] but there is a considerable gap between Philo's Abraham and Ambrose's. For Philo, Abraham's chief virtue is not trust in God but zeal for piety.[32] He is exemplary because he shows that the law of God is compatible with the law of nature.[33] He leaves his native land because he is a model contemplative whose soul must leave his body behind; he shows that the contemplative life is the consummation of virtue.[34] Not tied to a particular earthly abode, Abraham is a citizen of the ideal cosmopolis.[35] Philo does not see Abraham's departure from Chaldea as a test of his faith, and he treats Abraham and his activities primarily on an allegorical level.

Still, Philo regards Abraham as pursuing the good through teaching;[36] and for Ambrose as well all of Abraham's virtues except faith are acquired and must be learned. As Ambrose says of Abraham, "In the beginning, even he was not perfect" (in principio et ipse inperfectior).[37] In his first educational exercise, Abraham must reject the gods of Chaldea, his native land, and substitute monotheism, the worship of the unseen God, for the Chaldeans, in addition to being polytheists, identified their gods with the stars, a confusion between the Creator and the creation. On this point, Ambrose and Philo are decidedly in accord. But Ambrose goes beyond Philo, noting that, although God is invisible, Abraham comes to "see" and to "know" God—but only after he sets aside Chaldean astronomy: "Scripture thus teaches that Abraham could see God only after he abandoned the observations of the stars" (Hoc ergo scriptura docet, quia Abraham stellarum obseruatione dimigrans deum uidit).[38]

Abandoning Chaldean theology is part and parcel of abandoning pagan religious beliefs and practices more generally. One such practice, which the ancient Jews shared with their Gentile neighbors and which diaspora Judaism and Christianity abandoned, was animal sacrifice. Ambrose is delighted to

---

31. Berton, "Abraham dans le *De officiis*," 313.

32. Philo, *On Abraham* 13.60–14.67, 17.77, 18.85; although Philo does refer to Abraham's faith at 45.262–46.276.

33. Ibid. 1.4–6.

34. Philo, *On the Migration of Abraham* 1.1–7.33, 8.36–42; idem, *On Abraham* 18.88; idem, *Questions and Answers on Genesis* 4.21, 4.48, 4.138.

35. Philo, *Questions and Answers on Genesis* 3.39.

36. Philo, *On Abraham* 11.52.

37. Ambrose, *De Abr.* 1.3.12; Tomkinson trans., 12. See also ibid. 1.2.4, 2.6.26.

38. Ibid. 2.3.8–9; the quotation is at 2.3.9; my trans. Cf. Philo, *On Abraham* 15.68–72; idem, *On the Migration of Abraham* 33.184–36.197, 39.219–222; idem, *Questions and Answers on Genesis* 3.1.

note that, at the first altar Abraham erects to God, as with the sacrifice of the priest Melchizedek, no animals are offered—types of Christian worship, Christian priesthood, and of Christ, the one true offering to come.[39] But then Ambrose has to confront the animal sacrifices that Abraham offers later— worse yet, at God's command—which involve splitting in two a heifer, a nanny goat, and a ram, as well as sacrificing birds in one piece. Ambrose's handling of this difficult passage follows Philo closely. Both authors are concerned with objectors to this text who argue that Abraham, like the pagans, split the first three animals offered so that he could examine their entrails for the purpose of divination. Both Ambrose and Philo repeatedly deny this charge in very strong terms, and both interpret the animals and the way in which Abraham offers them in elaborate allegorical accounts explaining how the animals represent different parts of the created universe, the elements, the geographical subdivisions of the earth, and various human faculties. Ambrose adds a moral and etymological analysis of the animals as well.[40]

Another major subdivision of paganism that Abraham must abandon is the false learning represented by "Egypt." This is one of the major reasons why Ambrose's Abraham must pass through and then leave Egypt; another is that these events are a type of the Israelites' later sojourn in Egypt and escape from that land under the leadership of Moses. As we have noted above, what Egypt signifies for Ambrose is everything with which he disagrees in the Greek philosophical tradition.[41] Egypt is by no means identifiable with philosophy as such, an evident fact, considering Ambrose's acceptance of a number of philosophical teachings from a variety of schools as correct and as compatible with Christianity. Here Ambrose's accent differs notably from Philo's. While Philo identifies Egypt with sophistry, a point with which Ambrose agrees, Philo also identifies Egypt with the school disciplines, disciplines that Ambrose finds unproblematic. Philo's primary definition of Egypt, however, is sensuality, luxury, and attachment to the body, a notion that Ambrose does not emphasize.[42]

If Abraham has to learn monotheism, and the distinction between admissible and inadmissible Greek philosophical teachings, he also has to learn

---

39. Ambrose, *De Abr.* 1.3.16, 2.3.10.
40. Ibid. 2.7.39, 2.8.50–59; cf. Philo, *Questions and Answers on Genesis* 3.3, 3.8.
41. Ambrose, *De Abr.* 1.4.31, 2.10.73; for the typological reference, see ibid. 1.9.62–65.
42. Philo, *On Abraham* 21.103–22.107; idem, *Questions and Answers on Genesis* 3.16, 3.20–25, 3.33, 3.35.

monogamy and marital chastity.[43] His problem here is Hagar again. Her importance as a marker in sexual ethics is just as salient as her identity as false Egyptian wisdom. In this area, Ambrose's exegetical assignment is complicated not only by the marital conventions of the ancient Near East but also by those of Roman law, which permitted prostitution, concubinage, and the sexual use of slaves by their masters, and which also drew a sharp distinction between the status and inheritance rights of free-born children, the offspring of a legitimate wife, "as we accept according to our law" (et nos hunc morem accepimus),[44] and the offspring of slaves, who inherited nothing but their mothers' servile status irrespective of the status of their fathers.

As Ambrose presents it, the Hagar episode is rich with lessons on marital ethics. He in no sense denies Abraham's relationship with Hagar: the fact that they cohabit, that he has a son by her, and that he later sends mother and son away. The patriarch, he notes, is not made of rarer stuff than we are; he does not, initially, breathe a purer air; he is a man subject to the frailties common to human nature as well as an example of one who eventually overcomes them.[45] Basically, Ambrose argues, Abraham prefers the marriage bed to his relationship with Hagar, and he agrees to sleep with her only at the insistence of his barren wife, Sarah. In urging him to do so, Sarah, for her part, is willing to cede her own private rights as a wife for the sake of the public good; she acts the part of a "well-disposed wife" (uxori bonae cordi").[46] The key point that Ambrose wants to make, in assessing the motivations of Abraham and Sarah alike, was their shared view that he needs to sire offspring, which exculpates his infidelity to his wife's bed. As Ambrose puts it, "The merit of performing a duty to the public excuses an individual wrong" (Et ideo publici muneris gratia priuatam culpam praetexuit).[47]

This episode, Ambrose goes on to argue, conveys lessons for Christian husbands, wives, and concubines alike.[48] Christian husbands, he insists, have exactly the same marital responsibilities as wives. A single standard of marital

---

43. Scholars who have flagged this aspect of Abraham's conversion include Stenger, "Das Frömmigkeitsbild des hl. Ambrosius," 3; Berton, "Abraham est-il un modèle?" 353–54, 359; Satterlee, *Ambrose of Milan's Method,* 76–77.

44. Ambrose, *De Abr.* 2.11.89; my trans.

45. Ibid. 1.4.22.

46. Ibid. 1.4.24; my trans. As Clark, *Reading Renunciation,* 157, notes, John Chrysostom also argues for Sarah's righteousness in this connection, but not her public spirit.

47. Ambrose, *De Abr.* 1.4.24; my trans.

48. Ibid. 1.4.22–27. Noted by Chadwick, *The Church in Ancient Society,* 357.

fidelity prevails for Christians, and husbands must conform to it. Here we should note that in Roman law adultery (*adulterium*) was regarded as a crime gender-specific to women. A different term, *stuprum,* was applied to the illegal sexual activities of men; and the illegalities in their case were not isomorphic with those of women. Ambrose is well aware of this distinction and seeks to annihilate it, extending the sanctions of adultery to husbands as well as to wives. As he puts it, "Every *stuprum* is adultery; nor is it lawful for the man what is unlawful for the woman" (Omne stuprum adulterium est, nec uiro licet quod mulieri non licet).[49] Ambrose likewise applies the term *adulterium* to the remarriage of a man who divorces his wife and takes another, stating that such behavior, which is perfectly legitimate in Roman law, "is illegal" (non licet) for Christians. He attacks those men among his *competentes* who think that they have a right to act in this way: "This crime is more serious than adultery, which is a sin for which you should not think that you can invoke the authority of the law" (crimen est adulterii hoc grauius; quod putas peccato tuo auctoritatem lege quaerendam).[50] On this issue, then, Ambrose acknowledges what Roman law permits, and he adjures his audience to obey a higher law. He reminds the *competentes* that they are soon to be baptized. Whatever their past delicts in this department of human behavior may have been, they will now have to live according to a new and more rigorous standard: "You committed adultery as a Gentile; you committed it as a catechumen. It is forgiven you; it is remitted by baptism. Go, and see that you sin no more" (Fecisti gentilis adulterium, fecisti catechumenus: ignoscitur tibi, remittitur per baptismum, uade et post haec uide non pecces).[51]

If husbands have much to learn from the Hagar episode, so also do wives and concubines. If, indeed, husbands have consorted with concubines, wives,

---

49. Ambrose, *De Abr.* 1.4.25; my trans. On the Roman legal terminology, see Berger, *Encyclopedic Dictionary of Roman Law,* s.v. *adulterium, stuprum.* The few studies that treat Ambrose and Roman law confine themselves to church-state relations or to civil law in relation to natural law and devote no attention to his references to private or criminal law in the patriarch treatises. See, for example, Maes, *La loi naturelle selon Ambroise de Milan;* Hebein, "St. Ambrose and Roman Law"; Gaudemet, "Droit séculier et droit de l'église chez Ambroise"; idem, *Le droit romain,* 78–90; Lenox-Conyngham, "Law in St. Ambrose"; Sargenti and Siola, eds., *Normativa imperiale e diritto romano.*

50. Ambrose, *De Abr.* 1.7.59; my trans. Clark, *Reading Renunciation,* 236–37, also notes Ambrose's strictures against divorce and his urging his hearers to go beyond what Roman law permits in this area.

51. Ambrose, *De Abr.* 1.4.23; Tomkinson trans., 13. I have altered her spelling and punctuation slightly.

unlike Sarah, should not be jealous; while concubines who are slave women, if they bear children while their mistresses remain childless, should not be insolent. If they are, the husband is likely to take the part of his wife, as Abraham does.[52] In any case, insolent or not, Hagar's fate is sealed by the fact that Abraham must repudiate her and Ishmael in favor of Sarah, his only legitimate wife, who prefigures the church, the mother-to-be of Isaac, the son of promise, who prefigures Christ. For their part, Hagar and Ishmael prefigure the synagogue.[53]

While typology combines with the ethics of marital chastity and the rejection of "Egypt" in explaining Abraham's repudiation of Hagar and Ishmael, in *De Abraham* Ambrose confronts other potential embarrassments flowing from the tension between Roman concubinage, which he rejects, and Roman inheritance law, which he supports. In one salient case he deals with the problem by invoking the tactic of strategic omission. The book of Genesis reports that after Sarah's death Abraham takes another concubine, Keturah, by whom he has six sons (Gen 25:1–5). Although as a widower he is free to marry, it was apparently not yet the moment in salvation history when it was appropriate for a patriarch to practice exogamy. Just before his death, in planning his legacy, Abraham assembles all his children and distinguishes sharply between Isaac, on the one hand, and Ishmael and his six half-brothers by Keturah, on the other. To Isaac, his one legitimate son, Abraham bequeaths all he has; to the sons of his concubines, he merely gives gifts before sending them away (Gen 25:5–6). Ambrose does not include any of these events in *De Abraham*. The full weight of illegitimacy must rest on the shoulders of Ishmael, as the binary opposite of Isaac, the next bearer of the covenant with God, through whom Abraham's descendants will become a great nation, as numberless as the sands of the sea. While "by Isaac as the legitimate son, we may understand the legitimate lord Jesus" (per Isaac legitimum filium illum uerum legitimum possumus intelligere dominum Iesum), we should also understand him as the ancestor of the line of Jesse from which Jesus descended.[54]

Another troubling aspect of sexual ethics with which Ambrose must grapple in *De Abraham* is the question of why behavior forbidden in later ages was permitted in the age of the patriarchs. In addition to concubinage and

52. Ibid. 1.4.26.

53. Ibid. 1.2.20, 1.4.28, 1.4.31, 1.8.71–72, 1.8.74–1.9.85, 2.10.72–75, 2.10.85–86.

54. Ibid. 1.3.19–21; the quotation is at 1.3.20; Tomkinson trans., 11. See also ibid. 1.4.31, 1.7.61–65.

polygamy, there is the incestuous union of Lot's daughters with their father. *De Abraham* has to do double duty here. Ambrose wants to explain these sexual practices in a manner applicable not only to Abraham and his contemporaries but also later to Jacob, who engages both in polygamy with legitimate wives and in concubinage. In *De Jacob* Ambrose offers no historical or ethical justification for that patriarch's sexual morés. There, in the single passage in which he refers to that topic, he immediately, and uncharacteristically, moves to an allegorical interpretation. Leah represents the synagogue; Rachel represents the church.[55] Here too, in *De Jacob,* Ambrose practices the art of strategic omission, never mentioning Jacob's two concubines, Zilpah and Bilhah, the servants of his wives, who bear four of his twelve sons (Gen 30:3–13; 35:23–26). Nor does Ambrose treat any of Jacob's sons as different in legal status from each other or as differing in their inheritance rights. To be sure, not all of the sons receive the same legacies. But Ambrose presents these legacies as appropriate indices of the moral character of each son or of Jacob's ability to foresee the future history of the twelve tribes of Israel of which these sons are regarded, equally, as the legitimate progenitors.[56]

The rationale for the patriarchs' multiple consorts and for the behavior of Lot's daughters at which Ambrose arrives in *De Abraham* is a historical one, an explanation which, by implication, rationalizes departures from monogamy on the part of other Old Testament worthies.[57] Ambrose makes two points. First, the age of the patriarchs was close in time to the age of the great flood that had depopulated the world except for Noah and his descendants. The patriarchs take multiple consorts, not out of lust, but out of a recognized duty to repopulate the world. Second, the patriarchs lived before the law of Moses. Where there is no law, there is no sin. We should not impute guilt to the patriarchs for behavior that was not yet forbidden by God. Taking a cue from Philo, Origen, and John Chrysostom, Ambrose invokes a similar rationale to exculpate Lot's

---

55. Ambrose, *De Iacob et uita beata* 5.25, ed. Schenkl, trans. Palla.

56. Ambrose, *De patriarchis*, ed. Schenkl, trans. Banterle. On this work and on Ambrose's sources for it, see Argyle, "Joseph the Patriarch in Patristic Teaching"; Hollander, *Joseph as an Ethical Model;* Hollander and De Jonge, *Testaments of the Twelve Patriarchs: A Commentary.*

57. Ambrose, *De Abr.* 1.3.19–1.4.24. Noted by Berton, "Abraham est-il un modèle?" 363–73. Ambrose does try to bring the concubines of Leah and Rachel under the umbrella of the patriarch's consorting with women other than his wives in order to have offspring in *De Abr.* 1.4.24, although in Leah's case she has already borne children, a point he ignores.

daughters.[58] These daughters had been virgins, although betrothed, before their family left Sodom. However, their fiancés, not giving credence to Lot's warning about the impending punishment of their city, remain there and perish when Sodom falls. So disastrous is the destruction of Sodom and Gomorrah that Lot's daughters labor under the misapprehension that Lot is the sole remaining male person left on earth. So their post-diluvian and post-Sodom reproductive zeal explains and excuses their incest. The reasoning that the sisters offer to each other is that they are obliged to conceive offspring by their father lest the human race perish altogether. What guilt exists, Ambrose suggests, rests with their fiancés, a point that both Philo and Origen omit. Ambrose's implication is that, had the fiancés fled along with Lot's family, they would have duly married Lot's daughters, who would then have been able to contribute to the world's repopulation within the bonds of matrimony. As it is, lack of faith on the part of the disbelieving fiancés, which leads to their own deaths and pushes Lot's daughters into incest, can be compared with the guilt and punishment of Lot's wife for failing to heed Lot's warning not to look back. As an aside, Ambrose capitalizes here on the moral lesson to the *competentes* taught by Lot's wife: "If you want to escape, do not look backward, but forward" (Si uis ergo et tu euadare, ne respicias retro, sed ante te).[59] As for Lot himself, Ambrose exculpates him of incest because his daughters make him drunk; he is unaware of what he is doing when he sleeps with them. Still, his story points to the dangers of drink.[60] With these exegetical knots unraveled, Ambrose stresses to his *competentes* that they, today, can offer no similar justifications for failing to observe Christian standards of sexual ethics.

Chastity is clearly a theme to which Ambrose devotes sustained attention in *De Abraham*. In contrast to Philo, who sees the body as a bond or a fetter alien to the sage, from which he must detach himself as fully as possible,[61] Ambrose sees marriage, not abstinence, as the sexual norm for Abraham and the other patriarchs. Important as it is in its own right, and vital as it is for him

---

58. Ambrose, *De Abr.* 1.6.54; cf. Philo, *Questions and Answers on Genesis* 4.56; Origen, *Homily on Abraham* 5.4 in *Homilies on Genesis and Exodus*, trans. Heine. This view is shared by John Chrysostom, as is noted by Clark, *Reading Renunciation*, 156–57.

59. Ambrose, *De Abr.* 1.6.55; my trans.

60. Ibid. 1.6.57–58.

61. Philo, *Questions and Answers on Genesis* 3.10–11, 3.45, 4.11, 4.77.

to explain to his *competentes* what will now be required of them, he sees in chastity an ethical function that goes well beyond governing what transpires in—or outside of—the marriage bed. For according to Ambrose, chastity gives rise to a number of other virtues. These include temperance, modesty, selflessness, moderation in the use of food and drink, and the power to set aside dissolution, petulance, and insolence. Chastity inspires the vigilant attention needed to discipline the self against these and other temptations that would draw the aspirant to virtue away from the right path.[62] This observation suggests that, by practicing moderation and unselfishness in the use of marital sex, a Christian will be able to develop moderation with respect to other physical needs and with respect to the virtues of the soul as well.

While marital chastity is thus one of Ambrose's main concerns as a virtue that Abraham must acquire, it seems acceptable to him, as well as to Moses, the putative author of Genesis, for Abraham to place the chastity of his wife Sarah at risk both in Egypt and in the land of Abimelech through which they pass. In Egypt, Abraham dissimulates concerning Sarah's status, claiming that she is his sister, not his wife. He reasons that, if the Pharaoh knows that she is married, he will put Abraham to death in order to marry her himself. As he had envisioned, the Egyptians, impressed by Sarah's beauty and demeanor, do present her, passed off as Abraham's sister, to the Pharaoh. Abraham's reasoning thus seems flawed on two levels. First, his lie does not prevent the Pharaoh from taking Sarah into his household. Second, given God's promise that Sarah is to become the matriarch of the people of Israel, traveling with her husband to the land that God will show them, the presumption is that God will watch over Abraham and Sarah during their wanderings, protecting them from any *contretemps* that would jeopardize these outcomes.[63] Abraham's dissimulation thus suggests that he lacked full confidence in God, which stands in sharp contrast with faith, his paramount virtue.

Despite its initial failure in Egypt, Abraham invokes the same stratagem in the vain effort to dissuade Abimelech from taking Sarah into his household when the couple arrives in that ruler's territory, where Abraham acknowledges that Sarah is indeed his half-sister as well as his wife. While both rulers are thus prepared to marry Sarah, they both discover that she is already married and return her to Abraham unsullied. This development suggests that Abra-

---

62. Ambrose, *De Abr.* 2.4.17–18.

63. A point flagged by Berton, "Abraham est-il un modèle?" 353–54, and Clark, *Reading Renunciation*, 157–58, following John Chrysostom.

ham's assumption that the rulers would put him to death in order to marry Sarah is without foundation. Without pausing to comment on whether Abraham's reasoning is sound and whether his dissimulations are either effective or justifiable, Ambrose moves swiftly to the moral he wants to draw from these episodes: although the rulers in question were Gentiles, they knew that adultery was forbidden by the "natural law" (ius naturae).[64] This conclusion offers yet another opportunity to impress upon his *competentes* the fact that they have no excuse for practicing adultery: "And so, you who are aspiring to the grace of baptism, and striving for faith, learn the sober lesson of chastity" (Discite enim qui ad gratiam baptismatis tenditis uelut quidam fidei candidati continentiae disciplinam sobriam).[65]

While Abraham's acquisition of theological correctness and sexual propriety receive much attention in *De Abraham*, the patriarch develops and displays a host of other virtues as well. Sages seek to redeem others. In Abraham's case, he saves his nephew Lot, who becomes embroiled in a war among the kings of his region and is led captive to Sodom. The fact that Abraham goes to war on Lot's behalf reflects his courage and his willingness to undertake risks. It also suggests that Abraham possesses considerable military prowess, since the 318 men he takes with him into battle are vastly outnumbered. But this small band are of the elect, showing that the righteous will triumph over larger forces. The number 318 also had a traditional Trinitarian or Christological reference. In any case, Abraham humbly attributes his victory to God, displays magnanimity to the vanquished, a lack of worldly ambition despite his military success, and generosity to Melchizedek, to whom he lavishly donates a tenth of his booty at the priest's offering of bread and wine in celebration of Abraham's victory.[66] Abraham saves Lot again when God destroys Sodom and Gomorrah.[67] He tries to intercede with God in order to save Sodom as well, mercifully if unsuccessfully.[68] Abraham is thus a model for the later saints, "for their faith

---

64. Ambrose, *De Abr.* 1.2.6–9, 1.7.59, 2.4.15–18. The quotation is at 1.2.8; my trans. Noted by Berton, "Abraham est-il un modèle?" 353–54.

65. Ambrose, *De Abr.* 1.7.59; my trans.

66. Ibid. 1.3.14–15, 2.7.42. On the significance of the number 318 and its equation in Ambrose and his predecessors with the cross of Christ or the Trinity, or with the number of council fathers at Nicaea in 325, or as an anagram of the name of Jesus, see Rivière, "'Trois cent dix-huit'"; he notes that, while Origen was one of Ambrose's sources on this point, he did not follow Origen's lead, 357–61.

67. Ambrose, *De Abr.* 1.2.17–1.4.22, 1.6.53–55, 2.8.45–47.

68. Ibid. 1.6.46–48.

preserves us and their righteousness protects us from destruction" (illorum etenim nos fides seruat, illorum iustitia ab excidio defendit).[69]

Abraham's would-be intercession on behalf of Sodom can be linked to another episode in the patriarch's life that Ambrose ignores, unaccountably, although it illustrates the patriarch's virtuous efforts to engage in peaceable relations with his neighbors even when provoked. The book of Genesis relates that, after restoring Sarah to her husband, Abimelech makes a pact with Abraham in which they agree to deal honestly with each other in the future. But subsequent to that agreement, servants of Abimelech fill in some wells that Abraham had dug. Although Abraham is clearly the offended party here, he diplomatically arranges a peaceful settlement of the matter with Abimelech, sealing it by giving him gifts (Gen 21:22–32). This gesture could easily have been cited by Ambrose as an illustration of Abraham's observance of the sage's four principles of behavior with respect to his neighbor offered by the natural philosophers, which he cites early in the treatise. But he does not do so, omitting this passage of the biblical text in his account of Abraham's life.

Another virtue that Ambrose highlights in Abraham is his hospitality. In developing this theme, Ambrose distances himself both from Philo and from the classical tradition. While Philo sees Abraham's hospitality as flowing from his piety, he also stresses that Abraham's welcome of the three angelic strangers signifies the fact that Abraham has attained an incorporeal nature.[70] Hospitality, to be sure, was seen as a virtue among the Romans. Cicero, for example, treats it as an expression of dignity that enhances one's esteem and glory; on the other hand, Ambrose treats hospitality as a virtue in its own right, not as a means to the end of worldly reputation. It is rather an expression of kindness, fraternal love, and the duty that any honorable person owes to a stranger, whose physical needs a Christian must supply.[71] Ambrose also treats hospitality as a social obligation that is mandatory and unequivocal. At the same time, he suggests that people in his own day were seeking to shirk this obligation, pleading hard times. In his view, there are no extenuating circumstances whatsoever that excuse Christians from welcoming guests and attend-

69. Ibid. 1.6.48; Tomkinson trans., 25.

70. Philo, *On Abraham* 22.107–23.118; idem, *Questions and Answers on Genesis* 4.8.

71. This contrast is brought out well by Berton, "Abraham dans le *De officiis*," 319–21. The distinction is not noted by other authors who comment on Abraham's hospitality; see Kellner, *Der heilige Ambrosius*, 102; Dassmann, *Die Frömmigkeit des Kirchenvaters Ambrosius*, 20; Vasey, *The Social Ideas in the Works of St. Ambrose*, 47.

ing to their physical needs. We are all guests on this earth, he observes, and so we must welcome those who visit us. Christ, he notes, confirms this Old Testament rule and this contemporary requirement; those who welcome guests, welcome Christ himself.[72]

Both Abraham and Sarah are prompt and gracious in receiving their angelic visitors; their example should be imitated. While preserving her modesty by remaining in her tent, Sarah makes her own important culinary contribution to the entertainment of their guests; in addition, the three loaves of bread she prepares stand for the Trinity.[73] And while Sodom's sins include wantonness and extravagance,[74] the chief moral failing that triggers God's wrath against the city is the Sodomites' violation of the rules of hospitality. They seek to entertain the angelic emissaries who have just visited Abraham and Sarah in order to subject them to sexual abuse.[75] By contrast, Lot invites them to his own house, even offering them his virgin—and betrothed—daughters as an inducement. As we have seen, Ambrose places a high valuation on chastity, and he would certainly agree that it is a father's sacred duty to guard the honor of his daughters. But it is better for Lot to propose even this extreme gesture of hospitality than to allow the visitors to be forced "to sin against nature" (aduersus naturam delinquere).[76]

Prudential household management and marital and filial piety also mark Abraham's dealings with his servants and relatives. Highly illustrative of the virtue of prudence is Abraham's handling of the division of land with Lot. It is their respective servants, Ambrose notes, who provoke dissent. In order to forestall a falling-out with his kinsman, Abraham, the more powerful of the two, divides the land and then invites Lot, the less powerful, to choose the portion he prefers. Abraham thereby preempts the possibility of future objections on Lot's part. As we have already had occasion to observe, Ambrose thinks that in making moral decisions reason chooses in the light of what is intrinsically good and also in the light of what is useful.[77] Abraham's settlement

72. Ambrose, *De Abr.* 1.5.32–44.

73. Ibid. 1.5.38. John Chrysostom also praises Sarah's hospitality, as is noted by Clark, *Reading Renunciation*, 183–84.

74. Ambrose, *De Abr.* 1.3.14, 1.6.52.

75. Ibid. 1.6.44–53.

76. Ibid. 1.6.52; my trans.

77. See chapter 3, 36, and n. 17 above. Philo also praises Abraham for his good judgment in dealing with other men but omits filial piety and the norm of the good and the useful; cf. Philo, *On Abraham* 37.208–41.244.

of the land dispute with Lot is an exercise in utilitarian conflict resolution before the fact worthy of John Stuart Mill.[78] Abraham also displays prudence in selecting a burial plot when Sarah dies. He manifests temperance in his mourning for her as well as "marital affection" (maritalis adfectus), the term of art in Roman law denoting the fidelity, honor, and respect owed to a legitimate spouse with whom one intends to procreate legitimate heirs, as distinct from the attitude one might have toward a more casual partner.[79]

Abraham takes seriously his paternal obligations toward his son Isaac as well. "As is the duty of a good father" (Itaque quod boni est patris),[80] Abraham seeks a suitable bride for Isaac. It is important for Isaac, as for Abraham himself, to avoid exogamy, a point that inspires Ambrose to adjure his *competentes* to avoid mixed marriages. So Abraham sends a trusted servant to find a suitable spouse for Isaac from among his own kin back in Chaldea. The servant's punctilious execution of this charge reflects Abraham's ability to train his household staff well. Ambrose calls this point expressly to the attention of the *patresfamiliae* among his *competentes:* "Observe, now, the virtue of a good head of household, and consider first what his responsibility is, and to whom he should entrust it, so that you, too, may train your servants to bestow paternal affection on your children and perform their duties" (Aduerte nunc uirtutes boni patris familias et considera primum quod munus et cui mandet, ut et tu ita instituas seruulos ut liberis tuis paternum adfectum deferant, officia exsequantur).[81]

Abraham instructs his servant that Isaac's future wife will be recognizable by her kindness and generosity in offering water to him and his mounts, suggesting that parents should seek virtue in the spouses they select for their children.[82] We have seen that hospitality is a virtue that Ambrose values highly. He does not specifically ascribe this virtue to Rebecca by name, although she certainly manifests it. While Ambrose notes that she receives Abraham's servant courteously at the well, he omits the passage in Genesis in which she takes the initiative in offering the servant lodging for himself and stabling for his mounts at her family home (Gen 22:25). This omission is strange since it sup-

---

78. Ambrose, *De Abr.* 1.3.10–13.
79. Ibid. 1.9.80; my trans. Noted by Gori, intro. to his ed. and trans. of *De Abr.*, 113 n. 1; see Berger, *Encyclopedic Dictionary of Roman Law*, s.v. *affectio maritalis*.
80. Ambrose, *De Abr.* 1.9.81; Tomkinson trans., 39.
81. Ibid. 1.9.83; Tomkinson trans., 40. I have altered her wording slightly.
82. Ibid. 1.9.87–88.

presses a dimension of Rebecca's character that would have been useful to Ambrose's argument in *De Abraham* and, *a fortiori*, in *De Isaac* as well.

As a prudent earnest of the good faith of the marriage offer, Abraham has provided his servant with valuable jewelry and clothing as gifts to Rebecca. In the Septuagint, this jewelry consists of bracelets and a nose ring (Gen 24:22; 24:30; 24:47). But, presumably because the nose ring would have been regarded as barbaric in first-century Alexandria, Philo discreetly transforms the nose ring into earrings. Origen agrees with Philo, and Ambrose follows suit, despite what he finds in the Septuagint text, nose rings being equally out of fashion in fourth-century Milan. Unlike Philo and Origen, however, he hastens to explain to his female *competentes* that this gift of jewelry does not give them license to rush to the marketplace and stock up on items of personal adornment. For, he explains, the jewelry given to Rebecca signifies her virtues: the bracelets stand for her willingness to do good deeds, while the earrings stand for the openness of her ears to receive true doctrine.[83]

Rebecca also possesses the virtue of filial piety. As Ambrose presents the decision to accept Abraham's marriage proposal on behalf of Isaac, Rebecca plays no role in it at all. She defers entirely to her elders, he says. At this juncture Ambrose quotes the one literary passage that he regards as having a positive ethical content, Euripides' *Andromache* 987–988, where the poet makes the same point about maidenly passivity and self-abnegation with respect to the parents' choice of a daughter's husband. Ambrose cites the Euripides text in Greek, also supplying a Latin translation.[84] Consistent as it may have been with Roman law, and gratifying as it may have been to the ears of the *patresfamiliae* among Ambrose's *competentes*, in making this point he chooses to ignore both the text of Genesis (24:57–58) and Philo.[85] For in that biblical passage, and seconded by Philo, Rebecca's elders specifically invite her response to the marriage proposal. And she, just as expressly, gives her firm consent. It is on the basis of Rebecca's free choice that her mother and brother agree to the union. Here, in supporting the Roman legal view of how marriages should be made

83. Ibid. 1.9.87, 1.9.89. Cf. Philo, *Questions and Answers on Genesis* 4.104–110, 4.118; Origen, *Homilies on Genesis* 10.4.

84. Ambrose, *De Abr.* 1.9.91. Other literary references in this treatise are mere *scholia* with no doctrinal point, as with Vergil, *Ec.* 1.45; Vergil, *Georg.* 4.208; Homer, *Odd.* 14.258 (untrans.) at *De Abr.* 1.9.82, 2.1.4, and 2.10.68, respectively. The Homer citation, dealing with the navigability of the Nile, is also found in Philo, *Questions and Answers on Genesis* 3.16.

85. Ambrose, *De Abr.* 1.9.92. Cf. Philo, *Questions and Answers on Genesis* 4.132–133.

and whose consent was necessary in making them, Ambrose misses an important opportunity. For in the next patriarch treatise, *De Isaac*, Rebecca's moral education is to be the theme. She would not be educable unless she freely wanted to be. Her free will, a topic soon to receive increasing attention from Ambrose in the patriarch treatises, is a critical factor in the process. And he has already described her, in accounting for the nose ring turned into earrings, as possessing ears open to instruction. Furthermore, he interprets Rebecca's acceptance of the marriage proposal typologically as Christ's call to the nations to enter the church; she represents those who respond positively to this call,[86] an act that also requires free will. Instead, Ambrose gives priority to his own chosen delineation of Rebecca as a model of virginal reticence. On her arrival in Canaan, when she approaches Isaac, she puts on a veil. Ambrose sees this event as an opportunity to address the unmarried girls among his *competentes*: "So, virgins, learn to cultivate modesty and not to show yourselves to strangers with your head uncovered" (Discite ergo, uirgines, quemadmodum seruetis uerecundiam, nec intecto capite prodeatis ante extraneos), neatly linking the theme of modesty with the fact that Roman brides were veiled, a practice perpetuated by the early church.[87] In any case, the mission to Rebecca having been concluded successfully and his son's wedding duly celebrated, Abraham can die in peace, his duties as a father consummated.[88]

Important as these other virtues are, it is still faith that Ambrose returns to again and again as Abraham's outstanding moral attribute. While Abraham manifests faith from the beginning of his story, not having had to learn it, and while he displays this faith through all the tribulations he experiences, including the repeatedly deferred divine promise of a son by Sarah, two events stand out as the most paradigmatic test cases of Abraham's faith. The first is his acceptance of circumcision as a necessary sign of his membership, and that of his male household, in the covenanted people of God, a totally new idea, as Ambrose, unlike Philo, presents it. Outlandish as this rite may have appeared to Abraham, he accepts it without hesitation, even though, as Ambrose acknowledges, circumcision was not strictly necessary in Abraham's own personal case. Ambrose does agree that circumcision is important for the Israelites.

---

86. Ambrose, *De Abr.* 1.9.90, 1.9.92–93; noted by Argal Echarri, "Isaac y Rebeca," 138–40. Abraham's servant stands for the apostle who brings the Good News, *De Abr.* 1.9.94.

87. Ibid. 1.9.93; my trans. On the veiling of Roman brides, see Gori, intro. to his ed. and trans. of *De Abr.*, 125 n. 23.

88. Ambrose, *De Abr.* 1.9.94.

While circumcision is physical, its effects are also spiritual. It promotes chastity and removes vicious desires, thus testifying to the fact that both the body and the soul are to be saved. While the other Israelites may have needed circumcision, however, Abraham did not. For he was called by God and granted the covenant before he was circumcised. To be sure, Ambrose holds that circumcision is perfected, in the Christian dispensation, by Christ's sacrifice of his whole body and by the baptism without which his *competentes* cannot be saved. Nonetheless, he sees the rite as problematic for Abraham himself, and his acceptance of it as a major test of faith which the patriarch passes with flying colors.[89]

By all accounts, however, the climax and the *locus classicus* for Abraham as our father in faith is the sacrifice of Isaac.[90] In ordering him to sacrifice Isaac, the long-awaited child of promise, born to the aged and barren Sarah by a miracle, and the necessary link between Abraham and the many descendants God has told him that he will have, God seems to be acting at cross purposes to his own promises and to his own divine plan. On the face of it, the command appears to make no sense at all, to be counterintuitive and counterproductive. Another problem is that God apparently expects Isaac to be complicit in his own execution despite his own awareness of the role he has been chosen to play in the covenant. Ambrose observes that all the tests that Abraham has met already, each more difficult than the last, have strengthened his faith and enabled him to overcome the ultimate temptation to spare his son. It is a double temptation: the temptation to put his paternal love for Isaac first, and the temptation to question the coherence of God and his plans for Abraham and his descendants. Ambrose acknowledges the point that God never intends that Isaac should actually be killed. In the end, God provides the sacrificial ram before Abraham's knife can fall. But Abraham does not know this. Nonetheless, he responds to God's command without question and without hesitation.

---

89. Ibid. 1.4.29–31, 2.11.79. Cf. Philo, *Questions and Answers on Genesis* 3.47–48, who, while agreeing that circumcision curbs lust and has a spiritual significance, also observes that it is a hygienic practice used widely for that reason by African and Near Eastern peoples.

90. Ambrose, *De Abr.* 1.8.66–79. Cf. Philo, *On Abraham* 32.167–176, 33.177, 35.199, 36. 200–207, who, unlike Ambrose, finds it necessary to distinguish the sacrifice of Isaac from child sacrifice as practiced by some pagans, who emphasizes Abraham's Stoic equanimity more than his zeal, and who allegorizes the event as a case of the mind transcending the passions. Cavadini, "Exegetical Transformations," offers another account of Ambrose's departures from Philo and also from Origen.

Next, as his behavior on the day he sets forth to the site of the sacrifice indicates, having committed himself to obedience to God, Abraham carries out what needs to be done with dispatch and zeal. He rises at dawn and is ready to do the hard work necessary in preparation for the sacrifice, not delegating it to the servants who accompany him and Isaac. When the party approaches the sacrifice site, Abraham dissimulates with his servants: "He spoke deceitfully to his servants" (Captiose autem loquebatur cum seruulis).[91] This is a deception that Ambrose finds acceptable. By telling the servants that "we" will return from the sacrifice, Abraham obscures the fact that he thinks that he will be the only one returning. He does so justifiably, so that his servants will not know what is about to happen and will not try to prevent him from following God's orders. Christological typology is involved here, embracing both Isaac, the intended sacrifice, son of a miraculous birth, carrying the wood on which he is to be immolated on his own shoulders, as well as the ram, the lamb of God that serves as his substitute.[92] When Abraham has passed this ultimate test, he receives God's third and final confirmation of the covenant.

When Isaac asks Abraham where the animal for the sacrifice is, Abraham answers that God will provide. His words prove prophetic in the short run. But in a wider sense, Ambrose wants to develop the theme of Abraham as a prophet in Bk. 2 of De Abraham.[93] Abraham's story forecasts a number of future events beyond his own personal development; he also prophesies concerning the later history of the Israelites as well as concerning the Christian revelation to come. In sharp contrast with Origen, who disavows any interest in biblical history as such,[94] Ambrose yokes history and typology together. And while he says in the prologue to Bk. 2 that he is now moving on to the "higher sense" (altiora sensum) of persons and events in Abraham's life "in order to explain the progress of ideal virtue" (uirtutis formas . . . processum explicare) so as "to reveal the mysteries of the prophetic Scriptures" (ad reue-

---

91. Ambrose, De Abr. 1.8.71; Tomkinson trans., 36.

92. Ibid. 1.8.71–72, 1.8.74, 1.8.77–78, 1.9.85, 2.8.49; noted by Argal Echarri, "Isaac y Rebeca," 132–38.

93. Noted by Stenger, "Das Frömmigkeitsbild des hl. Ambrosius," 27–33; Lazzati, Il valore letterario della esegesi ambrosiano, 72–73; Gori, intro. to his ed. and trans. of De Abr., 19–20; Van der Lof, "The 'Prophet' Abraham," 17–18, 26–27; Jacob, "The Reception of the Origenist Tradition," in Hebrew Bible/Old Testament, 1:692–93.

94. Origen, Homilies on Genesis 10.4: "I have often said already that in these stories history is not being narrated but mysteries are interwoven"; idem, On First Principles 4.2.1–4, 4.2.5–9, 4.3.1–3, 4.3.5, trans. Butterworth.

landa propheticarum scripturarum aenigmata),[95] the "higher senses" do not ignore ethics and history but return to selected events in Abraham's life in order to show that he was a prophet as well as a virtuous man.

The key event in Abraham's life that points ahead is his sojourn in Egypt during the course of his wanderings. Here, Abraham forecasts the subsequent emigration of the Israelites to Egypt, their enslavement there, their liberation by Moses after four generations, and their wanderings in the desert until they reach the promised land. Morally, that liberation forecasts Christ's liberation of us from sin, enabling us to cultivate the four cardinal virtues, which inform and temper each other.[96] Once again, Ambrose brings forward Hagar to stand for the sinful "Egypt" we must set aside, for the synagogue, and now for heresy as well; while Sarah once more stands for the church. Sarah's initial barrenness signifies the fact that the time must be ripe for the coming of Christ. So the wisdom Abraham possesses includes the knowledge of these future events, which is why his story is a sign of the mystery of the church to come.[97]

The second major theme in Bk. 2 of *De Abraham* is the recasting of Abraham as mind, signifying the rational faculty. The emphasis on Abraham as a man of faith in no sense means that he is a fideist who thinks that reason has no contribution to make to the moral and religious life.[98] The very fact that Abraham's project is the governing of the irrational aspect of human nature by the rational, in fact, privileges human reason.[99] Reason helps Abraham overcome both physical temptations, theological and philosophical errors, and mental distress.[100] Once the mind, and through its efforts, the body, have been purified, Abraham shows us that we can attain immortality, which is what the covenant truly signifies: our spiritual regeneration as children of God, who, with face unveiled, can contemplate the splendor of beatitude and the face-to-face encounter with God.[101] The spiritual regeneration and the encounter with God that Abraham enjoys are a function of his moral growth; they are far from the mystical ecstasies of Philo's Abraham.[102] Rather than advocating

---

95. Ambrose, *De Abr.* 2.1.1; my trans.
96. Ibid. 2.9.16–2.10.71.
97. Ibid. 2.6.34, 2.8.48, 2.10.72–77.
98. See, on the other hand, Madec, *Saint Ambroise et la philosophie*, 226, 240.
99. Ambrose, *De Abr.* 2.1.2–2.2.5, 2.6.26, 2.6.28–33.
100. Ibid. 2.3.8, 2.4.13–2.5.19.
101. Ibid. 2.1.3, 2.1.4, 2.2.5, 2.3.8–9.
102. Cf. Philo, *On Abraham* 3.9; idem, *On the Migration of Abraham* 8.36–42.

contemplative exercises, Ambrose advises his *competentes* to go to church daily, to read the Bible, to pray, and to meditate; their objective is a good conscience, not visionary transports.[103] Abraham's travels through dangerous lands signify the fact that we must all confront exposure to evil as we seek to know the good. But we do so as strangers passing through foreign lands, not as immigrants seeking citizenship. For all Christians, life is a pilgrimage; and in this respect, we are all the children of Abraham, whose true citizenship is in heaven.[104]

Ambrose comments on the fact that Abraham became wealthy in lands, flocks, and servants. These possessions signify not worldly wealth but the riches of virtue attained by those who triumph over the temptations that assail even the just. Agreeing with the Stoics, Ambrose maintains that only the sage is truly rich. The lands that Abraham acquires signify the promise of blessedness, the fullness of good deeds. This happy state involves three types of goods: the goods of the body, the goods of the soul, and external goods. The goods of the body are chastity, patience, and temperance. The goods of the soul are prudence and justice, which in turn entail courage. The external, or accidental goods, are the rewards of labor as well as health, beauty, strength, and vigor, which may come and go according to one's age. These principles, Ambrose avers, are shown clearly by the example of Abraham and later by the explicit teachings of the Ten Commandments and the New Testament.[105]

Ambrose also returns, in Bk. 2, to two episodes that he had discussed in Bk. 1 of *De Abraham,* in each case providing them with a somewhat different gloss. The sacrifice of Melchizedek, after Abraham's victory over the kings of Sodom, which he treats from a typological perspective in Bk. 1 as a forecast of the Eucharist, with Melchizedek standing for Christ the celebrant, recurs, with a strictly moral message, in Bk. 2. To be sure, in Bk. 1, Ambrose praises Abraham's generosity in granting a tithe of his booty to Melchizedek. In Bk. 2 he reframes that point. Abraham's generosity now reflects his virtues of unselfishness and lack of worldly ambition, qualities he can manifest because his righteous mind is sustained by grace. He is satisfied with what he has, since virtue is its own reward.[106] Circumcision is also a topic that Ambrose casts in a different light in Bk. 2. There, he describes circumcision as standing even more strongly for the circumcision of the mind and heart. Now, he observes,

103. Ambrose, *De Abr.* 2.5.22.
104. Ibid. 2.4.13, 2.9.61–65.
105. Ibid. 2.5.20–21, 2.7.37–39, 2.10.68–71.
106. Ibid. 2.8.45–49; cf. ibid. 1.3.16–17.

"humankind" and "mind" are equivalent. Hence, this concept of the circumcised mind and heart, purified and freed from all superfluous thoughts and desires, cleansed of luxury and unchastity, applies to persons of both sexes, for Christians. Yet, Ambrose again reminds his *competentes*, even circumcision, so redefined, does not suffice, since no one is saved without baptism.[107]

In his summation, Ambrose states that of all Abraham's attainments, the greatest is wisdom. He has learned how to rise above vice with a "steadfast mind" (mens . . . ualidior), the mark of a sage. His wisdom includes an honest recognition of his personal limitations and the self-knowledge needed for a good conscience, for composure, for prayer, and also for philosophy: "Fittingly rich is he who also enriches the disputations of the philosophers" (Merito diues, qui etiam disputationes philosophorum diuitis facit).[108] Ambrose ends Bk. 2 with a general description of the Christian sage. In all areas, "his moderation should be strict" (acuta sit moderatio).[109] He possesses all the cardinal virtues, with temperance paying particular attention to chastity. He possesses a hospitality of wisdom as well as of goods.[110] Ambrose moves from the declarative to the hortatory mode in his final peroration:

> Moreover, let him . . . know only how to live according to nature, . . . to choose the bond of wisdom alone; through the commandments of God, let him know not to prefer the glory of this age and the inheritance of present praise, and let him sacrifice his advantage on the altars of the Lord. Thus, he will not incur, or fear, the fire of judgment, but rather toil for the rescue of others.

> preterea nesciat nisi secundum naturam uiuere, . . . solius sapientiae praeoptet copulam, mandatis dei saeculi istius gloriam et quandam praesentis laudis hereditatem praeferre nesciat atque ut altaribus domini suas immolet utilitates, ita iudicii ignem non excipiat neque reformidet, sed magis etiam ut alios eripiat elaboret.[111]

---

107. Ibid. 2.11.78–93; the point about baptism occurs at 2.11.82.

108. Ibid. 2.5.19–23, 2.10.77. The quotations are at 2.5.19 and 2.5.23, respectively; Tomkinson trans., 56, 58.

109. Ibid. 2.11.82; my trans. For more on counsels of moderation in *De Abr.*, see ibid. 1.4.26, 1.7.59, 2.2.7, 2.6.31, 2.6.34, 2.8.46, 2.10.68, 2.11.82.

110. Ibid. 2.11.78–93.

111. Ibid. 2.11.93; Tomkinson trans., 103. I have altered her spelling, capitalization, and word order slightly. See also ibid. 2.8.60.

All the virtues of the philosophers and then some. Despite Abraham's rough start and repeated trials, and despite Ambrose's view that Abraham, like everyone else, has limits that he must recognize, the first of the patriarchs emerges as a Christian sage with marked affinities to Stoicism and Aristotelianism. He has made his moral choices with an eye to the useful as well as to the intrinsically good, and he has followed the four precepts of the unnamed natural philosophers in his interactions with others, displaying a friendly disposition and taking up the sword only in the defense of his kinsman. Abraham's conversion has worked its way not only in his private life but also in his role as a leader of men. The second convert in the patriarch treatises, Rebecca, begins her moral education with decided moral advantages. In comparison with Abraham, she undergoes a more domestic *paideia,* in *De Isaac,* but not an exclusively private one.

CHAPTER 5

Isaac

Of all the patriarch treatises, *De Isaac* has engendered the most controversy. Not only is Ambrose's dependence upon, or independence from, his exegetical sources—above all Philo and Origen—and his treatment of Greek philosophy—above all Platonism and Neoplatonism—an issue, but so is the very structure and argument of the work. The compositional problem that Ambrose faces in this treatise is acute, for unlike the *uitae* of the other patriarchs, which he can approach in a more or less narrative manner, narrative is inapposite to the agenda he sets for himself in *De Isaac*. Narrative is also impossible. Activities and events that exemplify virtue on Isaac's part are few in number in the text of Genesis.

This limitation is even more stringent in the case of Rebecca, given that her conversion is Ambrose's focus. In contrast with Abraham, the primordial convert, Rebecca does not undergo adventures or trials that bespeak immoral practices or incorrect beliefs that she must abandon, and her gradual acquisition of virtue and knowledge. Before her marriage to Isaac, as we have seen in *De Abraham*, Rebecca is depicted as modest, courteous, generous, and filial, endowed with good works and ears open to instruction, even if Ambrose chooses to ignore her hospitality and her exercise of free will in deciding to accept Isaac as her husband sight unseen. She does not appear to have any vices in need of correction. For its part, the book of Genesis is silent on what transpires in either her inner or her outer life between her marriage to Isaac and her pregnancy some time later.

Since a biographical approach to Rebecca's conversion cannot really be based on the book of Genesis, Ambrose takes a literary tack in *De Isaac* quite different from the rhetorical strategies he adopts in the other patriarch trea-tises. He draws his basic account from the Song of Songs, casting Rebecca as the Bride and Isaac, the type of Christ, as the Bridegroom. From the Bride's side of the dialogue in the Song of Songs he extracts a four-part scheme for Rebecca's progress as a convert. This tactic has been recognized by previous scholars, although there is some disagreement among them on where, in *De Isaac,* the dividing lines among the four parts should be drawn. What has not been noted heretofore is the fact that Ambrose also uses as an organizing prin-ciple the three precepts of the Delphic Oracle: know thyself, nothing in excess, thou art. How he relates this classical scheme to the Christian ethics derived from his biblical sources does much to illuminate Ambrose's attitude toward Greek philosophy.

Aside from its biblical intertextuality, which has baffled and irritated scholars who approach *De Isaac* with the canons of classical rhetoric as their chief analytical tools, two other features of the structure of this work that have inspired discussion and disagreement are its redundancies and its apparent organizational confusion. Medievalists addressing themselves to this text are less likely than classicists to be bothered by its intertextualities; as has been noted, Ambrose's method in *De Isaac* resembles the exegesis and preaching of monastic authors who, like the audiences they address, are steeped in the rumi-native and reduplicative technique of *lectio diuina.*[1] Even if that insight can clarify this particular aspect of Ambrose's literary strategy in *De Isaac,* other compositional problems remain. While some scholars hold that, on the basis of his biblical and other sources, Ambrose offers a five-part scheme, a three-part scheme, or a combined three- and four-part scheme in his account of Re-becca's progress,[2] the vast majority of commentators maintain that his scheme is a fourfold one. Their points of agreement and disagreement on where the four parts begin and end have been anatomized carefully in recent scholarship.[3]

---

1. Nauroy, "La structure du *De Isaac,*" 220, 225.

2. See, respectively, Dörrie, "Das fünffach gestufte Mysterium"; Sagot, "La triple sagesse dans le *De Isaac*"; Madec, "L'Homme intérieure selon saint Ambroise."

3. The fullest examination of previous literature on this point is by Sanders, *"Fons vitae Christus,"* 16–21, 76–94; she gives her own formula for the four-part scheme at 95–98. The prede-cessor with whom she agrees the most is Nauroy, "La structure du *De Isaac,*" 210–36. See also Jacob, *"Arkandisziplin," Allegorese, Mystagogie,* 234–54, for another recent reprise of the scholarship on this issue. Also worth consulting are Piccolo, "Per lo studio della spiritualità ambrosiana," 36–38; Iacoangeli, "Anima ed eternità nel *De Isaac,*" 115–37; Pasini, *Ambrogio di Milano,* 217–19, 222. On the other hand, Fitzgerald, "Ambrose at the Well," 80, 85–86, sees no organizational scheme at all in this work.

Only one scholar has noted Ambrose's appeal to the Delphic Oracle.[4] But he confines himself to the first precept, "know thyself," displaying no interest in Ambrose's use of the second and third precepts. Nor is he interested in coordinating the appeal to self-knowledge with Ambrose's larger agenda in *De Isaac*.

Our own reading of this treatise leads us to propose a structure for the work that correlates the progress marked by Rebecca's passage through the stages delineated by the first two precepts of the Delphic Oracle with the first three stages of the Bride's quest for the Bridegroom, leading to the final stage of union with him which the two schemes share but on which the biblical scheme improves. This reading also proposes that, after a preface dealing briefly with Isaac himself and indicating why he is a worthy consort and guide for Rebecca the convert, Ambrose presents a discussion of human nature which shows that he has developed considerably the anthropology he presents in *De Abraham*. He now espouses a position that squares Aristotle, and to a lesser extent the Stoics, with St. Paul. Ambrose then offers an elaborate introduction to Rebecca's story, an overview of what is to transpire during the convert's development. This section of the work extends from *De Isaac* 3.7 to 5.49. It is only at *De Isaac* 6.50 that Ambrose summarizes the Bride's four stages from the Song of Songs succinctly and specifically. He then doubles back, illustrating each stage anew, a section found in *De Isaac* from 6.53 to 8.77, before concluding the treatise with his exhortation to his *competentes* at 8.78–79. In short, the main section of the work needs to be read symphonically: Ambrose first states the main themes, then recapitulates them concisely, and then develops variations on them at length, enlarging and focusing on the central themes in each *ritornello*, before transposing them into a new key in the coda that concludes with the moral lessons that he wants his *competentes* to learn from Rebecca's conversion.

The figure of Isaac that Ambrose presents at the beginning of *De Isaac* as Rebecca's appropriate teacher and spouse recalls the Isaac he presents in *De Abraham*. Ambrose rehearses Isaac's role as a type of Christ while also sketching an abbreviated profile of his moral character as a man. Noting that he has already "described sufficiently both the origin of holy Isaac and the grace he received in my discussion of his father" (In patre nobis sancti Isaac uel origo

---

4. Courcelle, *Connais-toi toi-même de Socrate à Saint Bernard*, 1:122–23, 125; idem, "Saint Ambroise devant le précepte delphique."

satis expressa est uel gratia),[5] Ambrose reprises Isaac's status as a Christ-figure: he is the long-awaited child of promise, born miraculously to an aged and barren mother, offered as a sacrifice; he thus prefigures the birth of the long-awaited Messiah to the Virgin Mary, sacrificed in such a way as not to be lost to his Father. Isaac's name, meaning "joy" etymologically, stands for the joy of Christians forgiven their sins and granted the grace of salvation.[6]

In addition, Isaac possesses his own personal virtues. In *De Joseph*, where Ambrose indicates each patriarch's paramount virtue, the one he assigns to Isaac is "the purity of a sincere mind" (sincerae mentis puritatem).[7] But in *De Isaac*, he ascribes a wider range of virtues to him. The Isaac of this treatise is mild, humble, gentle, good, and true, a man who knows how to live in this world with innocence and without reproach.[8] In preparation for Rebecca's arrival, he displays wisdom by withdrawing to meditate, Ambrose notes, an observation that triggers the first of his numerous remarks in this text about the importance of detachment from physical pleasures so that the mind can focus on the things of heaven.[9] At the same time, Ambrose clarifies what he means by detachment. A wise and perfect soul such as Isaac's, he observes, "shuns and rejects everything that is excessive or inconstant or wicked; . . . Its flight is not to depart from the earth but to remain on earth, to hold to justice and temperance, to renounce the vices in material things, not their use" (omne inmoderatum mobile malignum refugit ac respuit; . . . Fuga autem est non terras relinquire, sed esse in terris, iustitiam et sobrietatem tenere, renuntiare uitiis, non usibus elementorum).[10] Ambrose's criteria for evaluating detachment, in short, are the cardinal virtues of wisdom, justice, and temperance—temperance interpreted as the avoidance of excess, maintained with constancy, a blend of Aristotelian and Stoic values.

Returning to typology, Ambrose observes that Isaac, like Christ, can be understood as the fountain of life, a well of living water. While we first encounter Rebecca at her own well, drawing water for Abraham's servant,

---

5. Ambrose, *De Isaac uel anima* 1.1, ed. Schenkl, trans. Moreschini; trans. McHugh in Ambrose, *Seven Exegetical Works*, 10.

6. Ibid.

7. Ambrose, *De Ioseph* 1.1, ed. Schenkl, trans. Palla; my trans.

8. Ambrose. *De Isa.* 1.1–2.

9. Ibid. 1.1, 3.6, 3.7. On virtue as detachment from physical pleasures, see also ibid. 1.2, 2. 3, 2.4, 2.5, 3.8, 4.11, 4.13, 4.16, 4.23, 4.25, 4.27, 4.32, 4.34, 5.46, 6.52, 6.54, 7.59, 7.60, 8.78, 8.79.

10. Ibid. 3.6; McHugh trans., 14. Noted by Sanders, *"Fons vitae Christus,"* 25–27, 99–102. Cf. Philo, *Questions and Answers on Genesis* 4.187, trans. Marcus, who treats Isaac as a contemplative.

Isaac is the new well to which she will now go to fill her water jar. This association of ideas leads Ambrose in three directions. First, representing Christ as the source of saving doctrine, it also clarifies the status of Rebecca. As Isaac's wife, she signifies both the individual soul in relation to Christ, and the church as his bride. And, as a type of the church, Rebecca has a double significance. Since she is of Abraham's kin, she represents those of Israel who will be saved in the New Dispensation; equally, Ambrose identifies her with the Samaritan woman who converses with Christ at her well (John 4:1–5), who represents the Gentiles who will be brought into the church.[11] It has been widely recognized that this individual and ecclesiological significance of Rebecca in *De Isaac* derives from Origen, who sees the double resonance of Rebecca as the church gathered from Jews and Gentiles alike as Ambrose does.[12]

The second direction in which Ambrose takes the theme of Isaac as a fountain or well is sacramental. He notes that water washes away impurity. So too, he reminds his *competentes,* their own imminent baptism will remove past sins. To be sure, Christians who suffered in the age of the martyrs were cleansed thereby of all their faults; but equally "strong, too, is that death through the bath through which every sin is buried and every fault forgiven" (Est et mors illa ualida per lauacrum, per quam peccatum omne sepelitur et culpa dimittitur).[13]

---

11. Ambrose, *De Isa.* 1.2, 4.20, 4.25, 8.78; see ibid. 4.28 for his reference to the Samaritan woman.

12. Origen, *Commentary on the Song of Songs,* prologue 1, 2.1; *Homily* 1.1, in idem, *The Song of Songs: Commentary and Homilies,* trans. Lawson, For scholarship on this point, see Kellner, *Der heilige Ambrosius,* 106; Thamin, *Saint Ambroise et la morale chrétienne,* 319, 326, 335; Daniélou, "La typologie d'Isaac," 376–80, 384–93; Lazzati, *Il valore letterario della esegesi ambrosiano,* 33–40, 73, 76; Dörrie, "Das fünffache gestufte Mysterium," 80–81; Hadot, "Explication du 'De Isaac' d'Ambroise," 150–52; Dassmann, "Die Kirche und ihre Gleider," 137–44; Argal Echarri, "Isaac y Rebeca," 146–60; Sagot, "La triple sagesse dans le *De Isaac*"; eadem, "Le 'Cantique des Cantiques' dans le 'De Isaac'"; Palla, "Temi del *Commento* origeniano del *Cantico dei Cantici*"; Iacoangeli, "Anima ed eternità nel *De Isaac*"; Jacob, *"Arkandisziplin," Allegorese, Mystagogie,* 69; Sanders, *"Fons vitae Christus,"* 23. On the other hand, Parodi, *La catechesi di sant'Ambrogio,* 363, and Clark, *Reading Renunciation,* 112 n. 58, think that Ambrose focuses mainly on Rebecca as signifying the church, while Piccolo, "Per lo studio della spiritualità ambrosiana," 38–50; Jacob, "The Reception of the Origenist Tradition," in *Hebrew Bible/Old Testament,* 1:693–97; Pasini, *Ambrogio di Milano,* 217–19; and Fitzgerald, "Ambrose at the Well," 87, think that he views her as representing primarily the individual soul. Lucchesi, *L'Usage de Philon,* 64, 66, 82, 83, sees Philo as the major source for Ambrose's Rebecca as representing the religious community.

13. Ambrose, *De Isa.* 8.76; McHugh trans., 60. Other references to baptism occur at 4. 24 and 8.77. Ambrose's baptismal focus is noted by Sanders, *"Fons vitae Christus,"* 202–9; that being the case, however, at 15 and 94 she joins Kellner, *Der heilige Ambrosius,* 105, and Piccolo, "Per lo studio

Ambrose also uses the theme of the wells as a vehicle for shedding light on Isaac's moral character. Indeed, in this connection there is a passage in the book of Genesis which, had he exploited it fully, would have enabled Ambrose to show Isaac teaching by example, instead of confining himself to stating that Isaac had this or that virtue without illustrating it in action. Genesis 26:17–22, 26–31 relates that men of Gerara, in the neighboring land of Abimelech, filled in wells that Abraham had dug, subsequent to his settlement of his earlier dispute with Abimelech on just that issue. These neighbors, clearly, have not adhered to their ruler's agreement; or at any rate, they act as if it does not apply to Abraham's heir. Isaac follows his father's example in response to this act of hostile and unprovoked trespass. In so doing, he also follows the advice on the sage's proper behavior toward his neighbors given by the unnamed natural philosophers to whom Ambrose refers in *De Abraham*, as Abraham himself did. Rather than initiating a quarrel by insisting on his rights or seeking to enforce them by taking up arms, Isaac simply digs new wells, without protest. When Abimelech discovers what has happened, he hastens to make a new agreement with Isaac concerning their respective water rights, a pact that they seal by eating a meal together. Had Ambrose chosen to comment on this passage of Genesis, most of which he omits, he would have been able to amplify the topic of Isaac's wisdom. For if the meditative Isaac displays theoretical wisdom, the Isaac of the wells displays prudential wisdom in his peaceable, diplomatic, and utilitarian mode of dealing with his neighbors. He also displays, in his behavior toward them, the Stoic maxim, "bear and forbear."

But this is not what Ambrose does in his treatment of Isaac's opening of new wells. Rather, he observes, these wells represent Isaac's moral, natural, and mystical wisdom, the wisdom imparted by Solomon in Proverbs, Ecclesiastes, and the Song of Songs, respectively. Moral wisdom teaches us that we should be satisfied with what is our own. Natural wisdom teaches us that if we suffer worldly setbacks we should take comfort in God's abundance, which

---

della spiritualità ambrosiana," 35, in arguing, unconvincingly, that *De Isaac* was aimed, not at the *competentes,* but at the neophytes following their baptism. Equally unconvincing is Palanque, *Saint Ambroise et l'empire romain,* 441, who sees Ambrose's references to the Easter liturgy as irrelevant to the argument of *De Isaac,* which he thinks was written as a treatise from the outset. Following Sanders on the theme of Isaac as a type of Christ, the well of living water, Fitzgerald, "Ambrose at the Well," 84, 89–94, 96–99, likewise ignores the liturgical and baptismal aspect of this image in *De Isaac.*

overrides the cares of this life. Mystical wisdom teaches us that charity is the greatest of virtues.[14]

As a number of scholars have noted, this passage in *De Isaac* is heavily dependent on Origen.[15] Yet Origen handles the same topic rather differently. To begin with, Origen's remarks do not occur in the homilies he devotes to Isaac. He makes no reference to Isaac's well-digging or to his conduct toward his neighbors. Origen discusses the modes of wisdom conveyed by Solomon's books in the prologue of his commentary on the Song of Songs. There he observes that the Greek philosophers divided knowledge into four disciplines. One of these is logic. But since logic is intimately connected with the other three branches of knowledge, he notes, he will not treat logic separately. The other three modes of knowledge are ethics, physics, and contemplation. According to Origen, ethics teaches us seemly behavior and the acquisition of habits conducive to virtue. Physics teaches us the nature of individual things, which we need to know in order to live virtuously, that is, in accordance with nature. Contemplation takes us from earthly things, which we grasp with our physical senses, to heavenly things, which we perceive with the mind alone. Origen also argues that these three modes of knowledge are typified by Abraham, Isaac, and Jacob, respectively.[16] Origen is not concerned with applying this doctrine either to the moral education of Rebecca or to a well-rounded description of Isaac's virtues. Rather, his concern in this text is to argue that the goal of the Bride in the Song of Songs is to attain contemplative wisdom, that is, her mystical union with the Bridegroom.[17]

Given these discrepancies between Origen's definitions of the three modes of knowledge to which Solomon's books give access and the way he ascribes them to the patriarchs, and Ambrose's handling of the same issues, some scholars have raised questions about the function of this Origenic material in *De Isaac*. For some *Quellenforscher*, Origen's lack of interest in the themes that concern Ambrose directly in *De Isaac* is irrelevant; they are interested only in

14. Ambrose, *De Isa.* 4.20–29.

15. Sagot, "La triple sagesse dans le *De Isaac*," 109; Savon, *Saint Ambroise devant l'exégèse de Philon*, 1:71–77, 78–81; idem, "Ambroise lecteur d'Origène"; Palla, "Temi del *Commento* origeniano al *Cantico dei Cantici*," 72; Nauroy, "La structure du *De Isaac*," 228; Sanders, *"Fons vitae Christus,"* 33–40.

16. Origen, *Comm. on the Song of Songs* prologue 3.

17. Noted by Lawson, intro. to his trans. of Origen, *Comm. on the Song of Songs* 6, 10–12, 14–16; Trigg, *Origen*, 203–4.

locating Origen, or Philo and Origen, as Ambrose's source.[18] A leading commentator on the organization of *De Isaac* regards the passage about the wells and the three modes of knowledge as "un bloc erratique" in its overall composition; as she sees it, this material pertains neither to the characterization of Isaac, which it follows, nor to that of Rebecca, which it precedes.[19] Against this view, from another analyst of the work's structure, comes the claim that *De Isaac* is not a mere bricolage of sources organized haphazardly;[20] still, this account leaves unclarified the role of the material on the modes of knowledge that Ambrose takes from Origen.

The real problem with this section of *De Isaac*, which extends from 4.20 to 4.29, is not its content but its placement. For, in between this passage about the wells and the modes of knowledge and the opening section of the treatise describing Isaac, we find Ambrose inserting his discussion of human nature. That subject is extremely important in its own right. It is also vital as the foundation on which Rebecca will take up her assignment to attain self-knowledge as the first step in her moral education. Editorially, it would have made more sense had Ambrose done three things that he does not do with the passage about the wells. First, as just noted, he truncates his own ability to delineate Isaac's moral character by omitting the account in Genesis in which the patriarch resolves his dispute with his neighbors over his water rights. Second, given the fact that Ambrose's definitions of the three modes of knowledge differ from Origen's, had Ambrose included Isaac's pact with Abimelech, he could have underscored how his own definitions of moral, natural, and mystical wisdom apply to that incident. Satisfaction with what one has is a principle that is manifestly, and wrongly, rejected by the sinful Gerarans. But the maintenance of forbearance and tranquillity in the face of unprovoked hostility on the part of others, and charity or love of neighbor however the neighbor behaves, not returning evil for evil, illustrate the character of the virtuous Isaac. Isaac's handling of the matter certainly yields practical advice for getting along with one's neighbors that is useful to Ambrose's *competentes*. The passage, in short, could have been amplified in order to put flesh on the bones of Isaac as a moral example had Ambrose developed it along these lines. The

18. See, for example, Madec, *Saint Ambroise et la philosophie*, 193–95; Savon, *Saint Ambroise devant l'exégèse de Philon*, 1:71–77, 78–81.

19. Sagot, "La triple sagesse dans le *De Isaac*," 109.

20. Nauroy, "La structure du *De Isaac*."

third editorial change that would have clarified the function of this material as an illustration of Isaac's moral character and typological significance alike would have been its repositioning, its placement before and not after the passage on anthropology. For this material makes the most sense as the conclusion to the preface on Isaac, who is Rebecca's source of saving doctrine, sacramental initiation, and ethical instruction. The passage on human nature, had it followed the passage on the wells and the modes of wisdom, could have served as a smooth and logical transition from the preface, on Isaac, to the main body of the treatise, on Rebecca, dealing, as it does, with the human nature that they share.

Before proceeding to that transition, it is worth noting that Isaac's settlement of the dispute with Abimelech over the wells is not the only passage of Genesis touching on the patriarch's relations with this ruler that Ambrose omits. He also bypasses another locus in the biblical account in which Isaac is likewise shown to be imitating his father's example: the episode in which he places the chastity of his wife at risk. As Genesis 26:6–11 reports, owing to a famine in their own territory, Isaac and Rebecca travel to the land of Abimelech. As Abraham had done before him both there and in Egypt, and despite the fact that his dissimulation involves the same faulty reasoning and also proves futile, Isaac claims that Rebecca is his sister, not his wife. The only difference between this incident in Isaac's life and the parallel ones in Abraham's is that what Isaac fears is that one of Abimelech's subjects, not the ruler himself, will kill him in order to marry Rebecca. As it happens, this threat is averted by Abimelech, who sees through Isaac's ploy and orders his subjects to leave Rebecca alone since she is already married. Had he wished to do so, Ambrose could have capitalized on this event in Isaac's life to remind his *competentes*, as he does in *De Abraham*, that adultery is intrinsically evil and that it is recognized to be so under the natural law, even by the Gentiles. His disinterest in seizing this opportunity in *De Isaac* may reflect the fact that these dissimulations of Abraham and Isaac have, on balance, exegetical embarrassments that outweigh their positive uses. Or, Ambrose may have hoped that he had exhausted the topic of monogamy and marital chastity in *De Abraham*.

In any case, Ambrose takes up the subject of anthropology immediately after Rebecca's meeting with Isaac, a sensible idea since self-knowledge is to be the first step in her conversion. Following Origen, Ambrose maintains that Rebecca does not come empty-handed to the task of self-knowledge. For Origen, the Bride brings betrothal gifts of her own, matching those given to her by the Bridegroom. These gifts are natural law, reason, and free will. Further-more, he sees Rebecca, instructed in stages by Isaac, as moving from good deeds to better, from things holy to things holier.[21] For her part, Ambrose's Rebecca arrives with the gifts given to her by Abraham's servant in recognition of her existing virtues; she is "already endowed with heavenly mysteries" (cae-lestibus iam dotata mysteriis), by which he means three things: the earrings signifying the openness of her ears to instruction, the bracelets signifying her good works, and a soul that can and will "subdue the bodily passions and turn them to the service of the virtues" (quae passiones corporis subigit et ad uirtu-tum officia conuertit).[22] As with Isaac himself, Rebecca is not expected to extir-pate her passions. Rather, her education will show her how to reorient them to virtue so as to avoid excess and to reject "worldly vanities" (saecularium uani-tatem) and "unreasonable self-indulgence" (luxuriam inrationabilem).[23] To this task Rebecca must bring the rationality and free will that Origen ascribes to the Bride. Free will is essential. Just as the sinful soul "is the author of her own evils" (ipsa sibi auctor malorum est),[24] so also free will, in collaboration with grace, harnesses the passions leading to vice to the exercise of virtue.[25] Along with free will and grace, reason is also essential. For Rebecca cannot discover the particular way in which "nothing in excess," the governing of the irrational by reason, pertains to her without a knowledge of her own nature.

Rebecca's fulfillment of the Delphic injunction to know herself thus fol-lows the advice Origen gives to his Bride. But unlike Origen, Ambrose explains the methodology involved in self-knowledge and describes the substance of the anthropological enlightenment that results. Rebecca's recommended method of research is introspection, which yields a knowledge of both her imperfec-tions and her good qualities; this is the sense in which the Bride is both black and beautiful.[26] The conception of human nature at which she arrives through introspection represents a major advance over the anthropology that Ambrose outlines in De Abraham. At the same time, just as Abraham's education in-volves discrimination between philosophical doctrines that are acceptable and

21. Origen, *Comm. on the Song of Songs* 1.1, 2.11; idem, *Homilies on Genesis* 12.3 in *Homilies on Genesis and Exodus*, trans. Heine.

22. Ambrose, *De Isa.* 3.7; McHugh trans., 15. I have altered his wording slightly.

23. Ibid. 3.8, 4.16; McHugh trans., 15, 22.

24. Ibid. 7.60; McHugh trans., 50.

25. Ibid. 3.7. Noted by Hill, "Classical and Christian Tradition," 159, 161.

26. Ambrose, *De Isa.* 4.12–17, 8.64; cf. Origen, *Comm. on the Song of Songs* 2.5–6.

those that are to be rejected as incorrect, so also Rebecca must undergo a parallel philosophical *paideia*. Human beings, she learns, are made up of body, which is their "matter" (materia), and soul, which is their "form" (species). Furthermore, vices as well as virtues can arise in the soul as well as the body.[27]

Ambrose frames the hylomorphic principle already articulated in *De Abraham* in expressly Aristotelian terminology in *De Isaac*, although without naming its source. Neither does he name the philosophical sources for the doctrines he criticizes. With respect to the soul, he insists, it does not have a material composition of any kind: "For the soul is not blood; . . . nor is the soul harmony; . . . nor is the soul air; . . . the soul is not fire; nor is the soul an entelechy. Rather, the soul is the vital principle which made Adam a living being . . . in order to govern and vivify the body; [it is] the image of God" (Non ergo sanguis anima, . . . neque armonia anima, . . . neque aer anima, . . . neque ignis anima, neque entelechia anima, sed anima est uiuens, quia factus est Adam in animam uiuentem, . . . corpus anima uiuificet et gubernet; . . . imaginem dei).[28] Although it is the ruling principle of the human constitution, the soul can freely choose to detach itself from the golden chain of virtue and fall into sin by succumbing to irrationality, so that "it does not hold to the norm of moderation" (mensuram rerum non teneat).[29] For Rebecca, as for Isaac, Ambrose sees the problem of sin as the problem of excess brought on by the unreasonable use of free will, not as the problem of matter as such. His instruction that we should remain on earth, holding to moderation and justice, renouncing the vices in material things, not their use,[30] is the norm for her as well. In the act of renouncing vices and departing from excess, the soul can with equal freedom choose the rational and the good. While assisted by grace, this conversion of the soul is sparked by the soul's own capacity and desire, signified by the Bride's request for the kisses of the Bridegroom.[31]

27. Ambrose, *De Isa.* 7.61; my trans.

28. Ibid. 2.4; my trans. Noted by Loiselle, "'Nature' de l'homme," 39–40; Sanders, *"Fons vitae Christus,"* 23–25. For the classical sources of the theories Ambrose presents in this passage, see Moreschini, ad loc., n. 17.

29. Ambrose, *De Isa.* 3.5; my trans.; see also ibid. 3.6, 7.61, 8.65, 8.79.

30. Ibid. 3.6. On the other hand, some scholars maintain that, following Philo and/or Origen, Ambrose develops an educational program in asceticism or mysticism for Rebecca in *De Isaac*. See, for example, Daniélou, *From Shadows to Reality,* 144, 148; Clark, *Reading Renunciation,* 89.

31. Ambrose, *De Isa.* 2.6, 3.7, 3.8, 4.32, 6.50, 6.53.

But the soul, as Ambrose explains, is more than the form that specifies the body as a natural phenomenon. "Soul" also stands for "spirit," that is, the attitude of a person who is rightly oriented toward God, just as "flesh" stands not for our natural body but for our sinfulness, wherever in the human constitution it may arise: "Where 'flesh' is applied to a human being, a sinner is meant" (ubi autem caro pro homine nuncupatur, peccator exprimitur). It is free will, an intellectual faculty, that determines whether we incline toward "flesh" or "spirit." Here, citing specifically the doctrine of the tension between flesh and spirit developed by St. Paul in Romans 7:23, which he quotes, Ambrose stresses the point that the prison or cage of the soul is not the natural body, but "the flesh," as Paul describes it.[32] The body, he adds, should not be blamed for human sinfulness. For the body acts as the instrument of the soul, which is its ruling principle and in which can inhere the vices of ignorance and concupiscence.[33] The evils that are "deprivations of goods" (priuantur bonis) have the sinful soul as their source.[34] Far from being the soul's prison, the body can best be understood in terms of three other metaphors, Ambrose explains. The body is the house that gives the soul shelter. It is also the soul's clothing; it protects the soul and, in turn, it should be protected itself and kept in good repair.[35] And the body no less than the soul, so sheltered and protected, can be understood as a field, yielding a crop of virtue or vice depending on how we cultivate it.[36]

Enlightenment about her own nature and about human nature as such thus provides Rebecca with an anthropology that links an Aristotelianism tinctured by Stoicism with Pauline theology. Ambrose uses this amalgam to reinterpret decisively the Platonic and Neoplatonic ideas and imagery that he

---

32. Ibid. 2.3; my trans.; see also ibid. 6.52. Scholars who have recognized Ambrose's Christianizing of this theme in the light of Pauline theology include Dassmann, *Die Frömmigkeit des Kirchenvaters Ambrosius*, 41–44, 181–84; Otten, "Caritas and the Ascent Motif"; Madec, "L'Homme intérieure selon saint Ambroise," 296–306; Iacoangeli, "Anima ed eternità nel *De Isaac*," 108–11; Sanders, *"Fons vitae Christus,"* 23–25, 179–81. On the other hand stands the uncritical view that Ambrose is expressing untinctured Platonism here; see Courcelle, "L'Âme en cage"; idem, "Tradition platonicienne et traditions chrétiennes du corps-prison"; idem, "Le corps tombeau"; Loiselle, "'Nature' de l'homme," 32–34, 143; Tolomio, "'Corpus carcer' nell'Alto Medioevo," 5–6, 10–11, 13.

33. Ambrose, *De Isa.* 3.8, 7.27, 7.60.

34. Ibid. 7.60; McHugh trans., 51. On the privative theory of evil in Ambrose, Lenox-Conyngham, "Sin in St. Ambrose," interprets it, idiosyncratically, to mean that fallen humankind is afflicted only by the actual sins we commit and not by inherited original sin.

35. Ambrose, *De Isa.* 2.3, 7.62, 8.79.

36. Ibid. 3.7, 7.60, 8.68–70.

invokes. For Ambrose, the privative theory of evil does not equate the absence of virtue with non-being. The fall of the soul, when it sins, is not an unwilled metaphysical event, a fall of the soul into an alien material prison. Rather, it is the consequence of a freely willed choice on the part of the soul, which it uses the body to express. The soul's reversal of that unreasonable choice, in willing the good, assisted by grace, leads to a life governed by moderation, not asceticism. As the ruling principle of the moral agent, the mind is responsible both for that agent's folly and for its recall to virtue, which it can cultivate throughout the human constitution.

Armed with this understanding of human nature, Rebecca can proceed with the next phase of her learning experience. The Bridegroom's kiss, which the Bride seeks at the beginning of her quest for self-knowledge, conveys something else she seeks, a correct theology, which she also needs in order to engage in appropriate self-discipline. And so, in the second and third stages of the Bride's education, equivalent to the "nothing in excess" phase of the Delphic Oracle's program, she looks for the Bridegroom, first in her own chamber and then in the streets and public places of the city. Her quest is for the Word of God. Ambrose characterizes the theological advice which Rebecca asks for and receives and which, by implication, he gives to his *competentes,* by quoting Isaiah 48:20: "Go forth from Babylon, flee from the Chaldeans" (Exi de Babylone fugiens a Chaldeis).[37] Ambrose's citation of Isaiah in *De Isaac* is designed to remind his audience of two facts to which he thinks they need to pay careful attention but which the book of Genesis, regrettably, does not discuss specifically. Since Rebecca hails from the same Chaldea as Abraham, as a convert she too must set aside the Chaldean polytheism and star-worship in which she was raised as well as all forms of pagan religious practice. And, positively, she has to learn monotheism, the worship of the one, true, invisible God, by means of correct religious practice. She also has to be instructed in the covenant into which she will be incorporated by her marriage to Isaac, in whose history she will now play a critical role as the matriarch of the next generation, a mother whose sons will receive the distinctive badge of circumcision, setting God's people apart from everyone else. All of this theological instruction will have to take place after Rebecca arrives in Canaan, since Abraham's servant, when he explains his mission to Rebecca and her elders, says nothing about the

---

37. Ibid. 6.54; RSV trans., with "Chaldeans" in place of the text's "Chaldea" to square with Ambrose's Latin.

covenant and about Abraham's new religion when he describes his master's history and situation (Gen 24:34–44).

Ambrose makes use of several images in explaining Rebecca's quest for theological truth. Noting that, although invited to the wedding feast, guests must arrive wearing the proper wedding garments, he recalls Rebecca's modest veiling of herself when she first encounters Isaac in order to make the point that we must seek knowledge with the right attitude. Faith and love interact. Thus, the Bride's desire for the Bridegroom is, at the same time, a desire for the supreme truth as well as the supreme good. The Bride at first sees mere shadows; she seeks to replace them with the illumination of divine precepts. When she is ready to leave her chamber to look for the Bridegroom in the city, the watchmen take away her cloak. She no longer needs it, for she is now garbed in the mantle of the Holy Spirit, a mantle of faith and grace, revealing her good conscience and her imitation of Christ.[38] On another note, Ambrose compares Rebecca's quest for theological knowledge and virtue with a pilgrimage, a voyage to her new fatherland, where she is to become a "fellow-citizen of the saints" (ciuis sanctorum).[39]

In describing the virtues that Rebecca acquires, or perfects, at the conclusion of her quest for the Bridegroom, whom she eventually draws to herself by prayer,[40] Ambrose provides her with a large assortment of excellent moral qualities. She has been born again.[41] She possesses chastity and humility.[42] She possesses sincerity[43] and perseverance.[44] She has overcome the struggle between flesh and spirit, and her being manifests the harmony of the spheres, a doctrine that Ambrose now decides is a useful metaphor for the perfected convert's state.[45] The virtue that Ambrose mentions the most frequently in describing the perfected Rebecca is faith.[46] For the benefit of his *competentes*, he emphasizes the point that faith is more than a grasp of the basic tenets of Christianity, which, once accepted, can be allowed to lie inert in our minds.

---

38. Ibid. 4.12–17, 4.37, 5.43, 6.53–55, 8.68.
39. Ibid. 6.54; my trans. Cf. Eph 2:19; see also *De Isa.* 8.78–79.
40. Ambrose, *De Isa.* 6.50.
41. Ibid. 8.74.
42. Ibid. 4.17.
43. Ibid. 7.59.
44. Ibid. 5.48.
45. Ibid. 7.63.
46. Ibid. 4.37, 5.43, 5.47, 5.48, 6.55, 7.57, 7.59, 8.75–76.

Rather, faith must constantly be guarded against attack, constantly held fast, and deepened by zeal, piety, and continuing reflection on its message and its application to our lives.[47] Good works also ornament Rebecca's soul, as they had from the beginning; they are now revalued as expressions of her faith in action.[48] Patience is yet another virtue that Rebecca brings with her to Isaac and learns how to reinterpret. Noting that Rebecca did not become pregnant until she had been married for some time, Ambrose describes her fruitfulness as the reward for the patience with which she has undergone the entire conversion experience.[49] But the single most important virtue that the perfected Rebecca possesses is charity. Greater even than faith and hope, charity "tests whatever is pure and with its fire makes better whatever it has touched" (quicquid uero sincerum est probat et quod contigerit suo igne meliorat).[50]

These virtues now qualify Rebecca, as the Bride, for union with her Bridegroom. This consummation is a good index of how the Christian virtues test the classical virtues and improve on them while yet holding them fast. For the Delphic Oracle, "thou art," the encounter with the other, is the conclusion of the intellectual and moral *paideia* that she has to offer. Not so with Ambrose. To be sure, the Bride at last consummates her marriage to the Bridegroom. And while this union accomplishes her spiritual rebirth and its crown is her resurrection, a reference reminding the *competentes* of the Feast of the Resurrection that they are soon to celebrate with their baptism and with their first encounter with the resurrected body of Christ in the Eucharist,[51] the Bride does more than simply delight in her personal union with her divine spouse. She manifests a concern for others. Ambrose presents these others, initially, as the daughters of Jerusalem mentioned in the Song of Songs, who, as bridesmaids, accompany the Bride to her wedding, who follow her to her bridal chamber singing epithalamia in her honor, and who desire what she has but remain outside. For their sake, and for the sake of those still needing his help, the Bride encourages the Bridegroom to leave their nuptial chamber and go out to minister to those he can assist. The Bride herself wants to bring others with her so that they can ascend with her to God, and her joy in her

---

47. Ibid. 5.38–53.
48. Ibid. 3.7, 5.47, 5.48, 7.58, 7.62, 8.75.
49. Ibid. 1.1, 3.8, 4.18. Noted by Nauroy, "La structure du *De Isaac*," 234. Clark, *Reading Renunciation*, 183, also flags Origen as Ambrose's source for this virtue of Rebecca's.
50. Ambrose, *De Isa.* 8.77; McHugh trans., 61. For more on charity, see ibid. 4.25–29, 8.74–77.
51. Ibid. 1.2, 3.10–4.11, 5.47, 8.78.

Bridegroom is accompanied by her understanding that true love and a truly chaste conjugal union must also be unselfish. As a perfected soul, the Bride has all she needs, for the true good is sufficient. But if, like the Stoic sage, she is self-sufficient, she is not autarchic. Her spouse is always with her. For the Bride knows that Christ will remain at her side, even as he goes out to redeem his lost sheep and to teach those who lack instruction.[52]

Even viewing Rebecca as the individual soul in relation to Christ, Ambrose sees far more here than an individualistic kind of self-gratification in the bond signified by the consummation of the marriage. For at the same time, the individual soul functions as a member of a group. She seeks the salvation of others in her own time and place, as a precursor to the Great Sabbath that the entire church will celebrate in community. For Ambrose, the individual and ecclesiological understandings of Rebecca come together; her fellow-citizenship with the saints in the life to come begins with her intercessory role in this life.[53]

Circling back to a point made early in *De Isaac* about the delay between Rebecca's marriage and her eventual conception of offspring, Ambrose notes that she herself cannot bear until she is born again. But "now she is in labor who receives the spirit of salvation in her womb and pours it out to others" (parturit enim qui in utero accepit spiritum salutis et aliis infundit).[54] Or, again, "it was as if she had been made perfect, not for herself, but for others" (Ergo quasi perfecta non pro se, sed pro aliis interuenit).[55] It is for this reason that Rebecca can be called sister as well as wife, "because her gentle and peaceable soul enjoys a reputation for affection common to all rather than for union with one individual, and because she thought that she was bound to all rather than to one" (Quae non inmerito soror magis quam uxor adpelletur, eo quod mitis atque pacifica anima communis magis pietatis quam specialis copulae nomen accipiat et quia uniuersis magis quam uni se existimet obligatam).[56]

There is yet another index of Rebecca's moral perfection. Alone of all the wives of the patriarchs, she is granted direct communication with God. When she feels the infants moving in her womb during her pregnancy with Jacob and

52. Ibid. 4.11, 5.43–47, 7.57, 8.69.

53. Ibid. 6.53, 7.59. Dassmann, "Die Kirche und ihre Gleider," 144, notes the compatibility of the individual and ecclesiological aspects of Rebecca. The theme of unity in *De Isaac* more broadly is given an excellent analysis by Sanders, *"Fons vitae Christus,"* 179–202.

54. Ambrose, *De Isa.* 8.74; McHugh trans., 59. Noted by Nauroy, "La structure du *De Isaac,*" 226–36.

55. Ambrose, *De Isa.* 8.69; McHugh trans., 57.

56. Ibid. 4.19; McHugh trans., 23.

Esau, Rebecca is concerned and seeks advice about the phenomenon. Now the book of Genesis relates (24:59; 24:61) that when Rebecca left home to join Isaac she was accompanied by her nurse and her maids. Ambrose chooses not to mention this fact. Still, one might think that the pregnant Rebecca's first plan of action would have been to consult women in her household experienced in matters reproductive who could have advised her that the unusual amount of activity in her womb suggested the likelihood that she was pregnant with a multiple birth. But, in both the biblical text and in *De Isaac* as well, Rebecca bypasses this obvious means of assuaging her disquiet. Instead, she consults God alone. He tells her that she is indeed carrying twin sons, who are struggling with each other in the womb, as Ambrose reports. But he does not cite the second part of God's message to Rebecca in which God states that the obstetrical situation that she experiences forecasts the contest between her sons that will emerge once they are born, a contest in which the younger will triumph over the elder (Gen 25:23). With respect to the second half of this divine forecast, Ambrose states instead, and incorrectly, that it is Isaac who says that the elder will serve the younger.[57] But, in the text of Genesis, Isaac does not make this observation during Rebecca's pregnancy; God does. It is only much later, when the aged Isaac thinks he is blessing his firstborn, Esau, that he says that the son he is blessing will rule over his brothers (Gen 27:29), which is not the same thing. Ambrose's omissions and manipulations of the biblical text on this issue will, in the sequel, complicate the argument he develops in *De Jacob*, and unnecessarily so. But the point he wants to make about the perfected Rebecca is that, in addressing her concern about her pregnancy, she does not seek worldly advice. She "presumes nothing but invokes God as supreme protector of her counsels" (nihil sponte praesumat, sed in omnibus summum deum praesulem poscat suorum consiliorum).[58]

Ambrose presents a final delineation of the perfected Rebecca before offering the peroration to his *competentes* with which he ends *De Isaac*. For this purpose, he brings forward once more the image of the charioteer from Plato's *Phaedrus* that has drawn the attention of scholars concerned only with identifying Ambrose's Platonic and Neoplatonic sources or with viewing him primarily as a transmitter of them.[59] In comparison with his handling of the

57. Ibid. 5.45.

58. Ibid. 4.18; McHugh trans., 23.

59. Most notable is Courcelle, "Plotin et saint Ambroise," 31–35, 45; idem, "Anti-Christian Arguments and Christian Platonism," 165–66; idem, *Recherches sur les Confessions de Saint*

theme of the charioteer in *De Abraham*, Ambrose reworks this image in *De Isaac*. He also locates it at a different point in each of these works. In *De Abraham*, it will be recalled, Ambrose introduces Plato's charioteer, conflated with its appropriation by Philo and with the chariot of the prophet Ezekiel, early in the first book of the treatise, in order to specify the relationship between reason and the infrarational faculties that Abraham, as an incipient convert, will have to learn how to put into practice.[60] In *De Isaac*, he invokes Plato's charioteer image, framed by references both to Ezekiel's chariot and to the chariot of Aminadab mentioned in the Song of Songs, to illustrate, not Rebecca's path ahead at the beginning of her story, but the perfected convert's destination as she continues her journey.[61] The chariot motif, located at the end of *De Isaac*, is intended here to represent the soul already united to Christ in the fourth and final stage of the Bride's development. The chariot remains the soul. But it is now drawn by eight horses, four good and four bad. The good horses are the classical cardinal virtues: wisdom, temperance, courage, and justice, which now decorate Rebecca's soul.[62] The bad horses are the vices correlative to these virtues: wrath, concupiscence, fear, and injustice. The driver of the chariot remains reason.

It is instructive to note that Ambrose does not see, among the tasks of reason, the putting of the bad horses out to pasture while continuing to drive the good horses alone. All eight of the horses remain attached to the chariot. The message Ambrose conveys thereby is that the psychic energies that lead to the vices can, under the guidance of reason, be harnessed to the promotion of virtue. This is a position taught alike by Plato, Aristotle, and the Middle Stoic

---

Augustin, 106–17, 122; idem, "Ambroise de Milan, 'professeur de philosophie'"; idem, *Recherches sur Saint Ambroise*, 16. Courcelle's lead is followed by Taormina, "Sant'Ambrogio e Plotino"; Hadot, "Platon et Plotin dans trois sermons," 203–10; North, *Sophrosyne*, 365; Moreschini, intro. to his trans. of *De Isa.*, 9–13, 20–25; Iacoangeli, "'Humanitas' classica e 'sapientia' cristiana," 132–42; Moorhead, *Ambrose*, 172–73; Drecoll, "Neuplatonismus und Christentum," 107–9, 129–30. In sharp contrast to this view stand scholars who argue for Ambrose's complete rejection of philosophy in this work, notably Iacoangeli, "Anima ed eternità nel *De Isaac*," 107–8; Sanders, *"Fons vitae Christus,"* 25, 31–33, 110–14, 202. Neither is Sanders entirely consistent on this point, for at 66–68 and 108–10, she follows Piccolo, "Per lo studio della spiritualità ambrosiana," 44, in maintaining that Ambrose does use philosophical ideas where he deems them accurate and appropriate, recasting them in Christian terms.

60. See chapter 4, 45–46.

61. Ambrose, *De Isa.* 8.65–67; Ezekiel's chariot, representing the wings of charity, is mentioned at ibid., 8.77.

62. On justice, see also ibid. 5.48, 7.57; on temperance, see also ibid. 3.5, 3.6, 8.79.

Panaetius. Moreover, the classical virtues, thus enhanced, are yoked by faith, bound by charity, reined in by justice, and haltered by moderation. Like the natural moral excellence that Rebecca brings with her into her marriage, the classical virtues are to be retained. To invoke the Aristotelian terminology that Ambrose applies to the components of the human constitution, these virtues may now be the same in practice, materially. But in Rebecca's new fatherland, they are given new formal principles that explain the "how" and the "why" of the virtues. These new specifications and informing principles, Ambrose argues, are both classical and Christian. The driver keeps the horses together by means of justice and moderation no more and no less than by faith and charity. Equipped with these horses and these harnesses, reason drives the chariot to its destination, heaven, winning the prize of the race, Christ.[63] But now Christ emerges as the driver as well.[64] For it is the Word of God that guides reason as it wins its chariot's race; Christ, Ambrose indicates, is both the way and the end. And this is an end which the chariot races of the philosophers are incapable of attaining on their own: "From this source the philosophers portrayed those chariot-races of souls in their books; nevertheless they could not attain the victor's palm, because their souls did not know the summit of the Word and his height" (Hinc philosophi currilia illa animarum in suis libris expressere certamina, nec tamen ad palmam peruenire potuerunt, quoniam summitatem uerbi et altitudinem illorum animae nescierunt).[65] The philosophical virtues, by themselves, cannot lead us to the prize. But yoked in tandem with the theological virtues, the philosophical virtues are reinvigorated and revalorized, and are entrusted with making an important positive contribution to the Christian life of Rebecca and of Ambrose's *competentes*.

Ambrose focuses clearly on this point as well in the peroration of *De Isaac*. The message of Rebecca, the message of the Bride, is the same as the message of the virtuous Isaac portrayed at the beginning of the treatise. There, we recall, Ambrose also speaks of the soul's flight. It is not a Plotinian flight of the alone to the Alone, mediated, or not, by the mysticism of Philo or Origen.[66] Nor does Ambrose's appeal to the Song of Songs tradition in *De Isaac* advocate

63. Ibid. 8.65.

64. Ibid. 8.66–67.

65. Ibid. 8.67; McHugh trans., 55. I have altered his wording slightly.

66. See, on the other hand, the literature cited in nn. 30 and 59 above, to which may be added Pizzolato, *La dottrina esegetica di Sant'Ambrogio*, 68–75, 192–93, 320; Iacoangeli, "Anima ed eternità nel *De Isaac*."

an ascetic withdrawal from the world or a call to celibacy inspired by a venera-
tion for the Virgin Mary.[67] Rather, as we have seen, what Ambrose emphasizes
in *De Isaac,* along with the cardinal and the theological virtues, are the virtues
of diplomacy, constancy, equanimity, peacefulness, patience, humility, piety,
chastity, trust in God, service to others, the avoidance of excess, and the avoidance of the vices that may lie in material things, not their use.

The same perspective informs his treatment, for his *competentes,* of the
moral lessons they can take from Rebecca's conversion and apply to themselves. Here it is worth observing that there is a significant and underappreciated contrast in the way Ambrose uses the Song of Songs in *De Isaac,* on the
one hand, and in the works that he dedicates, not to his *competentes,* but to
Christians with a celibate vocation, on the other. In his treatises on virginity,
he cites the Virgin Mary as the consecrated virgins' model and inspiration and
certainly presents their calling, as brides of Christ, as one incompatible with,
and superior to, marriage.[68] What is truly striking about *De Isaac,* in this con-

----

67. See, on the other hand, the literature cited in n. 59 above, to which may be added Hadot,
"Explication du 'De Isaac' d'Ambroise," 150–52; Hill, "Christian and Classical Tradition," 5, 14, 16,
70, 153, 266; Clark, "The Uses of the Song of Songs," 401, 404–5. Matter, *The Voice of My Beloved,*
36, argues that Ambrose always cites the Song of Songs with a spiritual and Mariological interpretation; this claim clearly does not apply to *De Isaac,* where the Virgin is mentioned in passing
only three times: at 1.1 as the mother of Christ; at 5.46 as crowning him in heaven; and at 6.53 as
transfixed by a sword and as causing John the Baptist to leap in his mother's womb at the Visita-
tion. Clark and Matter confuse what Ambrose does with the Song of Songs and with Mary in *De
Isaac* with what he does with them in his other works, notably his treatises on virginity. But a clear
distinction between these contrasting uses has been made by Piccolo, "Per lo studio della spiritualità ambrosiana," 42–43.

68. For the Virgin, see Ambrose, *De uirginibus* 1.3.11–12, 2.2.6–2.3.19, ed. Cazzaniga, trans.
Gori; for the bride of Christ idea, see ibid. 1.3.11–12, 1.3.13, 1.5.21, 1.5.22, 1.7.32, 1.7.36–37, 1.8.52,
1.11.62, 1.11.65; Ambrose, *De uirginitate* 12.74–13.77, 13.79–80; Ambrose, *Exhortatio uirginitatis* 5.28,
9.58–59, 10.62, the two latter works ed. Cazzaniga, trans. Gori. The ascetic morality that Ambrose
deems appropriate to consecrated virgins has been extended uncritically to his ethics in general by
such authors as Clark, "The Uses of the Song of Songs," 401, 404–5, and Brown, *The Body and
Society,* 348–49, who do not take account of *De Isaac* or the other patriarch treatises. See also Courcelle, "Plotin et saint Ambroise"; idem, "Nouvelle aspects de platonisme chez saint Ambroise";
idem, "L'humanisme chrétien de saint Ambroise"; idem, "Anti-Christian Arguments and Christian Platonism," 165–66; idem, *Recherches sur les Confessions de Saint Augustin,* 106–17, 122, 124–38;
idem, *Late Latin Writers and Their Greek Sources,* 137–38; idem, "Ambroise de Milan, 'professeur de
philosophie'"; idem, *Recherches sur saint Ambroise,* 16; idem, *Connais-toi toi-même de Socrate à saint
Bernard,* 1:122–23, 125; idem, "Saint Ambroise devant le précepte delphique," 185–86. See also
Thamin, *Saint Ambroise et la morale chrétienne,* 324; Wilbrand, "Ambrosius und Plato"; Taormina,
"Sant'Ambrogio e Plotino"; Hadot, "Platon et Plotin dans trois sermons"; Solignac, "Nouvelles

nection, is that Ambrose does not present the spiritual union of the soul and Christ as in any way incompatible with the connubial love between husband and wife in a normal marriage—the calling, in this area of life, of the vast majority of the *competentes* for whose instruction he writes this and the other patriarch treatises. In the history of Song of Songs exegesis, Ambrose appears to be unique in his ability to read this text as pertaining to human marriage as it is experienced by spouses in historical time as well as to the spiritual relationship of any Christian, married or single, with Christ. His final advice, in his peroration, retains the ethical emphasis that he has orchestrated throughout *De Isaac:* an ethics of moderation governing the normal Christianity of lay people living active lives in the world. Their sacramental initiation into this normal Christian life, which is imminent, will begin for them, as her union with the Bridegroom begins for Rebecca, an ethical life that is a continuing process of conversion.[69]

In the end, the image of flight, which Ambrose invokes only to reinterpret in considering Isaac's virtues, is also an image that he invokes in order to reconfigure as he summarizes the lessons that Rebecca teaches at the close of *De Isaac.* The passage in which he does so also appears above in chapter 3, but its placement, as the conclusion to *De Isaac,* warrants its repetition here:

---

parallèles entre saint Ambroise et Plotin"; Seibel, *Fleisch und Geist beim heiligen Ambrosius,* 15–50, 97–99, 119–22, 129–45, 194–97; Dörrie, "Das fünffach gestufte Mysterium," 83–92; Dassmann, *Die Frömmigkeit des Kirchenvaters Ambrosius,* 17; Loiselle, "'Nature' de l'homme," 1–4, 12, 24–25, 31, 35–37, 44–46, 48–49, 77–78, 90, 117–20, 127, 143, 168, who also denies (8) that Ambrose's anthropology ever changed or developed; Brown, *The Body and Society,* 348–49; Markus, *The End of Ancient Christianity,* 34–38, 49; Clark, *Reading Renunciation,* 89; Moorhead, *Ambrose,* 172–73; Tolomio, "'Corpus carcer' nell'Alto Medioevo," 5–6, 10–11, 13. Although Hill, "Classical and Christian Tradition," generally portrays Ambrose as a Stoic, she sees him as teaching a Platonic body-soul dualism (153), and a doctrine of extreme asceticism (5, 14, 16, 70, 266). An alternative approach, emphasizing Ambrose's biblical anthropology to the exclusion of all else, is found in Szydzik, *"Ad imaginem dei";* idem, "Die geistigen Ursprünge der Imago-Dei-Lehre"; his strategy is to consider primarily Ambrose's *Hexaemeron* and *De paradiso,* ignoring the patriarch treatises.

69. This pastoral focus, emphasizing both ethics and sacraments for the normal Christian, has been noted by Dassmann, *Die Frömmigkeit des Kirchenvaters Ambrosius,* 98–99, 196–98; idem, "Die Kirche und ihre Gleider," 121–44; Piccolo, "Per lo studio della spiritualità ambrosiana," 38–39, 66–74; Nauroy, "La structure du *De Isaac,*" 226–36; Sanders, *"Fons vitae Christus,"* 19–21, 94, 99–102, 140–43, 179–81; Pasini, *Ambrogio di Milano,* 217–19, 222. On the other hand, Jacob, *"Arkandisziplin," Allegorese, Mystagogie,* 234–59; idem, "The Reception of the Origenist Tradition," in *Hebrew Bible/Old Testament,* 1:693–94, 695, 697, argues that Ambrose is concerned primarily and essentially with sacraments, not with ethics.

Let us flee, therefore, to our real, true fatherland. There is our fatherland and there is our Father, by whom we have been created, where there is the city of Jerusalem, which is the mother of all men. But what is this flight? . . . Let us not flee either with ships or chariots or horses, which are impeded and fall, but let us flee with our spirit and the eyes and feet that are within. Let us accustom our eyes to see what is bright and clear, to look upon the face of continence and of moderation, and upon all the virtues, in which there is nothing scabrous, nothing obscure or involved. And let each one look upon himself and his own conscience: let him cleanse that inner eye, so that it contains no dirt. For what is seen ought not to be discordant with him who sees, because God has wished that we be conformed to the image of his Son. Thus, the good is known to us and it is not far from any one of us, for "in him we live and move and have our being, for we also are his offspring," as the Apostle asserted that the Gentiles said (Acts 17:28).

Fugiamus ergo in patriam uerissimam. Illic patria nobis et illic pater, a quo creati sumus, ubi est Hierusalem ciuitas, quae est mater omnium. Sed quae est fuga? . . . Nec nauibus fugiamus aut curribus aut equis, qui obligantur et cadunt, sed fugiamus animo et oculis aut pedibus interioribus. Adsuescamus oculos nostros uidere quae dilucida et clara sunt, spectare uultum continentiae et temperantiae omnesque uirtutes, in quibus nihil scabrum, nihil obscurum et tortosum sit. Et ipsum spectet quis et conscientiam suam illum oculum mundet, ne quid habeat sordium; quod enim uidetur non debet dissonare ab eo qui uidet, quoniam conformes nos deus imaginis uoluit esse filii sui. Cognitum igitur nobis est illud bonum nec longe est ab unoquoque nostrum; *in ipso enim uiuimus et sumus et mouemur; ipsius enim et genus sumus*, ut apostolus gentiles posuit significare.[70]

This advice neatly concludes Rebecca's initiation, as it launches that of the *competentes*. Just as her conversion begins with her quest for self-knowledge, attained by introspection, so the ongoing life of Rebecca *in uia*, en route to a *patria* whose goals and values she has already internalized, is to be monitored by introspection. Her journey is not away from this world, by whatever means

---

70. Ambrose, *De Isa.* 8.78–79; McHugh trans., 63–64. I have altered his wording slightly.

of locomotion. It is, rather, a movement within, accomplished in the here and now, aimed at the integration of the self, whose virtues of moderation and self-lessness shine forth in the mirror of a good conscience. The Pauline struggle between flesh and spirit has been allayed; harmony has been achieved; she has recovered the image of God within her soul through the imitation of Christ.

The parallels between the ethical wisdom of the Greeks and the wisdom of the Old and New Testaments to which the Apostle to the Gentiles refers speak eloquently to Ambrose's success in combining both traditions in the lessons he presents to his *competentes*. This is his achievement in *De Isaac*, exemplified by Ambrose's Rebecca, reflecting his selective and often original use of his sources. His Rebecca has now been prepared to confront the challenges she faces and to impart the advice that she in turn gives, in *De Jacob*, the next of the patriarch treatises.

CHAPTER 6

Jacob

Ambrose's *De Jacob* takes a form quite different from that of his other patriarch treatises. While elsewhere in this corpus of works he argues that examples take precedence over precepts as an effective means of moral instruction, here he launches his treatise with a consideration of anthropology and ethics that is largely theoretical and, with minor exceptions, detached from exemplary events in the patriarch's life. It is only in the work's second book that he addresses himself systematically to the task of illustrating Jacob's virtues. Then, midway through Bk. 2, Ambrose switches gears rather abruptly, turning from Jacob to the martyrdom of the Maccabees. This move raises the question of whether there is any organic connection between the passage on the Maccabees and the rest of the treatise, or whether it was tacked on *ex post facto*. As with Ambrose's other patriarch treatises, *De Jacob* has drawn the attention of *Quellenforscher* interested in documenting his debts to Plato, the Neoplatonists, the Stoics, Philo, previous Christian exegetes, and in this case 1 and 2 Maccabees and Pseudo-Josephus as well, as a source for his 4 Maccabees material. On the other hand, his use of Aristotelianism has not attracted attention. What tends to pass unremarked is the independence with which Ambrose treats these philosophical, para-biblical, and exegetical sources and the way in which he reinterprets them in the light of Pauline theology. Equally noteworthy, and equally underappreciated, is his highly selective use of the book of Genesis in documenting Jacob's life and exemplifying his virtues. Ambrose omits much and alters much of what he includes of the biblical account of Jacob, even in cases where the material he leaves out could have been used to enhance his argument. The result of his handling of his sources, of whatever kind, is the emergence of a distinctive Ambrosian interpretation of anthropology, of ethics, and of Jacob himself.

Some of the *Quellenforscher* combine the wish to isolate Ambrose's borrowings with the desire to date *De Jacob* to 386, either because they want to make him the source of Augustine's Neoplatonism[1] or because they see the Maccabees section of Bk. 2 as a response to the Milanese basilica crisis of that year.[2] As we have already observed, this approach to the dating of *De Jacob* is basically flawed, owing to the fact that its supporters ignore the specifics surrounding the audience of *competentes* to which Ambrose addressed this and the other patriarch treatises, and the timing of the moral instruction he imparted to them. This means that, if one wants to place Augustine in the cohort of those who heard the preaching on which *De Jacob* is based, or if one wants to read the work as a response to the basilica crisis, the earliest possible date for the work in its present form is the beginning of Lent, 387.[3]

Leaving aside that question, those eager to view Ambrose as a transmitter of Platonism and Neoplatonism in this work have been concerned with trying to isolate particular authors and texts as his sources as well as with ascertaining whether his appropriation of them was direct or indirect.[4] Among those scholars seeking to trace Ambrose's dependence on Stoicism, some argue that he derived it by way of Plotinus, even while acknowledging that he had alternative modes of access to Stoicism, both direct and indirect.[5] Most commentators documenting Stoicism in Ambrose see him as more eclectic and as more

1. Hadot, "Platon et Plotin dans trois sermons," 215–20; Solignac, "Nouveaux parallèles entre saint Ambroise et Plotin."

2. Palanque, *Saint Ambroise et l'empire romain*, 154, 442, 514–15; Dassmann, *Die Frömmigkeit der Kirchenvaters Ambrosius*, 10–11; Nauroy, "Les frères Maccabés dans l'exégèse d'Ambroise," 215, 219–38; idem, "Du combat de la piété à la confession du sang," 49; Moorhead, *Ambrose*, 135–37.

3. See chapter 2, 25–27.

4. Hadot, "Platon et Plotin dans trois sermons," 215–20; Solignac, "Nouveaux parallèles entre saint Ambroise et Plotin," 148–56; Courcelle, "Plotin et saint Ambroise"; idem, "Nouvelle aspects du platonisme chez saint Ambroise"; idem, "De Platon à saint Ambroise par Apulée"; idem, "Tradition platonicienne et traditions chrétiennes du corps-prison," 426; idem, "Ambroise de Milan, 'professeur de philosophie'"; idem, *Recherches sur Saint Ambroise*, 16.

5. Palla, intro. to his trans. of Ambrose, *De Iacob*, ed. Schenkl, 216–20; Solignac, "Nouveaux parallèles entre saint Ambroise et Plotin," 149; cf. on the other hand, Felici, "Il *De Iacob et vita beata* di S. Ambrogio e il *De vita beata* di Seneca," who thinks that Ambrose takes a drastically anti-Stoic position.

concerned with combining Stoicism with Christianity,[6] or specifically with defending the position that the New Testament does not supersede the Old.[7] Scholars tracking Ambrose's use of Philo in *De Jacob* range from those who see straightforward positive influence,[8] to those who see Ambrose as modifying Philo's position,[9] to those who dismiss Ambrose's appeals to Philo as too fitful to be important.[10] The one study of the interpretation of Jacob in early Christianity to date sees Ambrose as sometimes aligning himself with his predecessors and sometimes not, predecessors who, in any case, take a far more preclusively typological line than he does.[11] 1 and 2 Maccabees and the 4 Maccabees of Pseudo-Josephus are the recognized sources for the Maccabees material in *De Jacob*,[12] with some commentators noting that these texts, especially 4 Maccabees, with its heavy appropriation of the Stoic doctrine of the sage in their portrayal of the martyrs, could easily have supplemented Ambrose's other sources for that philosophy.[13] No one discussing Ambrose's use of these sources for the martyrdom of the Maccabees has noted the changes that he rings on these materials.

Ambrose begins *De Jacob* by observing that virtue is teachable; that moral education involves discourse, reason, and examples of virtue; and that he intends to proceed in this order. Discourse, he notes, tells us what is right and wrong. It is useful as admonition but weak in persuasion; hence, it needs the assistance of reason. It is "the consideration of right reason" (rationis rectae consideratio)[14] that persuades us to do what is right, framing its advocacy either in terms of ends that are "according to nature" (de naturalibus)—that is,

---

6. Thamin, *Saint Ambroise et la morale chrétienne*, 313–14, 326, 328; Dassmann, *Die Frömmigkeit des Kirchenvaters Ambrosius*, 10–11, 19, 21, 22, 23–26, 29; Nauroy, "La méthode de la composition et la structure du *De Iacob*," 120–21, 125–40; Spanneut, "Le Stoïcisme dans l'histoire de la patience chrétienne"; Colish, *The Stoic Tradition*, 2:56–57.

7. Hahn, *Das wahre Gesetz*, 119–21.

8. Lucchesi, *L'Usage de Philon*, 64, 86.

9. Savòn, *Saint Ambroise devant l'exégèse de Philon*, 1:13, 350–76.

10. Palla, intro. to his trans. of Ambrose, *De Iac.*, 220–21.

11. Dulaey, "La figure de Jacob."

12. Kellner, *Der heilige Ambrosius*, 110–15; Palanque, *Saint Ambroise et l'empire romain*, 154, 442, 514–15.

13. Palla, intro. to his trans. of Ambrose, *De Iac.*, 218, 222; Nauroy, "Les frères Maccabés dans l'exégèse d'Ambroise," 215–45; idem, "Du combat de la piété à la confession du sang"; Niehoff, *The Figure of Joseph in Post-Biblical Jewish Literature*, 89–110; Rajak, "Dying for the Law."

14. Ambrose, *De Iac.* 1.1.1; my trans.

what is intrinsically good—or "according to what is "useful" (de utilibus).[15] Reason also enables us to govern our passions and to channel them in good, or at least neutral, directions.[16] Ambrose adds that reason's capacity to make use of these functions is inborn; God creates us with minds able to exercise "royal governance" (regale . . . imperium) over ourselves. God has also "implanted [in us] moral laws and feelings" (mores sensusque plantaret). Aside from these gifts that we enjoy as a function of our created nature, God has also given us his own precepts to follow. From both of these sources, human and divine, we can acquire wisdom, the knowledge of right and wrong, and the ability to choose the good.[17]

Thus far, Ambrose sounds much like the Middle Stoic Panaetius, except for the notion that we have innate ethical knowledge. Certainly the Stoics would agree that the mind is the ruling principle of the human constitution and that our prime goal is to attain wisdom, which this school placed at the head of the cardinal virtues since all virtues depend on correct intellectual judgments about the nature of things and about the moral value of what we experience. But Ambrose next makes a strongly Panaetian statement about these same cardinal virtues. Elsewhere in the patriarch treatises he shows his Aristotelian colors by treating justice as the paramount cardinal virtue, since its norm is the common weal; it is a supremely public virtue, while all the other virtues can have a purely private expression. In De Jacob, however, the cardinal virtue to which he gives pride of place is temperance. As we have seen in considering De Abraham and De Isaac, Ambrose proposes temperance, rather than asceticism, as the moral stance appropriate to his lay audience. To be sure, he reiterates this message in De Jacob, where his frequent appeals to detachment[18] treat this advice, not as a Neoplatonic flight from or repression of the body, but as moderation: "nothing in excess of what is needed" (nihil superfluum necessarium).[19]

But beyond that general orientation, in De Jacob Ambrose argues that, in the process of moral education, temperance is the virtue that comes first, even before wisdom. He thus reverses the relationship between "know thyself" and "nothing in excess" that he posits in De Isaac. Since the rational faculty no less

15. Ibid. 1.1.2; my trans.

16. Ibid. 1.1.4, 1.7.27, 1.7.29.

17. Ibid. 1.1.4; my trans.

18. Ibid. 1.4.15, 1.5.17, 1.5.19–1.6.20, 1.7.27, 1.7.29, 1.7.32–1.8.39, 2.3.12, 2.6.28, 2.6.29–2.7.30, 2.9.37–39, 2.10.42–2.12.57.

19. Ibid. 2.5.20; my trans.; see also 1.2.5–1.3.9, 1.8.37, 2.1.4, 2.4.15, 2.6.27, 2.10.43.

than the body is susceptible to the passions that arise from it, temperance is needed to moderate both the mind and the body: "Therefore, temperance comes before correction and is the mistress of learning" (Temperantia est igitur correctionis praeuia, disciplinae magistra).[20] Right reason also teaches us what and how to bear and forbear, counseling mercy and forgiveness.[21] If this lesson can be learned from the Stoics, it is also found in the Bible, in both the Old and New Testaments. The virtues that Ambrose flags, resulting from the exercise of right reason informed by temperance, are the other cardinal virtues of wisdom, courage, and justice, joined by humility, obedience, and fear of the Lord.[22] Of these three latter virtues, Ambrose singles out humility for more extended consideration. By way of his advice on how to acquire humility, he adds another ingredient to the list of sources of virtue along with right reason and temperance, namely, grace. We learn humility primarily as a response to the teachings of the New Testament, he explains. Neither the natural law nor the law of Moses suffices. Rather, it is the grace of Christ, forgiving our past sins and giving us the strength to struggle effectively against sin once we are reborn, that enables us to attain virtue in the here and now and eternal glory in the next life.[23]

Taught by Holy Scripture as well as by philosophy, we learn that the chief virtue of the sage, enabling him to attain and retain the happy life despite the vicissitudes of fortune, is equanimity. At the midpoint of Bk. 1 of *De Jacob*, Ambrose's injunctions to practice detachment undergo a shift. He no longer focuses on the need to disdain physical pleasures. Rather, he focuses on the constancy of the sage confronted by sufferings and misfortunes of all kinds. He presents his version of the Christian-Stoic sage, rehearsing the paradoxes surrounding the Stoic sage—a sage, however, whose self-sufficiency never translates into Stoic autarchy, since his natural virtues are united with grace. He is one of the Lord's elect, never lacking in God's assistance;[24] and he strengthens

---

20. Ibid. 1.2.5; trans. McHugh in Ambrose, *Seven Exegetical Works*, 123. As is noted by North, *Sophrosyne*, 224, "Sophrosyne becomes, for Panaetius, the psychological prerequisite for any virtuous activity; as such it achieves *de facto* primacy among the cardinal virtues." She does not, however, note Ambrose's appropriation of this idea in the section of her book dealing with his treatment of moderation (360–70).

21. Ambrose, *De Iac.* 1.2.8, 2.7.32.

22. Ibid. 1.3.8–9.

23. Ibid. 1.3.12–1.6.23.

24. Ibid. 1.6.26; Spanneut, "Le Stoïcisme dans l'histoire de la patience chrétienne," 108–9, offers a fine appreciation of the distinction between Ambrosian self-sufficiency and Stoic autarchy.

and consoles himself with the hope of resurrection and eternal life.[25] Still, like the Stoic sage, he is without fear; he can abandon things that are morally indifferent at will; he alone is truly rich and truly free; his virtues mutually coinhere in each other and in him.[26] Ambrose's sage also has some distinctly Christian, and Ambrosian, attributes. He rejoices in God's presence; he knows that nothing can separate him from the love of Christ, which will enable him to endure any hardships that life deals out to him. As a saint, he seeks to do good to everyone; he calms the fears of others, inspiring courage in them by precept and example; he is charitable to the needy, reckoning his own personal wealth as wealth held in common and as available to those needing support; he is a citizen of heaven.[27]

Ambrose offers a series of figures of speech to describe the sage. His soul is a richly cultivated field, yielding a crop of many virtues.[28] He is both an athlete and a lantern in a storm.[29] His soul sings sweet hymns of praise to God, even if his body, like a broken harp or cithara, is crushed by affliction.[30] Most frequently, Ambrose invokes nautical imagery. The sage pilots his way through the tempests of the world into a safe harbor, avoiding shipwreck, anchored against the storms of this life, his oars proof against the rising waves of suffering; he is an ark in the midst of the deluge.[31] Ambrose also offers an extended portrait of the sage:

> For the wise man is not broken by bodily ills nor is he disturbed by misfortunes, but he remains happy even amid troubles. Bodily adversities do not diminish the gift of a happy life or take away anything from its sweetness. For the happiness of life does not lie in bodily pleasures, but in a conscience pure of every stain, and in the mind of the man who knows that the good is also the pleasurable, even though it is harsh, and that what is shameful does not give delight, even though it is sweet. Therefore, the

---

25. Ambrose, *De Iac.* 1.7.31.

26. Ibid. 1.6.25–1.8.39.

27. Ibid. 1.7.27, 1.7.31, 1.8.36–39; for citizenship in heaven, quoting Phil 3:20, 1.8.39, 2.9.38.

28. Ambrose, *De Iac.* 2.1.3.

29. Ibid. 1.8.6. On Jacob as an athlete of God, Ambrose follows Philo, as is noted by Dulaey, "La figure de Jacob," 78–79.

30. Ambrose, *De Iac.* 1.3.39, 1.12.56, 2.9.39–40, 2.11.53.

31. Ibid. 1.6.24, 1.8.36, 2.6.28, 2.10.44, 2.11.53, 2.12.57. Courcelle, "De Platon à saint Ambroise par Apulée," 22–23, sees these themes as specifically Platonic, but they had become, by Ambrose's day, so commonplace as to have acquired a generic sense.

motive for living well is not bodily pleasure, but the mind's sagacity. For it is not the flesh, which is subject to passion, that judges but the mind, because nothing gives more pleasure than honorable counsels and noble deeds; that is why the mind is the interpreter of what constitutes the happy life. . . . And so the man who follows Jesus has within himself his own recompense, and in his [Jesus'] own love he has received grace.

Non enim frangitur sapiens doloribus corporis nec uexatur incommodis, sed etiam in aerumnis beatus manet. Neque enim aduersa corporis uitae beatae munus inminuunt neque de eius aliquid suauitate delibant, quia non in delectatione corporis uitae beatitudo est, sed in conscientia pura ab omne labe peccati et in eius mente qui cognoscit quia quod bonum est hoc delectat, etiamsi asperum sit, quod autem indecorum, etiamsi suaue, non mulcet. Ergo causa bene uiuendi non delectatio corporalis, sed mentis prudentia est. Non enim caro, quae subiecta est passioni, sed mens, quae iudicat, quia nihil melius delectat quam consiliorum honestas et operum pulchritudo; ea igitur beatae interpretes est uitae. . . . Habet ergo in se remunerationem suam qui sequitur Iesum et in suo affectu praemium est gratiam.[32]

In this formulation, divine grace and the Christian virtues empower the sage to practice the Stoic virtues, and correct intellectual judgment is the norm of good and evil. In this formulation as well, a key word for Ambrose is "flesh" (caro). For in attaining the detachment characterizing the happy life, the sage must come to understand the difference between body and mind on the one hand, and flesh and spirit on the other. The anthropology that undergirds the ethical ideal outlined by Ambrose involves a thorough rethinking on his part both of Aristotelian hylomorphism and of Stoic psychology in the light of St. Paul's doctrine of human nature as put forth in the Epistle to the Romans. In working out what emerges as the most fully developed anthropology found in the patriarch treatises in Bk. 1 of *De Jacob*, the two chief notions on which Ambrose focuses are free will and the passions. Without expressly mentioning any particular school of Greek philosophy, whether to assign praise or blame, Ambrose rejects Stoic psychological monism and redefines the Stoic theory of

---

32. Ambrose, *De Iac.* 1.7.28; McHugh trans., 137. Ambrose refers to conscience in the same vein at 1.8.39.

the passions while modifying the Stoic view of the mind as the ruling principle of the human constitution. He also distances himself from Neoplatonic asceticism and from the view that our sinful state, punished by our embodiment, is the result of a metaphysical fall of the soul over which we have no control. With Plato and Aristotle, and with Panaetian Middle Stoicism, he shares the view that we should not seek to quench the heat of our passions, but that we can and should redirect it so that it can fuel our development of virtue.

Ambrose insists on the principle that our free will is the source of both our virtues and our vices, a theme he connects with the contrast between slavery and freedom. As he puts it, "We are not constrained to obedience by necessity, as if we were slaves, but by the judgment of our will, whether we tend toward virtue or are inclined to vice" (Non enim seruili ad oboedientiam constringimur necessitate, sed uoluntate arbitra, siue ad uirtutem propendimus siue ad culpam inclinamur).[33] In a decidedly anti-Neoplatonic manner, Ambrose stresses the point that the source of our moral failings lies in our misuse of free will. Our problem is not the body, which is the agent of the will, and which, accordingly, can be the instrument of either virtue or vice:

> We cannot attribute our problem to anything but our will. No one is guilty of sin who has not turned to it by means of his own will. Actions imposed by others on the unwilling are not culpable; we regard as blameworthy only evil deeds committed voluntarily. . . . Why, then, do we accuse the body, as if it were weak? For our physical members are the weapons of injustice and the weapons of justice. . . . Therefore, mental disposition, not the body, is the author of guilt; the flesh is the servant of the will.

> Non est quod cuiquam nostram adscribamus aerumnam nisi nostrae uoluntati. Nemo tenetur ad culpam, nisi uoluntate propria deflexerit. Non habent crimen quae inferuntur reluctantibus, uoluntaria tantum comissa sequitur delictorum inuidia. . . . Quid carnem quasi infirmam accusamus? Membra nostra arma sunt iniustitiae et arma iustitiae. . . . Affectus igitur, non caro auctor est culpae, caro autem uoluntatis ministra.[34]

33. Ibid. 1.1.1; my trans.
34. Ibid. 1.3.10; my trans.

In the above instance, it is free will that is responsible for sin, and when this is the case, the will's external expression of itself is "the flesh." At the same time and by the same token, we can freely will to abandon sin, "the flesh," and seek virtue. When this occurs, "our will, following reason, calls us away [from sin]" (uoluntas reuocat rationem secuta).[35]

Therefore, Ambrose argues, we have the capacity to free ourselves from slavery to the vices, from slavery to sin. In so doing, we can attain self-mastery and the authority of a clear conscience, the freedom to act wisely in accordance with our own good will.[36] While our own initiative and effort are clearly required in this enterprise, Ambrose reminds his *competentes* that we are also assisted by Christ, who has redeemed us from slavery to sin. In elaborating this theme, he capitalizes on a Roman legal institution quite familiar to his audience. In ancient Rome, when a master manumitted a slave, the freedman did not acquire completely independent status and full civil rights immediately. Rather, he owed to his former master certain services, or *opera*.[37] Ambrose invokes this institution when he declares, quoting 1 Corinthians 7:22, that each of his *competentes* "is a freedman of the Lord" (libertus est domini).[38] Thus, he tells his audience, "You who have been redeemed by the Lord . . . owe servitude to him as your Lord and Redeemer. . . . You have received your freedom in such a way that you ought to remember your manumitter, so as to realize that lawful obedience is due to him, your patron" (redemptus a domino es . . . et quasi domino seruitutem debes et quasi redemptori. . . . Ita libertatem accepisti, ut meminisse manumissoris tui debeas, ut patrono tuo noueris legitimum obsequium deferendum).[39]

This slavery to sin from which the Christian is redeemed by the confluence of grace and free will—whose respective territorial rights Ambrose has no interest in delineating—is also equated by him with the conflict between flesh and spirit described by St. Paul (Rom 7:14–24). Ambrose agrees that the mind hates sin but that the flesh desires it: "With my mind I consent to the law and with my flesh I do what I do not want" (qui legi mente consentio et carne quod

35. Ibid. 1.1.1; McHugh trans., 119.
36. Ibid. 2.3.12–13.
37. Berger, *Encyclopedic Dictionary of Roman Law*, s.v. *manumissio, iurata promissio liberti*.
38. Ambrose, *De Iac.* 1.3.11; my trans.
39. Ibid. 1.3.12; McHugh trans., 128. I have altered his wording slightly.

nolo hac ago).[40] Ambrose's use of the term "flesh" (caro) in this context is quite deliberate and specific. It will be recalled that, in *De Isaac,* he argues that "the flesh" stands for human sinfulness as such, wherever in our constitution it may arise: "Where 'flesh' is applied to the human being, a sinner is meant" (ubi autem caro pro homine nuncupatur, peccator exprimitur).[41] Since it is human passions that lead us to sin, and since sin can be found in all the subdivisions of human nature, it behooves Ambrose to develop a theory of the passions accounting for that principle. He proceeds to do so in Bk. 1 of *De Jacob.*

Ambrose begins by noting that passions are a feature of the human condition which, while they can be governed and redirected, cannot be excised from our nature. The most powerful of the passions is concupiscence. He emphasizes the idea that concupiscence encompasses much more than sexual desire. What it means is unreasonable desire of any kind.[42] He hammers in this point by immediately citing, as his example of concupiscence, King David's desire for water from a well in Bethlehem currently behind enemy lines, which could be obtained by his troops only at great risk, when there was no lack of good water close to hand: "For David was subject to a human passion, so that he desired irrationally" (Humanum itaque passus est David, ut inrationabiliter concupisceret).[43] David did send men to bring him water from this well in Bethlehem. But, struck by compunction at the irrationality of his desire for the water, the selfishness of the orders that he had given to his men, and the unnecessary danger to which he had exposed them, he refused to drink it, pouring it out instead as a libation to the Lord. Ambrose presents David as a saint: "Among men, whom can we regard as better and stronger than holy David?" (Denique quem de hominibus meliorum et fortiorem adsumemus quam sanctum David?).[44] Nonetheless, David had to learn how to govern his passions rationally, even if after the fact.

40. Ibid. 1.4.15; McHugh trans., 130; see also ibid. 1.5.27. Noted by Palla, intro. to his trans. of Ambrose, *De Iac.,* 218–19.

41. Ambrose, *De Isaac* 2.3, ed. Schenkl, trans. Moreschini. Noted by Sanders, *"Fons vitae Christus,"* 179–81.

42. Ambrose, *De Iac.* 1.1.1–2, 1.2.5.

43. Ibid. 1.1.3; my trans. David's thirst in this episode is also described as an irrational desire in 4 Macc 3:6–17.

44. Ambrose, *De Iac.* 1.1.3; my trans.

With this introduction in place, Ambrose proceeds to analyze the passions under three headings.[45] Some passions arise in the body. The examples he gives are gluttony and wantonness. Some passions arise in the soul. Under this rubric, his examples are pride, envy, avarice, ambition, and strife. There are also passions that, according to Ambrose, arise in both the body and the soul. In this third category he places the Stoic quartet of pleasure, pain, fear, and desire. But he alters this Stoic doctrine significantly. In the first place, the Stoics were monists. For them, the fabled mind-body problem did not exist. What other schools of philosophy called mind and body, they viewed as a single phenomenon, merely containing within it a division of labor. The governance of this human entity by reason was not, for them, just a norm or a desideratum; it was also a description of the way they thought human beings actually function. Accordingly, the Stoics saw all four of the passions as arising from false rational judgments. Pleasure and pain reflect false intellectual judgments concerning what we currently experience. Fear and desire reflect false intellectual judgments concerning what we currently anticipate in the sequel. On the other hand, Ambrose, with Aristotle, sees mind and body as distinct if integrally united in the human person. Thus, mind alone, or body alone, or body and mind together, can be a source of the passions, passions which differ depending on the aspect, or aspects, of human nature in which they arise.

In addition to departing from the Stoics on the sources of the passions, Ambrose also expands the number of the passions from four to seven and invokes his own set of principles for analyzing them. Ambrose's approach to the passions is developmental. He considers them in the light of the sequence in which we experience them. Unreasonable desire leads to pleasure, which leads to joy. Fear leads to pain, which leads to sadness. Ambrose adds another passion, mental agitation, to joy and sadness, as the common outcome, with them, of pleasure and pain. This theory of the passions is not just an amplification of the Stoic doctrine on this topic; it is an original Ambrosian interpretation of the origins of the passions, and one that fits smoothly into his view of "the flesh" as sin, whether motivated by physical or mental passions, or both. This reformulation of Stoicism replaces the normative with the operational in the engendering of vicious states, which accords well with Ambrose's developmental approach to ethics more generally. Finally, it is worth noting how smoothly Ambrose integrates into his account, as passions of the mind, mental

45. Ibid. 1.1.1, 1.2.5.

states flagged as sins by New Testament authors. The sovereign remedy for all three kinds of human passions, according to Ambrose, is a "sober mind" (mens sobria), assisted by the virtue of temperance.[46]

Having outlined the anthropology and ethics that he develops in Bk. 1 of *De Jacob*, and having set before his *competentes* the image of the Christian-Stoic sage as its ideal embodiment, it remains, for Ambrose, to show that Jacob exemplifies this ideal. While he does move from discourse and reason to examples at some points in Bk. 1, Ambrose reserves his detailed consideration of Jacob for the first half of Bk. 2. In the assignment of each patriarch's paramount virtue at the beginning of *De Joseph*, he ascribes to Jacob the endurance of sufferings.[47] This quality is fully consistent with the equanimity of the sage, on which Ambrose focuses in the second half of Bk. 1. We recall as well the host of other virtues, Stoic and Christian, that Ambrose attributes to the sage. As the exponent of all these virtues and more, Ambrose's Jacob is a construct built with great selectivity. His Jacob is by no means isomorphic with the Jacob of Genesis. In fact, on occasion, Ambrose makes moral claims for his Jacob that are contradicted by the biblical text. At some points he rewrites the biblical text itself in order to strengthen his own case. And he omits much. Some of his omissions can be explained as an effort to avoid embarrassing or unwelcome topics, or exegetical questions for which he cannot find adequate answers. But in other cases Ambrose omits events and details mentioned in the book of Genesis which lack these problems and which he could have used to enrich the ethical instruction that he seeks to impart.

With *De Jacob* we have moved beyond the stage of patriarchal pedagogy devoted to converts and conversion. Ambrose now presents a protagonist deemed to have possessed moral excellence from his youth. The tribulations that he undergoes, and his interactions with God and his angels, are all occasions in which he displays his virtues. We first hear of Jacob when he is an infant in his mother's womb, struggling with his twin brother Esau. As we noted in considering this event in *De Isaac*, Rebecca appeals to God for an understanding of this phenomenon. According to Ambrose, God tells her that the prenatal tensions between her sons will continue in their postnatal lives. But Ambrose omits the second part of the prophesy, that the elder will serve the younger (Gen 25:23).[48] Had he included the full biblical phrase, Ambrose

---

46. Ibid. 1.1.4–5; my trans.; the quotation is at 1.1.4.
47. Ambrose, *De Ioseph* 1.1, ed. Schenkl, trans. Palla.
48. Ambrose, *De Isa.* 4.18; see chapter 5, 84–85.

could have simplified considerably his approach to the first set of problems he addresses at the beginning of Jacob's story: his acquisition of his brother's birthright and his masquerading as Esau in order to obtain his father's blessing, and the role of Jacob's parents, especially Rebecca, in these events. As Genesis 25:29–33 relates, Esau arrives from the field to find Jacob boiling pottage. He asks for the food, and Jacob's rejoinder is to ask for Esau's birthright in return. When Esau cedes it, Jacob immediately asks him to swear an oath reinforcing the cession, and Esau complies. However, this is not the way Ambrose reports the exchange between the brothers. First, Ambrose states that the food involved was prepared for Jacob—not that he prepared it himself—and that nonetheless he graciously accedes to Esau's request for it. More important, Ambrose's Jacob does not ask for Esau's birthright in exchange for the food, nor does he demand that Esau confirm the cession by an oath. Ambrose's Jacob merely "received from him the birthright of the firstborn" (a quo primatus benedictionis accepit).[49] The transfer of the rights of the firstborn becomes, in Ambrose's hands, a spontaneous offer initiated by Esau in which Jacob plays an essentially passive role.

Likewise, Jacob's reaction to Rebecca's advice that he substitute himself for Esau when it comes time for the aged Isaac to distribute blessings to his sons varies notably from the biblical account. Genesis reports that, when Rebecca divulges the impersonation scheme, Jacob's initial reaction is a purely practical one: since Esau is hairy, and he is not, how will he be able to fool Isaac? (Gen 27:11–12). On the other hand, Ambrose's Jacob is initially perturbed by his mother's advice and is unwilling to wrong his brother and deceive his father: "How respectful of God's commands he was! He refused to do wrong by his brother. How honorable! He refused to practice deceit upon his father" (quam religiosus, ut fratrem recusaret laedere, quam uerecundus, ut patrem timeret fallere).[50] In the end, what sways Ambrose's Jacob is his wisdom, mildness, and affection for his father and his filial piety toward his mother: "How respectful! He could not refuse his mother what she ordered" (quam honorificus, ut matri non posset quod iubebatur negaret!)[51]

---

49. Ambrose, *De Iac.* 2.1.4; McHugh trans., 148.
50. Ibid.; McHugh trans., 148.
51. Ibid.; McHugh trans., 148. While Ambrose follows his exegetical predecessors in justifying Jacob's deception as obedience to his mother, as is noted by Dulaey, "La figure de Jacob," 88–90, 95, he departs from tradition by noting Jacob's initial perturbation at the idea.

As for Rebecca, Ambrose's analysis of her behavior is unduly complicated. He wants to read this chapter of Jacob's story as a lesson in correct parent-child relations. In particular—and here he may reflect a Roman's discomfort with the very idea of a special legacy for the firstborn son, given that Roman inheritance law treated all children under *patria potestas* as entitled to an equal inheritance irrespective of sex or birth order—he is confronted with the fact of Rebecca's preference for the younger son, while Isaac clearly thinks that he should give the more important blessing to the firstborn. The major lesson concerning good parenting that Ambrose wants to convey is that parents should not play favorites among their children: "Children should be nurtured with an equal measure of devotion; . . . The norm of justice should be the same for all" (Eadem foueat prolem mensura pietatis; . . . par debet circa omnes esse forma iustitiae),[52] he urges. True, children as individuals have different traits, which may inspire their parents' love to a greater or lesser degree. Still, parents should not give their children preferential treatment, lest this policy lead to sibling rivalry, jealousy, and hatred, and the destruction of family life.[53] If, indeed, one parent is inclined to favor one of the children, Ambrose continues, the other parent should offset that favoritism by preferring another, the father's judiciousness tempered by the mother's soft-heartedness: "Let the one parent make good what the other has diminished" (Conpensat alter quod alter imminuit).[54] But Ambrose quickly abandons this kind of advice, and with good reason, for it continues to involve the preferential treatment of children by parents.

Ambrose eventually resolves the dilemma of Rebecca's behavior with three arguments, two elaborate and the last quite simple. Rather than preferring one son to the other, he states, she was preferring virtue to vice. Jacob was wise, just, and temperate; Esau, for his part, was unjust, wrathful, envious, and intemperate. Rebecca knew that Jacob was the more perceptive of the two; and in giving him Esau's clothes for the impersonation, she gave him the royal, priestly, and prophetic garments that the church makes more knowledgeable use of than the synagogue. In elaborating this theme, Ambrose takes a cue from Philo, who also says that Jacob and Esau represent virtue and vice, respectively. But in addition to typologizing the brothers, Ambrose names their

52. Ambrose, *De Iac.* 1.2.5; my trans.
53. Ibid.
54. Ibid. 1.2.7; McHugh trans., 150.

vices and virtues more specifically.[55] As the book of Genesis indicates, Esau manifests another kind of vicious behavior as well, which Ambrose passes over in silence. Esau's marital arrangements are profoundly offensive to Rebecca: he marries two Hittite wives (Gen 26:34–35; 27:46). The biblical text does not specify that these marriages were sequential, so the inference is that they were concurrent. Worse yet to Rebecca and Isaac, Esau also marries a daughter of Ishmael (Gen 28:9). As a polygamist, an exogamist, and a son who makes common cause with the outcast Ishmael, a potentially ominous compact between the deprived and the marginalized, Esau is viewed by his parents as anything but upright. Ambrose's reason for omitting this material is unclear unless it stems from an unwillingness to revisit the issue of monogamy and marital chastity in *De Jacob*, since it is impossible to defend Jacob's own marital practices on moral or historical grounds.

In any case, Esau's worst vice, of which Ambrose takes full cognizance, is his envious hatred of Jacob, whom he threatens to kill.[56] Yet and still, Ambrose claims that Rebecca interceded with Isaac on Esau's behalf after he had given the firstborn's blessing to Jacob so that Esau would receive a blessing as well, if a lesser one: "She took counsel also for her other son; she withdrew him from God's disfavor, lest he incur greater culpability if he lost the grace of the blessing he did receive" (et alteri consulebat, quem diuinae subducebat offensae, ne grauiore implicaretur reatu, si acceptae gratiam benedictionis amitterit).[57] Both this alleged intercession on Rebecca's part and the claim that she withdrew God's disfavor from Esau are sheer fabrications on Ambrose's part; neither of these events occurs in the text of Genesis.

Having argued both that Rebecca preferred not one son over the other but virtue over vice, and that she nonetheless sought the well-being of the vicious Esau, Ambrose returns to the simple point that could have cut through the Gordian knot represented by Rebecca's behavior in a single stroke. It is a move that Philo makes without having to embroil his account in the intricate web of argument that Ambrose weaves. As Philo sees it, in Jacob's deception of Isaac, it was God who was acting. Jacob—and, by extension, Rebecca—was simply carrying out the prophesy given by God during Rebecca's pregnancy. So too,

---

55. Ibid. 1.2.6, 1.2.8–10, 2.1.2–3, 2.2.6, 2.3.11; cf. Philo, *Questions and Answers on Genesis* 4.162, 4.165, 4.167, 4.170, 4.174, trans. Marcus.

56. Ambrose, *De Iac.* 1.4.14.

57. Ibid. 2.2.6; McHugh trans., 149.

Ambrose eventually agrees, Jacob was indeed given precedence over Esau by God, "preferred by the prophesy" (praeferabatur oraculo).[58] Rebecca's awareness of the fact that Jacob's superior moral qualities will enable him to make good use of his father's blessing and to serve as an appropriate bearer of the covenant in the next generation and her recollection, at length, of the divine prophesy, mean that the aid she gives to Jacob should be reckoned as an expression of her piety.[59] Another aspect of her piety can be seen in Rebecca's behavior: she functions as a corrective to Isaac's desire to give the firstborn's blessing to Esau, even though Isaac himself is aware of the prophesy. Despite that knowledge, Isaac seeks to place a human presumption concerning his elder son's rights, or his own gastronomic preference for the wild game that Esau hunts, over God's stated plans for his sons. It is Rebecca, not Isaac, who is more sensitive to the notion that God's will can override human conventions and presuppositions, and that his will must be done.

In any event, reminding his audience that patience is one of Rebecca's virtues and that she bequeaths it to Jacob, Ambrose notes that she sends him away to her brother Laban to escape Esau's fratricidal wrath. Patience, forbearance, and longanimity are indeed qualities that Jacob will need and that he displays in abundance as he enters the next phase of his life. Ambrose heightens the pathos of his parting from his parents and his homeland by describing his departure as an "exile" (exilium) he did not fear, a term that does not occur in Genesis in this context. Nor does Philo use this term either, telescoping Jacob's long stay with Laban as a swift passage through political life and the life of the senses endured before Jacob arrives at his true goal, the contemplative life.[60]

But before continuing with Jacob's subsequent adventures, Ambrose takes pains to address an issue that will recur repeatedly in this patriarch's life, namely, the problem of fraud and deception. In Jacob's story, there are two kinds of fraud and deception, admissible and inadmissible. Ambrose is careful to distinguish between them and to offer justifications for the deceptions that he regards as acceptable. Initially, he takes from Philo the idea that not all deceit is blameworthy; as Philo notes, all's fair in war, and military strategems such as ambushes are perfectly all right.[61] In Rebecca's case, as Ambrose has

58. Ibid. 2.2.8; my trans.; cf. Philo, *Questions and Answers on Genesis* 4.212.

59. Ambrose, *De Iac.* 2.2.3–8.

60. Ibid. 2.4.14; my trans.; exile is also mentioned at 2.4.18; on Philo, see Savon, *Saint Ambroise devant l'exégèse de Philon*, 1:350–76.

61. Philo, *Questions and Answers on Genesis* 4.228.

argued, her piety and zeal in facilitating God's prophesy inspire her to order Jacob to masquerade as Esau and to assist him in carrying out the impersonation. Her actions, and Jacob's in obedience to her, are therefore not merely excusable, but praiseworthy.

The language that Ambrose uses to describe the deception counseled by Rebecca and carried out by Jacob is, legally speaking, neutral; and under the circumstances, Ambrose's wording in that passage can scarcely be accidental. For in treating Isaac's reaction to Jacob's deception, Ambrose takes specific account of the criminal terminology that would describe such acts and addresses it squarely. Roman law had two technical terms for denoting actionable deception: *dolus* and *fraus*.[62] *Dolus* meant any wily contrivance aimed at defrauding, deceiving, or cheating someone else. If such activity were proved to a magistrate, he would dismiss any claims or defenses based on it. *Fraus* was understood, in the first instance, as an act designed to defraud or deprive someone of legitimate advantage. Also, in contractual relations, *fraus* meant the cheating of a creditor by means of alienations, that is, the diminution of the debtor's property, making it impossible for him to pay his debts. In discussing Isaac's response to Jacob's deception, Ambrose observes that, after Isaac recognizes it, far from criticizing Jacob for what Ambrose describes as *dolus*, Isaac praises him instead: "For deceit is good when the plunder is without reproach. Now the plunder of piety is beyond reproach" (Bonus enim dolus, ubi inreprehensibilis est rapina; inreprehensibilis autem rapina pietatis).[63] Here, Ambrose equates Isaac's paternal blessing with booty legitimately seized by a victorious warrior, and his justification of Jacob's *dolus* is in accord with Philo's military exception. But later in the same paragraph, Ambrose offers another case of deception expressed in Roman legal language whose perpetrator he likewise exculpates, although without a military rationale. When Joseph governed Egypt, Ambrose notes, he summoned his brother Benjamin, held back in Canaan by his father Jacob, "having fabricated a pious fraud" (piae conmento fraudis).[64]

Pious fraud, therefore, exists and is justifiable; but it has to be contrasted with the vicious kind of fraud and deception for which Romans would be

---

62. Berger, *Encyclopedic Dictionary of Roman Law*, s.v. *dolus, fraus*.

63. Ambrose, *De Iac.* 2.3.10; McHugh trans., 152.

64. Ibid.; my trans. Ambrose's justification of pious fraud has been discussed by Argal Echarri, "Isaac y Rebeca," 146–60, although without noting his use of Roman legal terminology.

legally culpable. There are four other episodes in the section of Genesis dealing with Jacob's life where fraud and deception occur, leaving aside Joseph's
ploy for getting Benjamin to Egypt. The single biggest culprit is Laban, who
cheats Jacob repeatedly. While Laban professes great joy in welcoming Jacob
as a kinsman, he insists that Jacob work for him for no wages, merely to be
rewarded after seven years by the hand of his daughter Rachel. As Genesis
29:13–28 relates, he then passes off his elder and less beautiful daughter, Leah,
as Jacob's initial bride. When Jacob discovers this deception, he is constrained
to work for another seven years for no wages in order to gain the hand of his
beloved Rachel. While elsewhere Ambrose describes the replacement of
Rachel by Leah as outright *fraus*,[65] and while Laban's action certainly matches
the first definition of fraud in Roman law, in *De Jacob* Ambrose chooses to
omit this important example of the crime. His only reference to Jacob's bigamy
is a typological one. In his two marriages, Jacob prefigures Christ, who shared
in both the law and grace; Leah and Rachel represent the synagogue and the
church, respectively.[66]

Rich as is this dishonesty in the substitution of brides as an indictment of
Laban, Jacob's bigamy and the exegetical problems it presents on a historical
and moral level outweigh, for Ambrose, its pedagogical advantages, which
accounts for its omission in *De Jacob*. Chastity is one of the virtues he ascribes
to Jacob,[67] so Jacob cannot be viewed as sexually involved with multiple consorts out of lust. Nor can his relations with these consorts, who include Zilpah
and Bilhah, the maids of Leah and Rachel, be justified, as Abraham's relations
with Hagar are initially justified, as necessary so that the patriarch can sire offspring, given a sterile wife. For Leah bears Jacob four sons before she gives Zilpah to him as a concubine; and she continues to bear further children, two sons
and a daughter, after he has taken up with Zilpah (Gen 29:31–35; 30:9–13,
17–21). The rationales that Ambrose develops to deal with sexual relations out
of wedlock in *De Abraham* simply do not work in *De Jacob*. Nor do the strictures, elaborated in his first patriarch treatise, for distinguishing between legitimate sons as true heirs, and illegitimate sons as no heirs at all, apply in

---

65. Ambrose, *De uiduis* 15.90, ed. Cazzaniga, trans. Gori.

66. Ambrose, *De Iac.* 2.4.16. This exclusively typological treatment of Jacob's two wives is
entirely consistent with the previous exegetical tradition, as is noted by Dulaey, "La figure de
Jacob," 127–30. See also Clark, *Reading Renunciation*, 84. Jacob also stands for Christ as a shepherd
at *De Iac.* 2.2.8, 2.4.17–2.5.20.

67. Ambrose, *De Iac.* 2.1.2.

Jacob's case. For he treats all twelve of his sons as equally qualified to serve as progenitors of the twelve tribes of Israel, although four of them are the off-spring of his concubines. Here he ignores the helpful interpretation of Justin Martyr, who equalizes the sons of Jacob under the rubric that, in Christ, slave and free are equal.[68] All in all, notwithstanding his awareness of the fact that Laban's deception in switching his daughters as Jacob's brides is a strong ex-ample of a *fraus* that any Roman would recognize as a crime that his *compe-tentes* should be counseled to avoid, the potential embarrassments surrounding Jacob's sexual arrangements are so great that they cancel, for Ambrose, the educational utility of this episode in the patriarch's life.

But, even after Jacob has been "paid" with the hand of Rachel, he contin-ues to work for Laban without being able to accrue any capital, in the form of livestock of his own from among the flocks he shepherds, and increases, for Laban. This situation continues for several years until Jacob decides it is time to end his exploitation at Laban's hands and to return to his native land. Gen-esis 30:25–31:16 describes the bargain that Jacob strikes with Laban when Jacob announces his decision, Laban's effort to undermine the agreement, and Jacob's circumvention of his would-be fraud. The agreement states that Jacob will continue in Laban's employ for one more year. His recompense, which he will take with him when he leaves, will be all those animals in the flock he cares for that are born in the next lambing season with speckled hides. In order to pre-vent any such lambs from being born, Laban removes all the speckled males from that flock and sends them to the flocks shepherded by his sons at a dis-tance of three days' journey. This action on Laban's part corresponds precisely with the second definition of *fraus* in Roman law.

In response, Jacob's action is comprehensible, not as fraud repaying fraud, but as an exercise of the virtue of wisdom. Both theoretical and practical wis-dom come into play, right reason being cognizant of the nature of things as well as what is useful. Jacob has observed that, when the sheep mate in the presence of a branch whose bark has been partially peeled, their offsprings' hides are speckled, even if the parents' are not. Genesis treats this phenome-non, not as a symptom of sympathetic magic, but as a matter of scientific fact, observable in nature and verifiable empirically. Having ascertained this key to

68. For loci and literature on this issue, see Ambrose, *De patriarchis*, ed. Schenkl, trans. Banterle; Argyle, "Joseph the Patriarch in Patristic Teaching"; Hollander, *Joseph as an Ethical Model;* Hollander and De Jonge, *Testaments of the Twelve Patriarchs: A Commentary.* On Justin's argument, see Dulaey, "La figure de Jacob," 131.

his own successful experiment in genetic engineering, Jacob places branches of poplar, almond, and plane, which he has partially peeled, at his flock's watering place during the mating season. He is careful to bring to this breeding site only the stronger among the flock, drawing the weaker away from it. The result is that Jacob's recompense in new lambs is a rich one. It is true that he displays humility after the fact, observing that it is God who has given him the increase. He avers, also after the fact, that God has sent an angel to him in a dream, showing him the speckled lambs (Gen 31:9–12). The biblical text also states that God then tells Jacob that it is time for him to leave the duplicitous Laban and return home (Gen 31:14). Yet a text earlier in the same chapter indicates that Jacob had already made the decision to leave and that he had already executed the plan of breeding the strong sheep under his care in the presence of the partially peeled branches. Furthermore, the Jacob of Genesis consults his wives before leaving Laban, noting expressly that their father has cheated him ten times over, a statement with which Leah and Rachel concur, giving their solid backing to the decision to depart (Gen 31:6–7, 15–16).

There is certainly much in this passage that would have been useful to Ambrose in documenting culpable fraud and deceit in contradistinction to pious fraud; in illustrating Jacob's wisdom both theoretical and practical; in delineating the fact that he acts with divine approval, being on intimate terms with God; and, finally, in exemplifying good husband-wife relations in his consultation with Leah and Rachel and his winning their concurrence before moving the household. This is not, however, the direction in which Ambrose chooses to take this episode, or at least those aspects of it that he decides to include. Indeed, despite the pedagogical utility of this passage and its comparative lack of exegetical embarrassments, he largely abandons the opportunity to make any of the above points. Ambrose omits Jacob's genetic engineering altogether. He interprets the branches taken from three trees of different species typologically and morally, and not altogether happily, as signifying the Trinity; the grace of priestly office betokened by Aaron's rod, the fruit of good works when undertaken by a devout mind, and the incense and evening sacrifice offered to the Lord. While some Christian predecessors of Ambrose also read a Trinitarian significance into the three branches, the focus of their exegesis had been to refute Celsus' criticism of Jacob's action as trickery, a concern of no interest to Ambrose.[69] Ambrose recognizes in Jacob's intimacy with God

69. Ambrose, *De Iac.* 2.4.19. On this issue, see Dulaey, "La figure de Jacob," 132–33, 137.

one of his moral gifts, vouchsafed to him also in the encounter with God that initiates his journey away from home.[70]

The more central points that Ambrose wants to make about Jacob's departure from Laban are two. First, harking back to the advice of the unnamed natural philosophers cited in *De Abraham* on how the wise man should get along with his neighbors, Ambrose presents Jacob as following the same rules in the face of Laban's hostility: "Now let us consider how the just man ought to behave if enmity arises. First, let him avoid it; it is better to go away without strife than to settle down with contention" (Nunc consideremus qualis uir iustus esse debeat, si inuidia fuerit extorta. Primum ut declinet eam; melius est enim sine lite abire quam desidere cum iurgio).[71] Notable here is Ambrose's use of the legal terminology for extortion and litigation, possibly suggesting the felt need to reprove litigiousness in his *competentes*. The second lesson he wants to draw from Jacob's departure is that it is prudent to possess property in the form of movable goods, especially goods clearly identifiable as the owner's, so that if one has to leave, one can do so swiftly and without confusion as to what one actually owns. Jacob's recompense was one that was justly and identifiably his; it was easy to transport; and its nature enabled him to counter Laban's bad faith charge that he was stealing Laban's own property.[72]

From this observation, however, Ambrose segues to a larger point, the need of the sage to be detached from wealth and to possess the riches of virtue which can never be extorted from him.[73] Ambrose closes this passage by citing Jacob's response to Laban's false claim that he is stealing Laban's goods. He uses language that resituates their standoff in Roman legal terms. As his Jacob says to Laban, "See if you recognize any of your vices and crimes. I have not carried out any of your frauds; I have no part at all in your deceits" (Quaere, si quid agnoscis uitiorum tuorum et criminum. Nihil mecum abstuli fraudum tuorum dolique consortia ulla non habeo).[74] This statement clearly reminds Ambrose's audience of the criminal as well as immoral nature of the *fraus* and *dolus* perpetrated by Laban, from which Jacob pointedly dissociates himself. Still, much more that is pertinent to his charge to his *competentes* could have

---

70. Ambrose, *De Iac.* 2.5.20.
71. Ibid. 2.5.21; McHugh trans., 157; see chapter 4, 45, 58, 68.
72. Ambrose, *De Iac.* 2.5.21–22.
73. Ibid. 2.5.23.
74. Ibid. 2.5.24; my trans.

been extracted from this episode had Ambrose engaged with the full text of Genesis and not subjected it to deletions that are difficult to explain.

The next incident in which deception occurs in Jacob's story follows on the heels of the one just discussed. As Genesis 31:17–35 relates, Jacob, still alert to the possibility that Laban may seek to prevent his departure with his flocks, wives, and household, leaves without announcing his time of departure, while Laban is preoccupied elsewhere. Unbeknownst to Jacob, Rachel has stolen Laban's household gods (Gen 31:19, 32). Jacob has clearly been successful in replacing the Chaldean polytheism and star-worship in which she was raised with his own monotheism, and the lesson extends to her father's personal devotions. When Laban finds that Jacob is gone and catches up with him, he accuses him of stealing the gods and searches his camp, arriving finally at Rachel's tent. She has placed the gods in her saddle-bags, on which she is seated. When her father enters her tent, Rachel apologizes for not rising in his presence, explaining that she is menstruating. The fact of the matter is not established, but her deceptive intention is clear; she makes this statement in order to prevent Laban from searching her saddle-bags. In any event, he does not find the gods. After another round of mutual recrimination, Jacob and Laban make a covenant establishing boundaries between them and finally part company (Gen 31:36–55). As for the household gods, in response to a divine message, Jacob buries them, on his homeward journey, at Bethel (Gen 35:4, 19). This is why, when Rachel dies, it is appropriate to bury her, as a type of the church, at Bethel, where the pagan gods were declared to be dead and buried. This burial also represents the *competentes'* imminent baptism, which will purge them of pagan error: "Every error of the Gentiles really is buried when one has been washed free of his vices, because our old man, fastened to the cross, now does not know how to be a slave to the old sin" (Tunc igitur uere absconditur omnis error gentilium, cum quis fuerit ablutis a uitiis, quia confixus cruci uetus homo noster nescit iam ueteri seruire peccato).[75] In dealing with this series of events, Ambrose is eager to emphasize for the benefit of his *competentes* that it is not just the public cults of pagan Rome that must be dead and buried for them but also the *lares et penates* of their own pagan ancestors.

In treating Rachel's role in this passage, Ambrose does two things that depart from the biblical text. He acknowledges that she has hidden the gods

---

75. Ibid. 2.7.33–34; the quotation is at 2.7.34; McHugh trans., 166. I have altered his wording slightly.

but does not mention the fact that she has stolen them. And, he provides Rachel with a rationale for her initiative in this connection: "Blessed was Rachel, who concealed the false gods of the Gentiles and declared that their images were full of uncleanness" (beata Rachel, quae abscondit cultus erroresque gentilium, quae simulacra eorum plena esse inmunditiae declarauit).[76] Rachel makes no such declaration, according to the biblical text. Ambrose gives Rachel much more agency than the book of Genesis does because she is Jacob's truly beloved wife and a type of the church, which will render the pagan gods obsolete. At the same time, he elides the matter of her theft and dissimulation, although her actions could easily have been classified and defended as a fully justifiable pious fraud. Instead, Ambrose makes a lateral move, distracting his audience from that issue by focusing on another one instead, Rachel's apparent lack of filial piety in remaining seated in Laban's presence. Delicately ignoring the matter of menstruation, he locates her action in the context of the cost of discipleship: "Let no one believe that she had betrayed the respect and devotion due her father because she sat while he stood, for it is written, 'He who loves father and mother more than me is not worthy of me' (Matt 10:37). When the cause of religion was at stake, faith had a just claim upon the judgment seat and unbelief like a defendant deserved to stand" (Nemo credat paternae pietatis laesam esse reuerentiam, quod stante patre sedit, quoniam scriptum est: *Qui plus fecerit patrem aut matrem quam me non est me dignus.* Ubi causa agebatur religionis fides debuit sedem habere iudicii et quasi rea stare perfidia).[77] While omitting the language of *dolus* and *fraus,* justified or not in Rachel's case, and while replacing these considerations with those of faith and justice, Ambrose still frames the matter in the legal language of the lawsuit, the courtroom, the judge, and the defendant.

There is one final instance in which, bending the text of Genesis to his own purposes, Ambrose confronts a situation in which deception is practiced, a double deception acknowledged to be such by the biblical text, but one that he conceptualizes under a different moral heading even though the biblical text as written offers rich opportunities for him to point moral lessons of use to his *competentes.* As Genesis 33:18–34:31 relates, when Jacob arrives in Canaan,

---

76. Ibid. 2.5.25; McHugh trans., 160–61. I have altered his wording slightly. On Rachel's theft of Laban's household gods, Ambrose follows previous Christian commentators and not Philo, who says that Jacob stole them, as is noted by Dulaey, "La figure de Jacob," 141–43.

77. Ambrose, *De Iac.* 2.5.25; McHugh trans., 161.

he sojourns in the land ruled by Shechem, son of Hamor. Jacob's daughter, Dinah, evidently a friendly and gregarious girl, with no female companions her own age in a family top-heavy with brothers, goes out to visit the women of the land. It appears that she does so unescorted and unchaperoned. She attracts the attention of Shechem, who seizes and rapes her. He then wishes to marry her. Hamor approaches Jacob with this proposal, which includes the arrangement of other marriages between his men and Israelite women. Jacob's sons are outraged at the wrong done to their sister. But, together with Jacob, they hear Shechem's suit and his willingness to accept any conditions they may impose enabling him to find favor in their sight. In thoroughly bad faith—as the biblical text indicates—Jacob's sons say that they cannot permit a union between Dinah or any other Israelite woman with the uncircumcised. Hamor and Shechem accept this condition, and they and all their men are circumcised. Without Jacob's knowledge or consent, two of the sons, Simon and Levi, lead an attack on Shechem's people, slaughtering all his men in their weakened state, plundering his city, and taking the women and children captive. When Jacob discovers what they have done, he chastises Simon and Levi. His reproach, in the book of Genesis, is based on utilitarian considerations. Jacob observes that his sons have placed the household in jeopardy in this land where they are surrounded by Gentiles. Their own numbers are few, and his sons' actions have earned them the hatred of their neighbors. But his sons object that it was necessary to avenge Dinah's rape; they will not allow their sister to be treated like a harlot with impunity. And there the matter rests.

Ambrose clearly has some choices to make in addressing the double deception—of Shechem and his men and of Jacob himself—carried out by Jacob's sons. One possible line of argument might have been the one based on Philo's distinction between admissible and inadmissible deception. The rape of Dinah could be construed as a declaration of war, in which case any stratagem that facilitates the punitive counterattack of the sons could be judged justified. On another level, such a reading of this episode would make good sense to a Roman audience, even if that audience might regard the punishment of Shechem as sufficient, for in Roman law rape was deemed a heinous crime. If the culprit was apprehended and convicted, the sentence was the death penalty. Moreover, the very notion that rape could be made the basis for a marital claim or proposal would have struck Roman ears as appalling and unthinkable.[78]

---

78. Berger, *Encyclopedic Dictionary of Roman Law*, s.v. *raptus*.

Both the crimes of *dolus* and *raptus* are involved in these events. And while Ambrose uses neither of these terms in describing them, he certainly acknowledges, in Roman legal language, that a crime has been committed. Dinah's brothers, he observes, "avenged the crime against their sister, who had been violated and whose modesty had been profaned, against the laws of their fathers"; and Jacob agrees that "the violation of chastity . . . had been committed" (ulti fuerat sororis iniuriam, quae contra instituta patria uiolato fuerat pudore temerata; . . . stuprum . . . commissum). Ambrose's use of the term *stuprum* expressly acknowledges the felonious nature of Shechem's wrongdoing.[79] Yet it is not in this Roman legal framework that Ambrose chooses to interpret the episode. Just as in *De Abraham* he urges the men among his *competentes* to adhere to a standard of sexual ethics more rigorous than what Roman law permits, so here too he appeals to a higher law. The principle he invokes in dealing with Dinah's rape is that right reason teaches us what and how to bear and forbear. It counsels mercy and the forgiveness of injuries. Jacob's forgiveness and temperance account for his treatment of his sons, whom he merely reproaches and does not punish for their violence and duplicity. It is not that Dinah's chastity and honor are unimportant. But it is more important to act rationally toward her defiler and his people. Reason, in Jacob's case, rightly moderates wrath. Furthermore, Jacob's willingness to forgive injuries is coupled with his foreknowledge that the church will be drawn from the Gentiles as well as the Jews. Since Shechem and his men were willing to accept circumcision, their intermarriage with Israelite women would have been, in principle, acceptable.[80]

In addition to sidelining the issue of deception, Ambrose's handling of Jacob's forgiveness of Dinah's rape bears comparison with his treatment of a theme that he addresses in *De Abraham* and *De Isaac*. In all three treatises, female chastity is put at risk, or is actually set aside, in support of moral considerations that Ambrose presents as more important. This fact is noteworthy not only because of the stress that Ambrose otherwise places on chastity but also because female chastity in particular was a value that Roman Christians shared with Roman pagans. With respect to married and unmarried women

---

79. Ambrose, *De Iac.* 1.2.7; my trans.; on *stuprum*, see chapter 4, 52.

80. Ibid. 1.2.7–8, 2.7.32. Cf. Ambrose, *De patriarchis* 3.10, ed. Schenkl, trans. Banterle, where Ambrose praises Simon and Levi for avenging Dinah's honor and where he states that Jacob did not criticize their action.

alike, chastity was the female virtue most desired and most highly praised in Roman literature.[81] In the case of Dinah, however, Ambrose subordinates that value, not to the pragmatic political concerns of the biblical Jacob, but to the moral principles of moderation, forbearance, and forgiveness. The one concern, or lack of concern, that he shares with the author of this part of Genesis has to do with the unfortunate Dinah herself. Her subsequent fate is of no interest to either of them.

Equally absent are some important moral lessons that Ambrose could have drawn from this episode but that he ignores, conceivably because they would suggest less than intelligent and responsible parenting on the part of Jacob and Leah, Dinah's mother. Friendliness in a young and unmarried girl may be well and good. But it is clear that Dinah's unaccompanied excursions into the countryside were extremely imprudent and that this was what gave Shechem his chance. A more circumspect approach to parental supervision of one's unmarried daughters is to be counseled, and it is an idea that contemporary Milanese parents, whether Christian or pagan, could be expected to approve. Also, Jacob and Leah do not seem to have given any thought to the matter of finding an acceptable husband for Dinah, given that their household is surrounded by Gentiles and that endogamy continues to be normative for bearers of the covenant and their children. Ambrose's omission of these considerations, pertinent as they may have been to the parents of unmarried daughters among his *competentes,* is understandable in the light of the fact that, in order to include them, he would have had to diminish the *paterfamilias* Jacob's stature as a perfect sage.

If forgiveness of injuries preempts other values in Ambrose's treatment of the Dinah episode, it is the ethical centerpiece of his reunion and reconciliation with Esau on his return to Canaan. Jacob's return home reflects his moral perfection. He needs nothing further from Laban. He has secured his fortune and he now seeks to make peace with Esau.[82] Ambrose's Jacob, like the Jacob of Genesis, approaches his meeting with Esau with humility and generosity. He bows before Esau seven times and sends him rich gifts. He freely forgives Esau for his envy, hatred, and fratricidal rage. In so doing, Jacob forecasts Christ's universal forgiveness of sin, the seven bows also signifying that Chris-

81. Treggiari, *Roman Marriage,* 105.
82. Ambrose, *De Iac.* 2.5.20–21.

tians should forgive those who injure them seventy times seven.[83] Ambrose adds that in preparation for his meeting with Esau Jacob displays the virtue of courage in the face of a reception whose amity or hostility he cannot predict. But above all, he manifests the equanimity of the sage, for "Perfect virtue possesses tranquillity and a calm steadfastness" (Perfecta uirtus habet tranquillitatem et stabilitatem quietis).[84]

Equanimity and tranquillity are also reflected in Jacob's encounters with God in dreams, visions, and direct speech; and these virtues continue to characterize him in old age as in youth and in the prime of life. Ambrose does not discuss all the encounters that Jacob has with God recounted in the book of Genesis. But in those he includes, he interprets God's communications with Jacob in his sleep as an index of his tranquillity of spirit as well as an index of his prophetic gifts. Prophesy, in particular, can be seen in the vision of Jacob's ladder, which forecasts Christ's descent from and reascent to heaven. The numbness in his thigh that Jacob experiences after wrestling with the angel foreshadows Christ's sufferings on the cross.[85] And just as Jacob was ethically precocious as a youth, so in old age he retains his spiritual energy and vigor and his mental tranquillity, which enable him to deal prudently with the needs of his household and to master the inescapable physical limitations that afflict humankind in the last stages of the life cycle: "There struggled within him the energy and vitality of youth and the tranquillity of old age" (certebant in eo inpigra uiuacitas iuuentutis et tranquillitas senectutis).[86]

The aged Jacob is a prophet not only in forecasting the coming of Christ but also in his blessing of Joseph's sons, when he meets them in Egypt. He discerns which is which and what the appropriate blessings are for each, although his eyesight is poor and Joseph has tried to organize the blessings differently. He prophesies as well in forecasting the future history of the twelve tribes of Israel whose progenitors are his own sons.[87] In Ambrose's final summation of

---

83. Ibid. 2.6.26–27. As Dulaey, "La figure de Jacob," 145, notes, the seventy-times-seven motif in this connection appears to be original with Ambrose; it is not found in previous Christian exegesis of this passage.

84. Ambrose, *De Iac.* 2.6.28; McHugh trans., 162; for the whole passage, ibid. 2.6.28–30; for courage, ibid. 1.8.36.

85. Ibid. 2.4.16, 2.7.30. In describing these two episodes, as noted by Dulaey, "La figure de Jacob," 107–16, 154–62, Ambrose follows his Christian predecessors, although, unlike many of them, he does not interpret the ladder in the Jacob's dream as the cross of Christ.

86. Ambrose, *De Iac.* 2.8.35; for the whole passage, ibid. 2.8.35–36, 2.9.40, 2.9.42.

87. Ibid. 2.9.36–37, 2.9.39–40, 2.9.42.

the virtues of Jacob, he highlights his temperance, courage, prophesy, wisdom, and forgiveness. But consistent with the presentation of Joseph that he plans to offer in *De Joseph* and with his more abstract delineation of the Christian-Stoic sage in Bk. 1 of *De Jacob,* Jacob's equanimity and tranquillity of mind hold pride of place.[88] It is this virtue, above all, that grants to Jacob his citizenship in heaven.[89]

Yet how fully does this Jacob, governed by equanimity from start to finish, actually compare with the Jacob of the book of Genesis? How accurately does Ambrose report Jacob's encounter with Esau? His encounters with God? It has to be said that in all these respects Ambrose takes notable liberties with the biblical text, not only in terms of what he omits but also in terms of how he reports what he includes. The Jacob of Genesis is not, as it turns out, the Christian-Stoic sage that Ambrose makes him. He does not maintain equanimity and tranquillity at all times. The biblical text states that Jacob's anger is kindled against Rachel when she berates him for her failure to conceive (Gen 30:2). Likewise, his calm breaks down in his final confrontation with Laban. He becomes angry and upbraids Laban for his dishonesty, and he leaves without informing his father-in-law of his time of departure because he is afraid that Laban will try to stop him and take back his daughters and the flocks that he claims Jacob has stolen from him (Gen 31:31, 36). As his encounter with Esau approaches, Jacob is told that his brother is coming to meet him, and he is both afraid and distressed (Gen 32:7, 11), although he masters these emotions. When Jacob later hears of the purported death of Joseph, he mourns effusively and refuses to be comforted; he says that he will continue to mourn until he dies (Gen 37:34–35). These outbursts of rage, fear, and distress and this excessive and intemperate mourning are scarcely consistent with the behavior of a sage who governs his passions by right reason. It is no surprise, then, that Ambrose makes a careful detour around these passages of Genesis.

In his dealings with God as well, the Jacob of Genesis betrays character traits that Ambrose has no wish to call to the attention of his *competentes*. One of the most striking of his many omissions of biblical material in *De Jacob* is the interaction of Jacob and God in his first dream-vision, just after he leaves

---

88. Ibid. 2.1.1, 2.8.35, 2.9.39–2.10.42. This picture of Jacob may be contrasted with Jacob elsewhere in Ambrose's writings as a model of industriousness, resourcefulness, and generosity, as is noted by Vasey, *The Social Ideals in the Works of St. Ambrose,* 154–55, 201.

89. Ambrose, *De Iac.* 1.8.39, 2.9.38.

home. In this dream, God confirms that the covenant he has made with Abraham and Isaac also extends to Jacob and his descendants. Specifically, God promises that the land will be theirs, that through them all the families of the earth will be blessed, and that he will remain with Jacob wherever he goes, protecting him and bringing him back to his own land. Reflecting on this message, Jacob imposes a condition. He offers a *quid pro quo*. If God delivers on these promises, then he will accept the Lord as his God, and he will give him a tithe of his wealth (Gen 28:10–16, 20–22). And following the episode in which he wrestles with the angel prior to his meeting with Esau, the Jacob of Genesis congratulates himself, since he has seen God face to face and yet lives (Gen 32:30). This Jacob, who boasts about his God-given gifts and who has the effrontery to try to bargain with God, is not the kind of example of virtue that Ambrose wants to place before his *competentes*. This Jacob does not make an appearance in his *De Jacob*.

Finally, does the Jacob whom Ambrose does present, the sage described by discourse and reason in Bk. 1 of *De Jacob* and by example in the first half of Bk. 2, have anything in common with the martyred Maccabees with whose fates he closes the work? At first glance, a negative answer to this question seems appropriate. While initially Jacob is threatened with murder at Esau's hands, he circumvents that outcome by leaving home. The numerous injustices heaped upon him by Laban in no sense threaten his life or his physical well-being. Furthermore, while the Maccabees are martyrs for their faith, no one attacks Jacob on account of his religious beliefs or practices.

And then there is the stylistic disjunction that opens the Maccabees section of Bk. 2 of *De Jacob*, which begins with an uncharacteristic lapse into the first person singular on Ambrose's part as he introduces the martyrdom of Eleazar, the Maccabees' priest: "I, who am a priest and will be helped by your prayers, O Eleazar, will not neglect to mention you" (Nec te, Eleazare, praetermittam, utpote sacerdotem sacerdos, sed, tuis iuuandus oratis).[90] His observation underscores two points that Ambrose makes frequently in the patriarch treatises: the idea that the prayers of the departed saints help the living, and the idea that Old Testament worthies are true saints. Here it must be noted that the texts on which Ambrose draws for his account of the Maccabees, 1 and 2 Maccabees and 4 Maccabees, although regarded as apocryphal by modern

---

90. Ibid. 2.10.43; McHugh trans., 173.

Scripture scholars who base their reconstruction of the Old Testament on the Hebrew Bible, were not so regarded by Ambrose. All versions of the Septuagint, the text of the Old Testament that Ambrose used, include 1 and 2 Maccabees. The Alexandrian version of the Septuagint includes all four books of the Maccabees as canonical. Jerome also includes these books as canonical in his Vulgate Bible, and 4 Maccabees forms part of the *Vetus Latina*.[91] Ambrose thus regards the Maccabees as fully legitimate Old Testament personages.

Eleazar, whose story is told in 4 Maccabees, the work of the first-century author Pseudo-Josephus, is indeed presented by him as a Judeo-Stoic sage. The fact that the author of a text regarded by Ambrose and his scriptural authorities as genuinely canonical feels free to draw so positively and so heavily on Stoic ethics makes problematic the view that Ambrose appealed to philosophy only to expose its shortcomings in comparison with biblical ethics. In the case of 4 Maccabees, biblical and Stoic ethics coincide. Pseudo-Josephus emphasizes the cardinal virtues and the primacy of reason as the rubrics under which Eleazar's martyrdom should be placed (4 Macc 1:1–18; 13:18). The issue triggering his ordeal is the desire of the tyrant Antiochus to force him to eat pork, in violation of Jewish dietary law, and to sacrifice food to idols (4 Macc 5:1–2; also 1 Macc 6:18–19). Ambrose reports Eleazar's martyrdom quite faithfully. He argues that Eleazar's virtue reflects not only equanimity in the face of torture and death but also moderation and obedience to God's law. Countering the tyrant's observation that pork tastes good, Eleazar replies that abstention from it is a training in self-restraint that serves to control concupiscence more generally. Moderation governs the other passions and helps us as well to develop other virtues such as prudence and justice. In mastering the pain inflicted by his tormenter, Eleazar also manifests courage. Ambrose sees his entire martyrdom as the triumph of reason over suffering.[92]

In moving next to the martyrdom of the seven Maccabee brothers and their mother, Ambrose retrojects the motivations of Eleazar in 4 Maccabees onto figures whose motives for resisting the tyrant are rather different. As 1 and 2 Maccabees relate, Antiochus' first offense is to rob the temple of Jerusalem of sacred liturgical objects and of its treasury, whose funds were set aside for

---

91. Metzger, ed., *The Oxford Annotated Apocrypha of the Old Testament*, xii (my thanks to Adela Collins for this reference); Tobin, in *HarperCollins Study Bible*, 1814; Fernández Marcos, *The Septuagint in Context*, 198; Wilson, in *The New Oxford Annotated Bible*, 362.

92. Ambrose, *De Iac.* 2.10.43–44.

the aid of widows and orphans. Next, he exacts tribute from the Jews and plunders Jerusalem, then burning the city and taking away many captives (1 Macc 1:21–31; 3:13–14; 5:19–21). Following that, Antiochus imposes idolatry, ordering any Jews who remain in the city to abandon their own religion, to sacrifice unclean animals, to desecrate the Sabbath, and to avoid circumcision (1 Macc 1:41–61; 2 Macc 6:1–11); 2 Maccabees 6:11 adds that he also installed temple prostitutes in the sacred precincts. Almost as an afterthought in 1 and 2 Maccabees is the tyrant's effort to force the Jews to eat pork, which the Maccabees refuse to do (1 Macc 1:62; 2:19–22; 2 Macc 7:1). In 1 Maccabees the hero, Judas Maccabeus, defeats the tyrant, cleanses the temple of pagan worship, and has new liturgical vessels made (1 Macc 4:36–58). It is clear that the desecration and subsequent purification of the temple, the destruction of paganism, and the restoration of the poor relief funds are the main issue in 1 and 2 Maccabees, not the dietary laws. But in Ambrose's hands, the one and only source of contention is the eating of pork.

The moral lesson that Ambrose draws from the Maccabees' martyrdom is twofold. First, echoing a point made about Jacob, the seven brothers indicate that perfect virtue is possible at any age. The virtues that they manifest, in addition to equanimity, are faith, courage, constancy, reason, obedience to God's law, and the love of holiness.[93] Second, the Maccabees illustrate another point made by Ambrose in Bk. 1 of *De Jacob*, the idea that obedience to God's law is freedom, while obedience to sin, of the sort that the tyrant seeks to enforce, is slavery.[94] The youths, their mother, and Eleazar alike foretell Christ's sacrifice and its effects; they are the seven-branched candelabrum lighting the liturgy of the church, recruited, like other Old Testament worthies, into the ranks of the Christian saints.[95]

If the Maccabees' story, as told by Ambrose, harks back to points he makes earlier in *De Jacob*, there are also notes he strikes early in that treatise that point ahead to the theme of martyrdom. As we have seen, in the second half of Bk. 1 Ambrose repeatedly argues that the constancy of the sage is proof against loss and suffering of all kinds, including physical afflictions. His treatment of Rachel's severance of her ties with her father accents the costs of discipleship for the Christian. Referring to the imminent baptism of the *competentes*, he associates their death to sin with their participation in the crucifixion,

93. Ibid. 2.11.45, 2.11.47–48.
94. Ibid. 2.10.43.
95. Ibid. 2.11.47, 2.11.53.

indicating that these new Christians will be expected to take up and carry their own crosses. They must be prepared to imitate Christ, as he notes, posing the following rhetorical question: "Why should we not endure hard and bitter sufferings for Christ, when he accepted such indignities for us?" (Cur nos pro illo non etiam dura et acerba toleremus, qui pro nobis tam indigna suscepit?)[96] He alludes to Old Testament worthies like Daniel in the lion's den, who remained calm in the face of suffering and imminent death, trusting in God.[97] And looking ahead to the Maccabees, he urges his *competentes* to remain steadfast in the face of sacrilege and religious persecution, asking, "ought we to be afraid of certain plots of our accuser?" (num metuendae sunt aliquae accusatoris insidiae?)[98]

Ambrose presents the commitment that his *competentes* are shortly to seal at the font in considerably starker tones than is the case in his references to baptism in his earlier patriarch treatises. In particular, as we have seen in *De Isaac*,[99] Ambrose speaks of the age of the martyrs as now past, observing that nowadays the ablution of baptism cleanses Christians of their sins as fully as did the martyrs' baptism by blood. But in *De Jacob*, it appears as if religious persecution, of a highly specific sort and from a highly specific quarter, may well be at hand. It is this that makes it likely that *De Jacob* in its present form was delivered, at the earliest, in 387, with reference to the basilica crisis of 386. A final point suggestive of that conclusion is Ambrose's peroration at the end of Bk. 2 of *De Jacob*, in which he yokes the spiritual triumph of the Maccabees to that of his own Milanese audience: "You have stood among the armies of the king, to which the whole world was subject—even India turned aside and fled from them into the remotest parts of the farthest sea—and you only, and without warlike combat, have achieved victory over the proud king" (Stetitis inter exercitus regios, quibus totus fuit orbis terrarum subactus, quos India quoque in extremi maris secreta refugiens declinauit, et soli de rege superbo sine bellico conflictu uictoriam reportastis).[100]

This suggestive equation of the Maccabees with the Milanese Christian community, withstanding the threats of the neo-Arian imperial court, requires, as we have seen, a creative rereading of 1 and 2 Maccabees in the light

---

96. Ibid. 1.7.27; McHugh trans., 137.
97. Ibid. 1.8.36.
98. Ibid. 1.6.26; McHugh trans., 136; see also ibid. 1.8.36, 2.5.22.
99. See chapter 5, 73.
100. Ambrose, *De Iac.* 2.12.58; McHugh trans., 184.

of 4 Maccabees. At the end of the day, however, Ambrose's independence in treating what he regards as canonical biblical texts should not be surprising, considering the freedom with which he treats the story of Jacob as told in the book of Genesis. This is a freedom that is matched by his adaptation of his philosophical sources, largely Stoic, in *De Jacob*. His modification of that tradition is particularly visible in his discussion of free will and in his theory of the passions, seen as arising in the soul, in the body, and in both. Retaining the cardinal virtues shared by many schools of Greek philosophy, he accents temperance, understood, in *De Jacob* as in *De Isaac*, as nothing in excess, not merely as a corrective of the Neoplatonic ethics of asceticism, which he dismisses, but also as the first step in the acquisition of knowledge and virtue. The anthropology of Stoicism and Aristotelianism alike he reinterprets in the light of the Pauline tension between the flesh and the spirit. That said, Ambrose retains much of the Stoic doctrine of the sage, accenting in particular his chief attribute of equanimity, but rejecting his autarchy.

While Ambrose does not name any of the philosophical sources he uses, he does advert specifically to the technical terminology of Roman law, particularly in dealing with the theme of deception and fraud, pious and otherwise, and with sexual delicts. As in *De Abraham*, the rules of Roman law sometimes support the argument he develops, while at other times he places them in a position subordinate to his moral message. Similarly, he sometimes follows the lead of Philo and of his Christian exegetical sources and sometimes does not. Compared with its predecessors among the patriarch treatises, *De Jacob* is notable for the increase in Ambrose's manipulation of his sources on all sides. And in comparison with the patriarch's story as told in the book of Genesis, there are a greater number of omissions and missed opportunities to point valuable moral lessons in *De Jacob* than elsewhere in the corpus of patriarch treatises. What Ambrose does choose to draw from his sources and to develop on his own initiative emerges in the depiction of his Jacob, and of his Maccabees, as ideal Christian-Stoic sages. Much the same can be said about Ambrose's goal and his achievement in the last of his patriarch treatises, *De Joseph*.

CHAPTER 7

Joseph

In many ways, Ambrose's *De Joseph* is the least problematic of his patriarch treatises. While this work has attracted the attention of *Quellenforscher,* commentators have focused less on Ambrose's debts to classical philosophy than on his place in the tradition of previous Jewish and Christian exegesis. Ambrose certainly displays familiarity with earlier interpretations of Joseph and makes use of his predecessors. But he also offers a personal approach to this patriarch as the culminating figure in the preparatory course in Christian ethics that he offers to his *competentes*. This treatise reflects a presupposition on Ambrose's part that his audience has already mastered the theological, anthropological, and ethical teachings that he presents in the first three patriarch treatises. He finds little need to revisit the theoretical underpinnings of these lessons in *De Joseph*. The pedagogy that the *competentes* have now received, he assumes, will enable them to understand any references he makes to Greek philosophy as well as to his earlier reformulations and reworkings of the doctrines involved.

While Ambrose presents Joseph's life and flags his virtues more or less in the order in which the book of Genesis recounts his story, amplified by biblical intertextuality of the type found in his other patriarch treatises, he does not hesitate to rewrite or gloss over passages in Genesis that fail to square with the portrait of Joseph he is constructing. In *De Joseph,* his treatment of the Bible as well as his other sources displays the flexibility visible in his earlier patriarch treatises. What emerges is a Joseph depicted as a Christian-Stoic sage and as the single most perfect example of virtue among the four patriarchs. Not only does Joseph possess, from his youth, the cardinal virtues that the patriarchs all manifest, but he also possesses the virtues of the statesman. He is thus able to save a wider assortment of people than the patriarchs before him, making him, in comparison with them, a type of Christ *par excellence*.

As we have noted, the dating of *De Joseph* has not escaped controversy any more than have the dates of the other patriarch treatises.[1] The most plausible *terminus post quem* for the work's composition is the end of the year 388, with the Lent of 389 as the earliest date for its initial airing in sermon form in its current version, given the internal references that Ambrose makes to the fall of the eunuch Calligonus, which took place in the autumn or winter of 388.[2] Ambrose alludes in *De Joseph* to Calligonus, "from whose end I shy away, at whose death I shudder" (cuius exitum refugio, mortem horresco).[3] He recalls his own interchange with Calligonus in 386, when the chamberlain of Valentinian II was sent to bid him to attend an imperial consistory as a means of settling the basilica crisis of that year, a request which Ambrose pointedly rejected. As he notes, "It does not please me to recall that discourse of mine which I poured forth in my sorrow and which was forced from me by the outrage done upon the church" (ne ipsius quidem sermonis mei meminisse delectebat, quem tunc temporis uel effuderit dolor uel extorserit ecclesiae contumelia).[4] These events, he observes, although they took place in the past, are still fresh in his mind.[5]

Also fresh in his mind, and in the minds of his *competentes*, are the stories of Abraham, Isaac, and Jacob, whose lives and virtues he has already conveyed to them and whose collective history he now completes with his account of Joseph: "While I have often preached about these patriarchs, today the story of holy Joseph comes up" (De quibus mihi cum frequens tractatus fuerit, hodie sancti Ioseph historia occurrit).[6] And, he reminds the *competentes*, the patriarchs' lives, lived in real historical time, are better than abstract ethical analysis in hammering home how virtuous people address the decisions and difficulties that face them: "The life of the saints is for others a norm of how to live"

1. See chapter 2, 23, 24–25, 27, 28–29.

2. Scholars supporting this analysis include Palanque, *Saint Ambroise et l'empire romain,* 197–99, 442, 552; Palla, intro. to his trans. of Ambrose, *De Ioseph,* 337–38; McLynn, *Ambrose of Milan,* 296–97; Moorhead, *Ambrose,* 155. Paredi, *Saint Ambrose,* 298–300, opts for the same date but without reference to Calligonus.

3. Ambrose, *De Ioseph* 6.30, ed. Schenkl, trans. Palla; trans. McHugh in Ambrose, *Seven Exegetical Works,* 209.

4. Ibid. 6.33; McHugh trans., 212.

5. Ibid. 7.38.

6. Ibid. 1.1; McHugh trans., 189.

(Sanctorum uita ceteris norma uiuendi est). Having indicated the paramount virtue of each of the patriarchs, he stresses that virtues in particular are more useful as examples than virtue in general; the former "are more precise and enter the heart more readily" (expressiora sunt eoque facilius mentem penetrant).[7]

In his identification of each patriarch's chief virtue at the beginning of this treatise, chastity is the particular moral excellence that Ambrose ascribes to Joseph, a point on which he has occasion to elaborate in recounting the patriarch's response to the would-be seduction of Potiphar's wife.[8] Taking Ambrose at his word here, a number of scholars have likewise focused on chastity as Joseph's salient virtue.[9] But if chastity is the virtue that Ambrose initially accords to Joseph, it is by no means his only or even his most important form of moral excellence.[10] Indeed, Ambrose shows Joseph displaying a wide array of moral qualities, which can be classified under the heading of the four cardinal virtues. Taking a leaf from his own book in *De Jacob*, where he calls temperance "the mistress of learning" (disciplinae magistra),[11] he treats Joseph's chastity in that work as the application of right reason to the self-discipline that enables him to resist sexual temptation in the face of the adulterous advances of Potiphar's wife, a position he reiterates in *De Joseph*. In the latter work, Ambrose notes that, in rejecting the invitation of Potiphar's wife, Joseph "first overcame her attack through a mental struggle, as it were, and drove her back with the shield of his soul" (Primum igitur mentis congressione superauit tamquam scuto animi inruentem repellens),[12] displaying the rational self-discipline that she so clearly lacks. Joseph's chastity is not a virtue to which he adheres as a proponent of asceticism, for in due course he marries and fathers two sons.[13] As with the other patriarchs, what Joseph exemplifies in his sexual life is moderation, not extremism.

7. Ibid.; for the first passage, my trans.; for the second, McHugh trans., 189.

8. Ibid. 1.2, 5.22–26, 6.28.

9. See, for example, Kellner, *Der heilige Ambrosius*, 116–18; Thamin, *Saint Ambroise et la morale chrétienne*, 326; Lazzati, *Il valore letterario della esegesi ambrosiana*, 73; North, *Sophrosyne*, 370. On this issue Dassmann, *Die Frömmigkeit der Kirchenvaters Ambrosius*, 294, is unique in seeing faith and devotion as the paramount virtues of Ambrose's Joseph.

10. Noted by Palla, intro. to his trans. of Ambrose, *De Ios.*, 337–38.

11. Ambrose, *De Iacob* 1.2.6, ed. Schenkl, trans. Palla; trans. McHugh, 123.

12. Ibid.; Ambrose, *De Ios.* 1.1, 1.2, 5.22–26, 6.31. The quotation is at 5.23; my trans. Joseph is also depicted as overcoming this sexual temptation, seen as well as a temptation to an act of ingratitude toward Potiphar in 4 Macc 2:1–3, as is noted by Gregg, "Joseph with Potiphar's Wife," 332, 336–41.

13. Ambrose, *De Iac.* 2.9.37; Ambrose, *De Ios.* 7.40.

If temperance enables Joseph to confine his sexual activity to marriage, it also informs the modesty that he possesses from earliest childhood[14] and his ability, as a mature man, to resist the temptations associated with the wealth and power accorded to him when he becomes the Pharaoh's prime minister. In elevating him to high office, the Pharaoh also gives him a ring, a gold chain, a fine robe, and a chariot. These endowments reflect, not a desire for wealth and status on Joseph's part, but the Pharaoh's recognition of his intelligence and competence.[15] As chief minister, Joseph inhabits a suitable residence and has the means to entertain guests in state. Receiving his brothers when they come to Egypt to buy grain, he does so, not out of ostentation or the desire to over-awe them by his munificence, but rather out of generosity and courtesy. Wining and dining them, "he is drunk with an inebriation, but a sober one" (inebriatur ebrietate, sed sobria). Following Philo, Ambrose's Joseph holds to the mean at this feast, maintaining a balance between deficiency and over-sumptuousness.[16]

With Joseph's temperance in mind as well as the anthropology that Ambrose develops in his earlier patriarch treatises, it is clear that his references here and there to the theme of the body as the cage of the soul should not be understood in a literal Platonic sense as bespeaking a dualistic conception of human nature.[17] Rather, Ambrose intends these references to be read in the light of his Pauline distinction between "the flesh" and "the body." Accordingly, for Ambrose the prison of our spirit is our irrational capitulation to sinful passions, whether they arise in the body, the mind, or both, and for which moderation and right reason are the antidotes, the position he develops in De Isaac and De Jacob.[18] At the same time, and in sharp contrast with his earlier patri-

14. Ambrose, *De Ios.* 1.2, 5.22, 5.25, 5.26.

15. Ibid. 7.40.

16. Ibid. 9.47–50, 11.60; the quotation is at 11.60; my trans. Cf. Philo, *On Joseph* 34.205–206, trans. Colson. On the theme of *sobria ebrietas*, Quasten, "'Sobria ebrietas' in Ambrosius *De sacramentis*," in *Miscellanea liturgica in honorem L. Cuniberti Mohlberg*, 1:117–25, follows Lewy, *Sobria ebrietas*, in treating this theme exclusively from a mystical perspective. Neither author discusses its reference in Ambrose's patriarch treatises.

17. Ambrose, *De Ios.* 6.31: we are "in hunc corporeum carcerem." Cf. Ambrose, *De Isaac* 2.3, 6.52, ed. Schenkl, trans. Moreschini; Ambrose, *De Iac.* 2.9.38.

18. See chapters 3, 5, and 6, 35–36; 71, 80, 91; 93, 99, 101–2, 125. For the literal understanding of this motif as reflecting straightforward Platonism and Neoplatonism on Ambrose's part in *De Joseph*, see Courcelle, "Anti-Christian Arguments and Christian Platonism," 165–66; idem, "L'Âme en cage"; idem, "Le corps-tombeau"; Loiselle, "'Nature' de l'homme," 32–34, 143; Tolomio, "'Corpus carcer' nell'Alto Medioevo," 5–6, 10–11, 13.

arch treatises, Ambrose's *De Joseph* is striking for its lack of multiple injunctions to flee physical pleasures and to observe moderation. His omission of such repeated advice suggests that, by the time he presented Joseph's story to his *competentes* in the course of their Lenten instruction, he assumed, or hoped, that they would have internalized that message sufficiently.

Joseph also serves as an exponent of the virtue of wisdom, a wisdom both suprarational and rational. His wisdom enables him to foresee the future and to know what is true and good as well as how to translate his theoretical knowledge into prudent and practical action. As Ambrose shows, Joseph enjoys intimacy with God from his youth. God favors him by granting him the grace of prophesy, sharing with him his own future plans for the covenanted people of Israel in dreams that give Joseph primacy over his elders, dreams that the young Joseph is able to interpret correctly.[19] This understanding of the mind of God, reflecting Joseph's supernatural wisdom, offends his brothers and even his father Jacob, who initially reproves him for lack of filial piety toward his elders.[20]

This biblical fact poses an ethical and exegetical problem for Ambrose for which he finds a solution only with considerable difficulty. Having opened *De Joseph* with the observation that Joseph is morally perfect from his youth, Ambrose notes that because of his virtue "he was loved by his parents . . . more than their other sons. But that fact gave rise to enmity" (a parentibus plus quam ceteri filii diligebatur. Sed ea res inuidiae fuit).[21] Here Ambrose reprises the theme of the preferential treatment of children by parents and why parents should avoid it, which he addressed earlier in *De Jacob*. There, we recall, God's prophesy to Rebecca while she is pregnant with Jacob and Esau provides the explanation for Esau's eclipse by his younger brother before their differences in moral character become evident. In *De Joseph*, however, Ambrose cites his parents' preference for Joseph before his prophetic dreams offer a divine rationale for his rule over his elders. As Ambrose continues to explore this topic, he notes that, while it is natural and pleasant for parents to love their children, recognizing their differing qualities, "parental love does harm to the children unless it is practiced with restraint; for it may give the beloved child free rein out of excessive indulgence or, by preference shown to one child, may alienate the others from the spirit of brotherly love. . . . Let the children be joined in

19. Ambrose, *De Ios.* 1.2, 2.7–3.9.
20. Ibid. 2.7, 3.8–9, 3.11–12.
21. Ibid. 1.2; McHugh trans., 189.

like favor, who have been joined in like nature" (amor ipse patrius, nisi mo-
derationem teneat, nocet liberis, si aut nimia indulgentia dilectum resoluat aut
praelatione unius ceteros ab adfectu germanitatis auertat. . . . Iungat liberos
aequalis gratia, quos iuncxit aequalis natura).[22] Ambrose's sage advice, however, is not followed by Jacob. He clearly does prefer Joseph, giving him the
coat of many colors.[23] This anomaly requires interpretation, lest Jacob be in-
dicted for bad parenting. As with Jacob's past preferential treatment by his
mother, Ambrose now explains, Jacob also can be excused in that he was preferring, not this particular son, but in him "the greater marks of virtue; thus
he would not appear to have shown preference so much as father to son, but
rather as prophet to a sacred sign. And Jacob was right to make for his son a
tunic of many colors, to indicate by it that Joseph was to be preferred to his
brothers with his clothing of manifold virtues" (in quo maiora uirtutum in-
signia praevidebat, ut non tam filium pater praetulisse uideatur quam propheta
mysterium, meritoque uariam tunicam fecit ei, quo significaret eum diuer-
sarum uirtutum amictu fratribus praeferendum).[24]

But if this is the case, if Jacob can legitimately prefer Joseph as virtuous
and as a sacred sign of a mystery to come, Ambrose is still left with the problem of explaining Jacob's annoyance when he first hears the interpretation of
Joseph's dream in which the sun and moon and eleven stars bow down to him,
betokening his rule over his parents as well as his brothers. Despite the analogous prophesy in his own history that gave him primacy over his elder brother,
Jacob nonetheless "reproved him" (obiurgavit illum).[25] Ambrose seeks to re-
solve this exegetical embarrassment by giving to Jacob a double typological
significance in this passage. Jacob is Israel twice over, he asserts. Jacob's initial
disapproval of Joseph's interpretation of his dream is a purely human response
to its overturning of hierarchy within the family. In this instance, Jacob represents the Israel that does not accept Christ as the Messiah. But he also represents believing Israel, the Israel that does accept Christ as the Savior. This
second Jacob acknowledges the divine message revealed in Joseph's dream
and sends him out to his brothers to observe how they are tending their sheep,

22. Ibid. 2.5; McHugh trans., 190. Cf. chapter 6, 106.
23. Ambrose, De Ios. 2.5–6.
24. Ibid. 2.6; McHugh trans., 191.
25. Ibid. 3.8, quoting Gen 37:10; my trans.

as a forerunner of the Good Shepherd.[26] This resolution of the dilemma of Jacob's treatment of Joseph, both the rationalization of his preference for Joseph and his initial resistance to, but later acceptance of, the idea of his primacy, appears to be Ambrose's own. If it enables him to explain this problematic biblical passage, the price it exacts from him is a high one. For it entails the treatment of Jacob, already portrayed as a type of Christ in *De Jacob,* as representing here the unbelieving as well as the believing Israel.

Joseph's wisdom is also reflected in his ability to interpret dreams that pertain to purely human events. This aspect of his prophetic wisdom, Ambrose shows, can be seen in his interpretation of the dreams of the eunuchs, Pharaoh's chief butler and baker, whom Joseph encounters in the prison to which he has been consigned as the result of the false accusation of Potiphar's wife. Joseph accurately reveals that these dreams mean that the baker has fallen permanently out of the Pharaoh's favor and will be put to death but that the butler will regain his master's favor and recover his former office. In agreement with Philo, Ambrose indicates that, although Joseph knows that the baker's dream portends misfortune, he does not fudge his words in interpreting it since, in conveying God's message, he is bound to tell the truth.[27] But Ambrose also adds a thought not found in Philo. This entire episode, he observes, reveals the fragility and arbitrariness of royal favor and the precarious state of those who enter royal service laboring under the delusion that they can thereby guarantee their own worldly success,[28] a sentiment that would certainly have rung true to an audience living under the rule of the late-fourth-century Roman emperors.

It is surprising that Philo does not make the same point, given the fact that, unlike Ambrose, he sees public service as such as a vast illusion. In commenting on Joseph's activities as the Pharaoh's prime minister after he succeeds in interpreting the ruler's dreams about the seven fat cows and seven lean cows, Philo says that the statesman is, indeed, the interpreter of dreams because political life, even politics as it might be lived in an ideal Stoic cosmopolis, and life itself, are dreams—fleeting and changeable, as are all external and physical realities. The statesman signifies the mind that sees through and past these illusions, perceiving and adhering instead to true spiritual realities. While Joseph's elevation by the Pharaoh is an appropriate reward for his merit, and while he does a capable job as prime minister, his statesmanship, for Philo, is

---

26. Ambrose, *De Ios.* 3.8–9.
27. Ibid. 6.29–30; see also Ambrose, *De Iac.* 2.9.42; cf. Philo, *On Joseph* 18.95.
28. Ambrose, *De Ios.* 6.29, 6.30.

not the crown of Joseph's career but a necessary, and from his standpoint, a mercifully brief phase that he must undergo before moving on to and attaining the contemplative life. This is an interpretation that, quite simply, is not to be found in Ambrose's *De Joseph,* despite the individual points on which Ambrose otherwise concurs with Philo.[29]

In Ambrose's treatment of Joseph's interpretation of the Pharaoh's dreams, Joseph tells the ruler that God is revealing thereby the future abundance and dearth of Egypt's agrarian resources. At the same time, he adds that the fat cows signify the neglect of reverence for God, which in turn leads to spiritual famine, a moral message more widely applicable and one not found in Philo.[30] Joseph's wisdom in grasping the divine forecast of what is to occur in the next fourteen years of Egypt's agricultural history is matched by his prudence in devising the policy of storing up the surpluses garnered in the good years against the dearth of the lean years. Accepting his wise counsel, the Pharaoh raises him to high office so that he can implement this policy and rewards him with wealth, power, and esteem. This circumstance enables Joseph to sell the grain he has stored up to the people of other nations who come to Egypt to buy it, including his own kin.[31] In describing Joseph's role as the interpreter of the Pharaoh's dreams and as the implementer of the policy that they suggest, Ambrose's accent lies squarely on Joseph's wisdom, both theoretical and practical, and on the executive ability as a statesman that enables him to render benefits more widely and to a greater number of people than is true of any of the other patriarchs, while at the same time rendering optimum service to his ruler.

In that sense, Joseph's service as a statesman can also be seen as the culmination of his exercise of the virtue of justice no less than of the virtue of wisdom. Justice, for Ambrose, means alleviating the needs of others as well as rendering to others what is fitting. Joseph manifests this virtue, as well, from his youth. He obeys his father in going out to seek his brothers and their flocks,

---

29. Philo, *On Joseph* 6.28–7.36, 14.67–79, 21.117, 22.125–24.147, 27.157. A number of scholars have noted Philo's downplaying of politics and of the active life in general and his disinterest in the ethics of the good statesman, in contrast with Ambrose's treatment of this issue. See, for example, Harrington, "Joseph in the Testament of Joseph, Pseudo-Philo, and Philo," 127–30; Palla, intro. to his trans. of *De Ios.,* 339–40; Piredda, "La tipologia sacerdotale del patriarca Giuseppe"; Feldman, "Josephus' Portrait of Joseph," 384–86; Niehoff, *The Figure of Joseph in Post-Biblical Jewish Literature,* 59–110. Hollander, "The Portrayal of Joseph," sees Ambrose as following Josephus, not Philo. On the other hand, Lucchesi, *L'Usage de Philon,* 64, does not see Ambrose as departing from Philo in his treatment of Joseph the statesman.

30. Ambrose, *De Ios.* 7.36–38.

31. Ibid. 7.38–43.

even though he is aware of their hostility.[32] Although he is sold into slavery through no fault of his own, he renders good service to Potiphar, his master, managing his household efficiently. His repudiation of the advances of Potiphar's wife reflects his sense of obligation to his master as well as his rejection of adultery as intrinsically sinful: "He flees the charge of ingratitude and the stain of sin as one who owes a debt to his master's kindness and his own blamelessness" (sed tamquam beneficii erilis et innocentiae suae debitor fugit crimen ingrati peccatique labem).[33] When he is jailed, Joseph also serves his fellow prisoners, counseling them as well as interpreting their dreams, in the case of the Pharaoh's chief butler and the baker.[34] When Joseph's brothers arrive in Egypt, not only does he offer them generous and courteous hospitality and fraternal devotion, but he also displays his brotherly love in counsel as well as by example.[35] He accords to them what kin deserve, whether they merit it or not, and this notwithstanding the pious fraud he perpetrates in persuading Jacob to let Benjamin come to Egypt, a subterfuge discussed in *De Jacob* if not in *De Joseph*.[36] Also in *De Jacob* but not in *De Joseph*, Joseph displays filial piety in promising that, when Jacob dies, he will not bury him in Egypt but will return his remains to Canaan where he can be buried with his ancestors. Ambrose's only allusion to Jacob's death in *De Joseph* is the remark that Joseph will be the one to close his eyes.[37] Most of all, however, Joseph exemplifies social responsibility and service to others in his sage policy as the Pharaoh's minister. The grain he has stored up enables him to feed the hungry, to save the lives of the nations who come to Egypt to buy grain no less than his own relatives. It is the function of the saints, Ambrose reminds his *competentes*, to look beyond their own needs to the needs of their fellows: "For this is the recompense and the life of the saints, that they have also brought about the salvation of others" (haec enim est merces et uita sanctorum, quod etiam alios redemerunt).[38]

32. Ibid. 1.2, 2.7, 3.9, 3.11–12.

33. Ibid. 5.23–24, 6.31; the quotation is at 5.23; McHugh trans., 204. Cf. Ambrose, *De Iac.* 1.2.6 and cf. also Philo, *On Joseph* 8.37–39, 9.40–11.57, who emphasizes Joseph's managerial skills and his chastity but who, on the latter point, ignores the theme of justice rendered to Potiphar and instead uses the occasion to expatiate on Jewish sexual ethics in contrast with that of the Egyptians. The theme of justice to Potiphar is noted by Gregg, "Joseph with Potiphar's Wife," 339–40.

34. Ambrose, *De Ios.* 6.29.

35. Ibid. 9.47–50, 10.53, 11.60, 12.69, 13.78.

36. Ambrose, *De Iac.* 2.3.10.

37. Ibid. 2.9.36; Ambrose, *De Ios.* 13.77.

38. Ambrose, *De Ios.* 7.41–42, 8.43, 9.49–51, 10.54, 11.63, 12.71; the quotation is at 12.71; McHugh trans., 123.

As an exponent of justice, Ambrose's Joseph also manifests the virtue of fortitude. He does not render evil for evil, but returns evil with good. As with his father, he faces injustice at the hands of others. At all times, following Philo's Joseph, he bears such treatment and the suffering it causes courageously, maintaining his calm, his equanimity, and his constancy, whatever his circumstances. Like the Stoic sage, he bears and forbears. Joseph displays these traits from the very beginning of his story. He does not chastise his brothers when they react with anger and envy at the dreams he interprets concerning their respective futures.[39] Joseph also bears without complaint the fact that his brothers seek to kill him. For Ambrose, even though the dismissal of that fratricidal intention, thanks to the intervention of Reuben and Judah, leads them to perpetrate another evil against him—"They sold him sinfully into slavery" (Male uendiderunt)[40]—Joseph does not protest.

As a slave in Potiphar's household, and subsequently in prison, Joseph maintains his constancy and forbearance. He does not accuse Potiphar's wife of trying to seduce him or seek to refute her false accusation against him.[41] In prison, his equanimity is such that it evokes from Ambrose a disquisition on the theme of moral freedom and slavery. As with the Stoic sage, he argues, the virtuous man is truly free whatever his circumstances, while the vicious man is the slave of his "flesh," that is, his vices. Moreover, low social or legal status does not prevent a person from acquiring virtue: "The flesh is subject to slavery, not the spirit, and many humble servants are more free than their masters. . . . Every sin is slavish, while blamelessness is free" (carnem seruituti subditam esse, non mentem multosque seruulos esse dominis liberiores. . . . Seruile est omne peccatum, libera est innocentia).[42] Hearers among Ambrose's *competentes* who are slaves can thus find consolation, and an important lesson, in Joseph's example.[43] When Joseph is unjustly cast into prison, he does not lose his blessed state, the inner freedom and constancy of the sage. As Ambrose puts it, "I may even say that Joseph was happier when he was imprisoned" (ergo beatiorem dixerim, cum in carcerem mitteretur).[44]

---

39. Ibid. 1.4; cf. Philo, *On Joseph* 41.246–250. On Joseph's manifesting the equanimity of the Stoic sage, see Hill, "Classical and Christian Tradition," 151–52, 160; Palla, intro. to his trans. of *De Ios.*, 338–39; Pasini, *Ambrogio di Milano*, 189–90.

40. Ambrose, *De Ios.* 3.11, 3.14; the quotation is at 3.14; my trans.

41. Ibid. 5.26, 6.31.

42. Ibid. 4.20; McHugh trans., 201.

43. Ibid. 4.21.

44. Ibid. 5.26; my trans.; cf. Ambrose, *De Iac.* 2.9.42.

Most importantly, Joseph forbears to exact vengeance upon his brothers when they are in his power on their arrival in Egypt. He forgives them for having injured him; and, with Philo's Joseph, he even places a providential construction on the fact that they were responsible for his enslavement and transportation to Egypt: God has sent him to Egypt so that, as events turn out, he can save their lives.[45] And this outcome is central for Ambrose:

This then is the whole point of the story, that we should know that a perfect man is not tempted to do wrong by avenging injuries or by returning evil for evil. . . . But this is admirable, if you love your enemy, as the Savior teaches. And he truly is to be admired who did this before the Gospel, who was compassionate when he was mistreated, and who forgave when he was harmed, who did not repay the injury when he was sold, but returned grace for offense, which all of us have learned after the Gospel but which we cannot observe.

Hinc argumentum totius historiae processit, simul ut cognoscamus perfectum uirum non moueri ulciscendi doloris iniuria nec malorum rependere uicem. . . . Sed illud mirabile, si diligas inimicum tuum, quod saluator docet. Iure ergo mirandus qui hoc fecit ante euangelium, ut laesus parceret, adpetitus ignosceret, uenditus non referret iniuriam, sed gratiam pro contumelia solueret, quod post euangelium omnes didicimus et seruare non possumus.[46]

In Joseph the Christian injunctions to love one's enemies and to turn the other cheek cohabit comfortably with the fortitude of the Stoic sage.

In manifesting all of the cardinal virtues as his story unfolds, Ambrose's Joseph is not only a Christian *avant la lettre,* he is also a type of Christ.[47] Like

---

45. Ambrose, *De Ios.* 1.3, 9.47, 9.50, 12.69, 14.84; cf. Philo, *On Joseph* 40.214. See also Ambrose, *De Iac.* 2.9.41.

46. Ambrose, *De Ios.* 1.3; my trans.

47. Although without connecting this theme with the cardinal virtues, a number of scholars agree on this point. While Kellner, *Der heilige Ambrosius,* 118, sees Origen as the single source for this idea, and Dulaey, "Joseph le Patriarche, figure de Christ," 86, 88–89, attributes it specifically to Tertullian, Argyle, "Joseph the Patriarch in Patristic Teaching," shows that this view was widely held in apologetic and patristic literature. See also Argal Echarri, "El patriarca José," in *Miscélanea José Zunzunegui,* 3:62–74; Palla, intro. to his trans. of *De Ios.,* 338–39; Pasini, *Ambrogio di Milano,* 189–90. Another possible source is the *Testament of the Twelve Patriarchs,* a Jewish text of the second century BC, reworked by Christian hands in the second century AD, and the basis for

Christ, Joseph possesses grace from his infancy and knows the mind of God, whose message concerning Joseph's primacy, in the dreams he sends the young patriarch, point ahead to the time when Christ will be lord of all.[48] Like Christ, Joseph obeys his father's mission to go out and tend his sheep.[49] Like Christ, Joseph is betrayed, sold, and stripped of his clothing; the blood on his coat of many colors points to Christ's crucifixion.[50] Joseph is truly tempted and, like Christ, he resists temptation.[51] Joseph asks to be remembered by the butler he has helped; and it is Christ who prompts the butler when he later remembers Joseph.[52] Joseph, like Christ, forgives those who have injured him and never accuses them.[53] Like Christ, Joseph feeds the hungry, nourishing them physically and, metaphorically, saving them spiritually as well. With respect to his brothers, he refuses to accept payment for the grain they buy and returns their money, giving them gifts instead. He saves the nations, not just Israel.[54] The power that Joseph wields in Egypt represents the power over all given to Christ. Like Christ, Joseph announces his identity as the savior of his people.[55] Like Christ, he takes the initiative with respect to those he intends to save. At Jacob's behest, he goes out to seek his brothers like the Good Shepherd seeking the sheep of his flock who have gone astray; and when his brothers return to Egypt with Jacob and their full households, he goes out to greet them, as Christ will greet the Jews who will be redeemed at the end of time.[56] Like Christ, Joseph is the new Adam. He makes himself visible rather than trying to hide from God and is willing to leave his garment behind him as he escapes from Potiphar's wife; his nudity in this case is a sign of virtue in contrast with Adam's clothing of himself when he becomes a sinner.[57] As with Christ, Joseph's sufferings are overcome by his resurrection. While the asses on

---

Ambrose's work by a similar title, *De patriarchis*, ed. Schenkl, trans. Banterle, as is noted by Hollander, *Joseph as an Ethical Model*, 13; Hollander and De Jonge, *The Testaments of the Twelve Patriarchs*, 42, 68, 82–85.

48. Ambrose, *De Ios.* 2.7, 3.9, 3.13.

49. Ibid. 3.8–9.

50. Ibid. 3.12–4.19.

51. Ibid. 6.31; noted by Gregg, "Joseph with Potiphar's Wife," 342.

52. Ambrose, *De Ios.* 6.29, 6.32, 6.34.

53. Ibid. 1.3, 3.13, 9.47, 9.50, 12.69, 14.84.

54. Ibid. 7.41–42, 8.45, 9.47, 9.49–51, 10.58–59, 11.63, 12.67, 12.70, 13.74–80, 14.83–84; cf. Ambrose, *De Iac.* 2.9.41.

55. Ambrose, *De Ios.* 12.67–70.

56. Ibid. 3.10, 14.84.

57. Ibid. 3.10, 5.25.

which his brothers return to Canaan to collect Jacob and their households recall the animal on which Christ made his entry into Jerusalem at the beginning of his passion, Joseph's restoration to life in the eyes of Jacob, who thought him dead, points ahead to Christ's resurrection.[58]

Ambrose strikes three other notes in presenting Joseph as a type of Christ, the savior of the nations. Alone among the patriarchs, he does not practice endogamy. He marries an Egyptian wife, a Gentile.[59] This marital practice is now acceptable for a patriarch, signifying as it does the ingathering of the Gentiles by the church. And, second, Ambrose makes much of the special love that Joseph bears toward his brother Benjamin, like himself a son of Rachel, a type of the church. When Joseph returns the money that his brothers have paid for the Egyptian grain, he places in Benjamin's sack a cup, representing the cup of salvation, Christ's sacrifice as the new high priest, the wine of the Eucharist.[60] Ambrose also refers repeatedly to the fact that St. Paul, the apostle to the Gentiles, was descended from the tribe of Benjamin.[61] And finally, notwithstanding Ambrose's depiction of Joseph as a Stoic sage possessing equanimity, he observes that he weeps on his meeting with Benjamin and again when he identifies himself to his brothers. Ambrose justifies these departures from Stoic *apatheia* by comparing Joseph with Christ, who wept for Lazarus.[62]

In presenting Joseph as a man who has mastered his passions completely, except for these two occasions when brotherly love lets loose his tears, Ambrose departs in notable ways both from the characterization of Joseph in the book of Genesis and from Philo's account of the patriarch. The Joseph of Genesis is a far more emotional person than Ambrose's Joseph. Far from displaying *apatheia* and self-mastery in his encounters with his kin when they arrive in Egypt, he is so overcome by his feelings that he cannot control himself. He sends everyone from the room and weeps so loudly that his Egyptian servants can hear him, even behind closed doors (Gen 45:1–2). When he meets Benjamin, Joseph falls on his neck and weeps (Gen 45:14). As for his other brothers, he not only weeps when he reveals his identity to them but also kisses them (Gen 45:15). Similarly, the biblical Joseph weeps when he reencounters Jacob (Gen 46:29). He also weeps in lamenting Jacob's death, although a

---

58. Ibid. 13.77, 13.80.
59. Ibid. 7.40.
60. Ibid. 11.63–64.
61. Ibid. 8.45, 9.46–47, 10.52, 10.58, 11.60, 11.63–66, 12.73, 12.75–13.76.
62. Ibid. 10.59, 12.66–67.

seven-day limit is placed on the mourning period (Gen 50:4, 10). After Jacob's death, Joseph's brothers ask his forgiveness, still thinking, in the teeth of the evidence, that he harbors hatred for them. He has already forgiven them, he reassures them, and weeps as he forgives them yet again (Gen 59:17; 60:21).

It is Philo who first tries to turn the Joseph of Genesis into a Stoic sage, claiming that he succeeds in mastering his feelings.[63] Nonetheless, he presents Joseph as weeping four times in his encounters with his kin. He weeps at his brothers' first visit to Egypt, when he greets Benjamin, when he is reconciled with his brothers, and finally when he is reunited with Jacob.[64] Philo could have accounted for these lachrymose passages, within the context of Stoic ethics, by portraying Joseph's repeated tears as manifestations of *eupatheia*, good feelings deemed acceptable because they are compatible with reason. But he does not do so. For his part, confining himself only to two episodes in which Joseph weeps, Ambrose Christianizes them as well as Stoicizing them even more fully than Philo does. Ambrose acknowledges that, at the prospect of greeting Benjamin, Joseph indeed weeps. But, he observes, retiring to his room, Joseph washes his face and recovers his composure: "Joseph was overcome by emotion but held it in check with deliberation. Reason was at a standoff with love. He wept, so as to temper with his tears the impulse of pious love" (Uincebatur adfectu Ioseph, differebatur consilio; ratio cum amore certabat. Fleuit, ut amoris pii aestus lacrimis temperaret).[65] Here, in a striking manipulation of Stoicism, instead of treating Joseph's outburst of weeping as a departure from *apatheia*, Ambrose depicts it as an act that itself moderates the fervor of his brotherly love. As with his weeping when he is reconciled with his other brothers, Ambrose describes Joseph's weeping before his meeting with Benjamin as Christ-like, comparing it, as we have seen, with Christ's weeping for Lazarus.[66] As for the other episodes of Joseph's weeping recounted in Genesis, most of which are also reported by Philo, Ambrose simply omits them.

There are other omissions or reworkings of the book of Genesis and of Ambrose's exegetical sources in his handling of two other major topics, the Egyptians and Joseph's brothers. Given the negative valency of "Egypt" in *De Abraham*, signifying as it does in that treatise both marital unchastity and false

63. Philo, *On Joseph* 28.166–29.168.
64. Ibid. 28.166–29.168, 30.175, 33.200–34.201, 40.237, 42.256.
65. Ambrose, *De Ios.* 10.57; my trans.
66. Ibid. 10.59, 11.66–67.

philosophy,[67] it is not surprising to find Ambrose presenting Egyptians in a negative light in *De Joseph* as well. Potiphar and his wife head the list of bad Egyptians. Following Philo with respect to Potiphar's profession, and in contrast with the book of Genesis, which describes him as the captain of the Pharaoh's guard (Gen 39:1), Ambrose presents him as the Pharaoh's chief cook. Unlike Philo, however, this thought launches, for Ambrose, a disquisition on food, raw and cooked. He segues from that idea to the observation that "there existed in Egypt a raw faithlessness, and no flame of awareness of God, no desire for true knowledge, had made it tender, no fiery words of the Lord had cooked it" (Erat . . . in Aegypto cruda perfidia, quam nullus diuinae cognitionis ardor et uerae scientiae cupiditas nulla molliuerat, non eloquia domini ignita dececserant).[68] If Ambrose adds this theological touch to Philo's characterization of Potiphar, he omits another point found in the text of the Hebrew Bible as well as in the Septuagint and repeated by Philo: the notion that Potiphar was a eunuch. This term, in fact, bears two meanings in both the Greek and the Hebrew Bibles; according to both texts, a eunuch can either be an official, irrespective of his state of physical integrity, or a *castrato*. For his part, Philo does not notice this double meaning and assumes that Potiphar was physically a eunuch; he raises the question, accordingly, of why he had a wife in the first place, an unreasonable situation, as he sees it.[69] This is a discussion that Ambrose omits. Eunuch or not, Potiphar is an incompetent manager. He cannot control his wife, and he cannot govern his own household, which is why he puts Joseph in charge of it.[70]

Furthermore, Potiphar is unjust. He imprisons Joseph "with his case unheard . . . as if guilty of a crime" (Inaudita causa, . . . tamquam reus criminis).[71] Moreover, he allows Joseph to languish in jail indefinitely, without any prospect of the determination of his innocence or guilt. Whatever may have been the situation in ancient Egypt, this practice contravenes Roman legal procedure. In Roman law, imprisonment was typically brief. An individual accused of a crime was imprisoned, pending the investigation of his case and its hearing by a magistrate. If convicted of a capital crime, he was imprisoned in

---

67. See chapter 4, 43, 44, 51–53, 65.

68. Ambrose, *De Ios.* 4.19; McHugh trans., 200–201. I have altered his wording slightly. Cf. Philo, *On Joseph* 5.27.

69. Philo, *On Joseph* 5.27, 12.58–60. See Young, *Analytical Concordance to the Bible*, s.v. *eunuch*.

70. Ambrose, *De Ios.* 5.21.

71. Ibid. 5.26; my trans.

between his sentencing and his execution. There was no such thing in Roman law as a jail sentence as itself a punishment for a crime.[72] Joseph's unjust treatment, his denial of a hearing, and his imprisonment with no end in sight are matters that deeply exercise and offend Philo.[73] As a person living in the first-century Roman world, he clearly expects the Roman legal system to work, and he retrojects his institutional and procedural expectations onto the practice of ancient Egypt. By contrast, Ambrose's comparatively matter-of-fact presentation of Joseph's treatment by Potiphar reflects the sensibility of a late-fourth-century Roman writing in an age in which political corruption and procedural irregularity were pervasive and frequently experienced facts of life, not seen as conditions about which it made much sense to complain.

If Potiphar is incompetent, unjust, and an index of Egypt's ignorance of and disinterest in theological truth, his wife is wanton, a seductress, a would-be adulteress, a person clearly ignorant or dismissive of appropriate sexual behavior and her own proper duty to her husband and to Joseph alike. She is a liar as well, laying a false charge against Joseph.[74] In this sense, she also bears some of the responsibility for his unjust imprisonment.

Another example of a bad Egyptian, and one whom Ambrose pointedly contrasts with Joseph, the good steward and helper of others, is the Pharaoh's chief butler, whose dream in prison Joseph successfully interprets. Joseph repeatedly asks the butler to remember his help and his plight when he is restored to his master's favor and to use his influence to assist him.[75] But in return, the butler displays forgetfulness and ingratitude. It is only when the Pharaoh despairs of acquiring an explanation of his dreams of the seven fat and seven lean cows that the butler remembers Joseph, still incarcerated. His plan of recommending Joseph to the Pharaoh is based on his judgment that it is in his own self-interest to do so. If he alone can provide an interpreter of the Pharaoh's dreams, he reasons, he will stand that much the higher in his master's esteem. Self-serving ambition is thus what motivates him to bring Joseph to the Pharaoh's attention. Ambrose offers an additional reason for the butler's behavior not found in Genesis or in any of his exegetical sources. He argues that the butler, having access to the Pharaoh's cellar, overindulges in his master's wine. His blame is attributable, in part, to his loss of sobriety. Ambrose

72. Berger, *Encyclopedic Dictionary of Roman Law*, s.v. *carcer.*
73. Philo, *On Joseph* 10.52, 15.80.
74. Ambrose, *De Ios.* 5.22–26, 6.28.
75. Ibid. 6.29, 6.32, 6.34.

compares the butler with Doeg and Aman, officials mentioned in the Old Testament who also rendered bad service to their masters,[76] comparing their behavior and that of the butler with Joseph's good service and gratitude to his own master.

If there is no lack of bad Egyptians in *De Joseph*, it is noteworthy that Ambrose finds a place for good Egyptians as well. Closest to Joseph is the Egyptian wife he marries, signifying that the time is now ripe for the ingathering of the Gentiles and their grafting onto Israelite stock. As Ambrose puts it, in the form of a rhetorical question, "Now who is he who took a wife from the Gentiles but he who gathered to himself a church from the nations?" (Quis autem est qui ex gentibus accepit uxorem nisi qui ecclesiam sibi ex nationibus congregauit?)[77] The two sons of this union receive their grandfather's blessing, even if he switches the blessings given to the elder and the younger. They will take their place, in turn, in the subsequent line of Joseph, as progenitors of one of the twelve tribes of Israel.

But the chief example of a good Egyptian is the Pharaoh whom Joseph serves. Ambrose is careful to exculpate the Pharaoh from the unjust imprisonment to which Joseph is subjected. Since this act was committed by someone else, namely Potiphar, the Pharaoh is innocent of it: "Thus the king is free from guilt, because the injury which the holy man suffered was done by another" (Ita rex uacat culpa, quia et id quod excepit uir sanctus iniuriae alienum fuit).[78] This depiction of the event gallantly leaves to the side the question of the Pharaoh's surveillance over his captain of the guard and his ultimate responsibility for the way in which the laws are enforced in his realm. Without giving that consideration a backward glance, Ambrose moves on, noting that when Joseph interprets the Pharaoh's dreams he tells the ruler, quoting Genesis 41:25, that God has favored him: "God has revealed to Pharaoh whatever he [God] is doing" (quaecumque facit deus ostendit pharao).[79] Furthermore, Ambrose presents the Pharaoh as a man of deep human sympathy. He empathizes with Joseph, expressing happiness when he is reunited and reconciled with his brothers. On that occasion, Ambrose does not hesitate to compare the Pharaoh with the church, rejoicing at the ultimate salvation of the Jews.[80] The Pharaoh

76. Ibid. 6.32–36; cf. Philo, *On Joseph* 19.99.
77. Ambrose, *De Ios.* 7.40; McHugh trans., 216. I have altered his wording slightly.
78. Ibid. 7.36; McHugh trans., 213.
79. Ibid. 7.37; McHugh trans., 214.
80. Ibid. 13.74.

also displays great generosity and hospitality in giving Joseph's brothers rich provisions for their journey back to Canaan to collect Jacob and their full households—a point noted by Philo—and in inviting the Israelites to return and settle in Egypt.[81]

Still, there are aspects of the Pharaoh's goodness and of Joseph's interactions with other good Egyptians recounted in the book of Genesis and in some of Ambrose's exegetical sources that he omits. When the Pharaoh makes him his prime minister so that he can provide grain in the lean years, Joseph sells the grain not only to his kinsmen and to the men of many nations who come to Egypt to buy it but also to the Egyptians themselves, thereby vastly enriching the Pharaoh and increasing his power over his own people (Gen 41:55–57; 47:14–20). This fact might well have been cited by Ambrose as an example of the prudent and farseeing service that Joseph renders to the Pharaoh. But he does not mention these grain sales to the Egyptians and the resultant shift in the power relations, to the ruler's advantage, within the Pharaoh's realm. With respect to the Pharaoh's generosity, Ambrose does not mention, as the book of Genesis and Philo do, that he grants the Israelites the land of Goshen in which to settle (Gen 46:34; 47:6, 10).[82] Nor does he note that, when the Pharaoh announces this cession of land, Joseph blesses him (Gen 47:10).

Also, while Ambrose merely alludes to Jacob's death in *De Joseph,* saying only that Joseph will be the one to close his eyes,[83] he omits the account of Jacob's death and of Joseph's fulfillment of his vow to return his father's body to Canaan for burial with his ancestors, placing this material in *De Jacob* instead.[84] According to Genesis, before Joseph essays this return to Canaan, he has recourse to the Egyptian embalmers, who prepare Jacob's corpse, the process taking forty days (Gen 50:2–3), a point noticed by Origen.[85] And the Pharaoh graciously grants permission to the Israelites to transport their father's body back to Canaan and then to return to Egypt (Gen 50:6). None of this material appears in Ambrose's account of Jacob's death and its immediate sequel, either in *De Jacob* or in *De Joseph.*

---

81. Ibid.; cf. Philo, *On Joseph* 42.251.
82. Cf. Philo, *On Joseph* 42.251.
83. Ambrose, *De Ios.* 14.83.
84. Ambrose, *De Iac.* 2.8.36, 2.9.38.
85. Origen, *On Joseph* 15.4, in idem, *Homilies on Genesis and Exodus,* trans. Heine.

His omission of Joseph's employment of the Egyptian embalmers, whose expertise in this area was legendary, is particularly striking. It is true that Ambrose also omits the passage in Genesis reporting that the wise men of Egypt were unable to interpret the Pharaoh's dreams (Gen 41:24), on which he might have capitalized had he wished to use this item in order to reinforce his characterization of "Egypt" as false philosophy. But having made his case for that position in *De Abraham*, Ambrose may have felt that it was unnecessary to repeat it in *De Joseph*. On the other hand, the Egyptian art and science of embalming is not something that he can dismiss or explain away as an example of false philosophy. And, had he included it under the heading of the good Egyptians, it would have appeared to undercut the very notion of Egyptian wisdom as somehow incorrect or deficient. The Egyptian embalmers constitute, for Ambrose, an exegetical embarrassment. His solution is simply to bypass them as well as the question of how Joseph and his brothers manage to transport Jacob's body back to Canaan undecayed.

A final inconsistency in Ambrose's handling of biblical material has to do with his treatment of the patriarch's brothers. The problem lies in the fact that he wants to make the brothers do double, or triple, duty, resulting in a certain amount of self-cancellation with respect to what they signify. Morally, Joseph's brothers are anti-types of virtue. Following Philo, Ambrose depicts them as examples of vice. They are angry and envious of Joseph on account of the primacy he will hold over them as foretold by his prophetic dreams.[86] They harbor fratricidal intentions toward Joseph; and the supersession of their murderous wrath by the decision to sell him into slavery instead is also sinful, in Ambrose's eyes.[87] Moreover, they deceive Jacob, lying to him when they explain that Joseph's coat of many colors is bloodstained because he was killed by a wild animal, although they know that this false testimony will bring their father grief.[88]

But side by side with their role as examples of vice, the actions of Joseph's brothers bear a number of typological meanings in Ambrose's hands. As the progenitors of the twelve tribes of Israel, the brothers can, in their own turn, be regarded as patriarchs themselves; and "the deeds of the patriarchs are

---

86. Ambrose, *De Ios.* 1.2, 2.7, 3.11–12; cf. Philo, *On Joseph* 2.5–5.22, who adds inhumanity to the list of the brothers' vices.

87. Ambrose, *De Ios.* 3.11, 3.13–14.

88. Ibid. 3.18.

symbols of events to come" (Gesta igitur patriarcharum futurorum mysteria sunt).[89] Some of these typological meanings, to be sure, reinforce the negative moral character that the brothers display in their treatment of Joseph. Ambrose compares the betrayal and sale of Joseph with the betrayal and sale of Christ by Judas. Collectively, the brothers represent the synagogue, unbelieving Israel, and the Jews who hand over Christ to the Roman authorities; while Reuben, the eldest brother, stands for the works of the law, which will be replaced by the gospel.[90]

At the same time, however, Ambrose wants to put a positive construction on the brothers' typological significance. Individually, Reuben, if he represents the law, also stands for humility.[91] Judah represents the gospel and the confession of sins.[92] Benjamin represents the church as well as serving as the ancestor of St. Paul, a point that Ambrose makes repeatedly.[93] Collectively, Joseph's brothers signify the Jews who will be redeemed at the end of time.[94] Also, he argues that all of the brothers, and not just Benjamin, stand for the apostles, who will evangelize both Jews and Gentiles, calling them alike to embrace the gospel and enter the church, apostles who, if they possess diverse gifts, receive the same Spirit.[95] Like their father Jacob, but even more confusingly so, Joseph's brothers display virtues as well as lapses from virtue and signify unbelieving as well as believing Israel no less than the mission to the Gentiles.

Whether or not Ambrose ascribes these multiple and frequently contradictory roles to the sons of Jacob in the light of the legacies that Jacob gives to them, in turn predictive of the later histories of the twelve tribes of Israel, his discussion of Joseph's brothers cedes, at the end of De Joseph, to Joseph's own treatment of these same brothers. The envoi of De Joseph reemphasizes the message of forgiveness and fraternal reconciliation central to this treatise and unites it with the theme of the incorporation of Ambrose's competentes into their new fatherland. Speaking of Joseph's brothers when they return to Egypt with their father and their full households, Ambrose has this to say: "For after such great hardness, after such great sins, they would be considered unworthy unless there were granted to them the remission of sins" (quia post tantam

---

89. Ibid. 14.85; McHugh trans., 237.
90. Ibid. 3.12–14, 9.46–48.
91. Ibid. 9.46, 14.84.
92. Ibid.
93. Ibid. 8.44–9.47, 10.58, 11.60–61, 11.64–65, 13.76.
94. Ibid. 14.84.
95. Ibid. 13.76, 14.82.

duritiam, post tanta peccata haberentur indigni, nisi donaretur his remissionem peccatorum).[96] As Ambrose has shown, the brothers do receive forgiveness, the remission of their sins—a phrase echoing the language of the baptismal liturgy that the *competentes* are soon to undergo and the language of the creed they are soon to profess in public.[97] In forgiving his brothers, Joseph stands for the Savior who forgives and receives his faithful people, Jew and Gentile, "not according to their merits, but according to the election of his grace" (non secundum illius merita, sed secundum electione suae gratiae).[98]

Ambrose's final exhortation to his *competentes*, as he completes their preparatory moral instruction in *De Joseph*, recapitulates the idea announced at its beginning in *De Abraham*, that they themselves have been elected to become members of God's covenanted people. Quoting Genesis 49:1–2, he adjures them as follows: "Gather yourselves together and hear Israel your father" (Congregamini et audite Israhel patrem uestrem).[99] This final line of *De Joseph* reinforces and orchestrates the fact that the patriarch treatises were meant to be absorbed and understood sequentially as building on each other in a progressive ethical *paideia*. Even though they are formally diverse, they are thematically interrelated.

Common methodological approaches, no less than themes, link *De Joseph* with the earlier patriarch treatises. Here as elsewhere in this corpus, Ambrose makes use of biblical intertextuality, both to underscore, with both Old and New Testament texts, the moral message of Joseph's example and to develop the typology attaching to him and to the other actors in his story. Here as well, he makes free use both of the book of Genesis and of his exegetical forbears. He places his own construction on the philosophical motifs to which he refers, be they the Platonic body as the soul's prison, revalued in the light of his hylomorphic anthropology and of his Pauline distinction between "the body" and "the flesh," or the Stoic doctrine of the sage. Ambrose's Joseph possesses more Stoic equanimity than does the Joseph of Genesis or the Joseph of Philo. At the same time, this Stoicism merges seamlessly with Joseph's prophetic gifts and with the Christ-like love of his brethren that enables him freely to forgive injuries. Joseph's hospitality, and that of the Pharaoh, recall the high valuation that Ambrose places on this virtue, while his good stewardship and public

---

96. Ibid. 14.84; McHugh trans., 236. I have altered his wording slightly.

97. See, for this language, Parodi, *La catechesi di sant'Ambrogio*, 117–18; Kelly, *Early Christian Creeds*, 172–73.

98. Ambrose, *De Ios.* 14.84; McHugh trans., 237. I have altered his wording slightly.

99. Ibid. 14.85; McHugh trans., 237.

service as an ideal statesman link his wide salvific role to a recognizably Roman tradition. As with the other patriarchs, Joseph possesses all the cardinal virtues and then some. He is a model of how the *competentes* are to live an ethical life in this world as lay people manifesting both private and public virtues, without succumbing to the temptations that beset the Christian in both private and public. The exalted office that Joseph holds enables him to wield more authority than the earlier patriarchs, and correspondingly, it enables him to do more good to more people, a clear message to the high-status members of Ambrose's audience. But to all his *competentes*, Joseph's Egyptian marriage and his feeding of the nations as well as his own kin convey the message of their Savior's firm assurance of his warm embrace and of the spiritual nourishment he will impart to them as they, the new Israelites, enter the Christian communion.

"And if you are Christ's, then you are Abraham's offspring, heirs according to promise."

—Gal 3:29 (RSV)

"Test everything, hold fast to what is good."

—1 Thess 5:21 (RSV)

"Nulla pudor est ad meliora transire."

—Ambrose, *Ep.* 73.7 (CSEL 82:3)

In the book which these remarks conclude, we have followed the course of pre-baptismal ethical instruction that Ambrose gave to his *competentes* in the Lenten sermons which he redrafted as his four patriarch treatises. In so doing, we have observed his development of the theory of human nature on which he grounds his interpretation of the patriarchs as *exempla uirtutis* for this lay audience of adult converts from Roman paganism. Neophyte Christians, for the most part they are or will be married, and they live active lives in the world of late-fourth-century Milan. Many of them are male heads of household who earn their livings in diverse ways, including public service. Ambrose is careful to point lessons to them on appropriate conduct in public life, with neighbors, business associates, competitors, and even enemies. He is equally interested in underscoring proper relations between husbands and wives, parents and children, masters and servants, and among siblings. He does not miss the opportunity to offer advice to unmarried girls, concubines, and slaves.

Ambrose begins to elaborate his theory of human nature in the patriarch treatises in *De Abraham,* giving it its fullest articulation in *De Jacob.* This anthropology, and the ethical corollaries that flow from it, serve as the templates that Ambrose imposes on the materials he selects from the wide range of sources—philosophical, literary, legal, biblical, and exegetical—on which he draws. He is highly selective in his use of all of these sources. He does not hesitate to do radical surgery where he finds it warranted or to transplant living tissue from one source to another. None of his sources holds a place of such privilege that it is exempt from this type of resectioning and recontextualization in aid of Ambrose's pastoral agenda.

What emerges, in the patriarch treatises, is a distinctive Ambrosian anthropology and an ethics of moderation. Both are worthy of recognition in their own right as his own creations. Together, they offer a stringent corrective to the image found all too frequently in previous scholarly assessments of Ambrose as an arch-Platonist and as a preacher of asceticism. His position in the patriarch treatises stands out in clear relief when compared with the ethical messages that he conveys to other audiences in the Milanese Christian community, audiences whose perceived vocational needs differ noticeably from those of his *competentes.*

The four legs of the platform on which Ambrose erects his anthropology in the patriarch treatises are his hylomorphic conception of human nature, his stress on free will, his theory of the passions, and his agreement with St. Paul's distinction between "the flesh" and "the body." Rejecting a Platonic or Neoplatonic understanding of the essence of a human being as a soul that makes use of a material body, seen as alien to its intrinsically spiritual nature or even as a prison to which it has been condemned as the result of a metaphysical fall over which it has no control, Ambrose sees human nature as an integral union of body and soul. For him, as for Aristotle, body and soul are both intrinsically human. Both are to be cared for in this life, and both are to be saved and glorified in the life to come. Following St. Paul, he does not see our physical nature, as such, as the source of our moral problems. Our problem is not the natural body but "the flesh," that is, sins into which we fall when we succumb to passions that may arise anywhere in the human constitution. Alternatively, body and soul alike are capable of conducing to virtue. It all depends on how we choose to use our natural endowment of reason and the infrarational aspects of our nature.

While Ambrose argues for a privative theory of evil, he distances himself from the Neoplatonic understanding of that doctrine. He does not regard matter as intrinsically evil or definable as non-being. He describes evil as the lack of virtue; he does not see it as a correlative of a lack of metaphysical status or of a negative metaphysical status. As they inhere in a moral agent, good and evil, virtue and vice, are functions of that moral agent's exercise of free will. Ambrose presents free will as equally capable of making the choice for virtue or for vice. What directs these choices is the decision to be guided, or not, by reason. Right reason, an Ambrosian notion compatible with the Stoic doctrine of natural law but one amplified by the moral agent's awareness of the duty to obey God's law as well, points us toward the good.

But reason, for Ambrose, is not infallible. This is because the mind no less than the body, and the mind in conjunction with the body, is subject to passions that arise in it naturally. In elaborating this position, Ambrose begins with the Stoic theory of the passions and reconfigures it decisively. He does not see the passions as arising exclusively from false intellectual judgments made by a mind that is not really distinct from the body, according to the monistic psychology of the Stoics. For Ambrose, while the human mind and body are integrally related, they can still be distinguished. They give rise to passions of different sorts: in the mind alone, in the body alone, and in body and mind together. The examples he gives of passions arising in the body alone have to do with sex and food: wantonness and gluttony, or excess in our ministering to these physical needs. He does not view concupiscence as specifically or exclusively sexual; for him it means any excessive and unreasonable passion. The passions that Ambrose sees as arising in the mind alone are pride, avarice, contentiousness, wrath, and envy. Some of these mental states are flagged as vices by classical moralists. All of them are flagged as vices by New Testament authors. They will subsequently take their place, in the Christian tradition, as the most intellectual, and hence the most heinous, of the mortal sins.

The Stoic quartet of passions—pleasure, pain, fear, and desire—survive in Ambrose's catalogue as passions that stem from both the mind and the body. In analyzing them, he departs from the Stoics not only in attributing them to a physical no less than a mental origin but also in two other ways. Instead of considering them as misjudgments about what we experience in the present and what we anticipate in the future, he considers them developmentally, in terms of how one passion leads to another. And he adds three other passions to the list: joy and sorrow as the respective outcomes of pleasure and pain, and mental agitation as the common outcome of joy and sorrow. This theory of the passions, coupled with the anthropology and psychology that undergird it, constitute an original Ambrosian position.

For Ambrose, mind and body alike are part of our integral humanity. Both are subject to passions that can deflect us from virtue if we succumb to them. And both can, at the same time, conduce to virtue if we are guided by right reason and moderation. Ambrose shares with Plato, Aristotle, and the Middle Stoic Panaetius the view that the passions cannot be extirpated. Rather, what we should seek to do is to reorient the psychic energies on which they feed, under the guidance of reason and the Word of God, so that they fuel our quest for virtue. It is in this sense that Ambrose invokes the image of the charioteer in Plato's *Phaedrus,* whose unruly horses of passion and spirit, and even the vicious antitheses of the cardinal virtues to which they lead, can be yoked by the Christian and classical virtues and driven by a rational charioteer to a destination that equates the happy life, not with the abandonment of this world or of material things as such, or of the lesser goods which, with Aristotle, he places on a trajectory that leads to the highest good. Rather, the immediate destination is a revalued here and now in which we abandon the vices in material things, not their use. Moreover, that destination is not upward or outward but inward. Introspection and inner purification are integral both to conversion and to the practice of the ongoing Christian life, with the life to come as its eternal reward.

As Ambrose sees it, the index of success in that Christian life is not contemplation or a mysticism that would draw his *competentes* away from the active life but a clean conscience, reflecting their awareness that they have lived out the cardinal virtues of wisdom, courage, temperance, and justice and the Christian virtues of faith and charity. By faith he means not only right belief but the abandonment of false philosophy and the public and private cults of pagan Rome. And charity includes unselfishness, generosity, hospitality, patience, conjugal chastity, corporal and spiritual works of mercy, and a Stoic forbearance and equanimity that merge seamlessly with the willingness to endure suffering, to forgive one's enemies, and to render good for evil.

While Ambrose portrays the protagonists of the patriarch treatises as displaying the constancy of the Stoic sage, he does not endow them with Stoic autarchy, for they are on intimate terms with God and are aided by his grace. So too, the *competentes* will need grace and the sacraments of the church. Ambrose places justice at the apex of the cardinal virtues, agreeing with Aristotle on the crowning importance of service to the common good. But he regards temperance as the virtue that must be acquired first, as the foundation of all moral education, and as the virtue that governs the exercise of all the others. He sees these virtues, Christian and classical alike, as incumbent on all his *competentes*, with their concrete reference in the lives of individuals proportioned to the nature and situation of those individuals themselves. In the application of rules to particular cases, he draws on both the injunction "Know thyself," the first precept of the Delphic Oracle, and the inheritance of Panaetian casuistry.

With these principles in mind, the ethics for the common man developed in Ambrose's patriarch treatises can be placed in a clearer perspective by comparing it with the ethical messages that he presents in hortatory works aimed at Christians in his flock with special callings in the church: priests, widows, and consecrated virgins. Ambrose also expects members of these groups to practice the cardinal as well as the Christian virtues, but with a different emphasis. In works directed to widows and virgins, Ambrose, as we might expect, accents sexual abstinence as what sets them apart, the primary way in which these women manifest the virtues of temperance and fortitude, with chastity defended by modesty and sobriety. At the same time, Ambrose thinks that their calling entails more than just physical integrity or continence. He sees the state of both groups of women as defined by their free choice of their calling, by an inner commitment to that choice, not by mere sexual abstinence.[1]

Ambrose also thinks that both sets of women need to display virtues other than chastity of mind and body and to engage in activities beyond those practices conducive to its support. While it is appropriate for widows to weep in mourning for their departed husbands and for virgins to weep as they reflect on Christ's sufferings,[2] widows, he urges, should not remain permanently in widows' weeds but should bestir themselves, engaging in works of mercy within the wider Christian community. In describing them, Ambrose focuses particularly on hospitality and almsgiving, activities in which wealthy Roman woman would normally participate as patronesses. And, although he envisions virgins as living quietly at home, except for their attendance at church services, as modest unmarried young Roman women of means were accustomed to do, he

---

1. Ambrose, *De uiduis* 2.11, 4.26; Ambrose, *De uirginibus* 1.4.15, 1.5.23, 2.2.7, 2.4.22–25, ed. Cazzaniga, trans. Gori; Ambrose, *De uirginitate* 3.13, 4.15, 7.40, 12.72–73, 14.88, 14.92, 16.98–99; Ambrose, *Exhortatio uirginitatis* 3.17, ed. Cazzaniga, trans. Gori. Noted by Gori in his intro. to *De uirginibus*, 14:1, 17–19.

2. Ambrose, *De uiduis* 6.35–36; Ambrose, *De uirginitate* 3.5.21–23.

enjoins them as well to aid the needy.[3] Also, while he warns virgins against participating in feasts at which there will be dancing and rich food and drink, he expects them to be cheerful as well as studious.[4] Predictably and traditionally, Ambrose advises both groups of women to abstain from wine. He urges them to observe the fasts of the church that are incumbent on all Christians and to confine their intake of food on other occasions to what meets their natural needs.[5]

Ascetics these women may be. But the lifestyle Ambrose envisions for them is comparatively moderate. If they follow his advice, they will not resemble the haggard wraiths with matted hair, with skin traumatized by scourges and hair shirts, dazed by lack of sleep, devoid of personal hygiene, and in danger of death by inanition, whom we meet in the ascetic writings of some of Ambrose's contemporaries.[6] These women may be ascetics in comparison with Christians not following celibate callings, but for Ambrose their sexuality is not the source of the major temptations that he sees as besetting either group. In the case of consecrated virgins, he enjoins silence. In his estimation, the principal temptation to which they are likely to succumb is the inclination to gossip and idle chatter, even during church services.[7] If virgins are tempted to be chatterboxes, the chief temptation of widows, as he sees it, is pusillanimity. What is most likely to incline them to contract second marriages, he thinks, is not the desire for a new sexual partner or the wish for additional children, but faintheartedness concerning their ability to manage their own property. He finds this claim a weak one, given the fact that many wealthy women in Roman society managed their own property. It is to offset this temptation that he sets before the widows the witness of Judith and Deborah, examples not merely of female enterprise and independence but even of female leadership in military and political activities typically conducted by men.[8] Widows, he argues, should not seek to excuse themselves as incompetent, pleading femi-

---

3. Ambrose, *De uiduis* 1.4–5, 2.11, 3.16, 4.26, 5.27–32, 9.53–54, 10.60, 10.66; Ambrose, *De uirginibus* 1.8.42. Noted by North, *Sophrosyne*, 363–64.

4. Ambrose, *De uirginibus* 2.2.9, 3.2.8, 3.5.25, 3.6.31 on the avoidance of feasts and dancing; ibid. 2.2.7, 3.4.16 on study and cheerfulness. On Ambrose's advocacy of study and reading for virgins, see Clark, *Reading Renunciation*, 56–57.

5. Ambrose, *De uiduis* 4.21–22, 7.38, 7.40–41; Ambrose, *De uirginibus* 1.8.53, 2.2.8, 3.2.8, 3.4.15; *De institutione uirginis* 17.109, ed. Cazzaniga, trans. Gori; Ambrose, *Exhortatio uirginitatis* 12.79.

6. See, in this connection, texts discussed in Colish, "Cosmetic Theology."

7. Ambrose, *De uirginibus* 1.3.10, 2.2.11, 3.2.10–3.3.14; Ambrose, *Exhortatio uirginitatis* 10.72–73.

8. Ambrose, *De uiduis* 7.37, 8.43–51, 9.52–59, 10.66, 11.67.

nine weakness. Rather, they should activate their own executive abilities in ministering publicly to others as well as in managing their own private affairs. Altogether, in his hortatory writings for widows and virgins, Ambrose stands out among previous and contemporary Christian writers addressing these audiences for not reducing the virtues of courage and moderation primarily or exclusively to sexual purity as the gauge of holiness.[9]

Ambrose also expects the priests for whom he wrote his *De officiis* to practice the Christian and cardinal virtues, suitably adapted to their clerical calling. As all commentators have noted, this means that arms cede to the toga; for them, courage and justice have nothing to do with the battlefield and are confined to magnanimity in their civic life and to their own self-mastery.[10] Ambrose pays little attention to the sex lives of his priests. If they are married when they enter the priesthood, they should remain in conjugal fidelity to their wives, and they should refrain from remarriage if they are widowed. If unmarried when they are ordained, they should maintain their premarital abstention.[11] Either way, they should conduct themselves with propriety and discretion in ministering to female congregants, visiting them only in the company of the bishop or an older colleague.[12] Ambrose's principal concern, however, is not with these matters but with the decorum of priests. This is the understanding of the virtue of temperance, taken from Panaetius, Cicero, and Horace, which he thinks is specifically apposite to them. For Ambrose, decorum involves not just the priest's inner life but his public performance, his presentation of self, the appropriateness and dignity with which he speaks or remains silent, and which he displays in all aspects of his behavior, including his demeanor, his carriage, his gestures, and his very gait. This topic receives most of Ambrose's attention, under the heading of the positive advice he gives to his clergy. Whatever their social origins, his goal is to show his priests how to manifest the *gravitas* of a Roman senator.

9. On Ambrose's predecessors and contemporaries, see North, *Sophrosyne,* 312–23, 328–60; Clark, *Reading Renunciation,* passim.

10. Ambrose, *De officiis* 1.35.175–1.42.209, ed. and trans. Davidson. On this point, a good recent account with a discussion of previous scholarship is provided by Becker, *Die Kardinaltugenden bei Cicero und Ambrosius,* 9–13, 116–60. Other useful assessments of the previous literature on this topic include Testard, "Le *De officiis* de saint Ambroise"; Davidson, intro. to his ed. of Ambrose, *De off.,* 1:45–50.

11. Ambrose, *De off.* 1.17.65, 1.18.69, 1.50.257–258. Noted by Gryson, *Le prêtre selon Saint Ambroise,* 296–97.

12. Ambrose, *De off.* 1.20.87.

At the same time, turning priests into Christian senators brings front and center the major temptation that Ambrose envisions as besetting his clergy, against which he warns them over and over again. Roman social and political life were bound together in his day, as they had been for centuries, by networks of patronage and clientage. As officers of the church whose public charge gives them a high social profile in the Milanese community, his priests, Ambrose warns, will have to learn how to avoid operating within this customary mode of interaction. He thinks that this is a problem most likely to arise in connection with money. By now many of the erstwhile social services of the Roman state had devolved onto the shoulders of bishops. The bishops were the fathers of the poor, and priests were their coadjutors in the day-to-day administration of poor relief. In this society, a secular personage with access to funds would normally use them to build up and maintain his own *clientela*. Priests with access to the diocesan funds set aside for poor relief must guard rigorously against the temptation to do likewise. Greed, Ambrose insists, in addressing this audience, is the root of all the vices, especially the lust for power that it is so frequently used to facilitate. Priests must transcend the social and institutional expectations and practices of their time and place. They must not use the funds at their disposal for networking but must make certain that they use them to serve the needy in strict proportion to their need.[13]

Three callings: virgin, widow, and priest. Three besetting temptations: talkativeness, faintheartedness with regard to the administration of property, and avarice as a means of obtaining funds with which to network. The widows must overcome their lack of courage. The priests and virgins must master the challenges to moderation, be they public or private, which they respectively face.

Moderation also has its own centrality and its own appropriate lineaments for Ambrose's *competentes*. The moral temptations that he sees them as most likely to confront, judging from the patriarch treatises, lie in a number of areas of both public and private life. They will have to learn how to deal prudently and charitably with people with whom they disagree, philosophically and theologically, people who may indeed treat them with hostility on that

---

13. Ibid. 1.4.14, 1.5.17, 1.6.23, 1.11.38–39, 1.16.63, 1.18.72, 1.20.86, 1.24.115, 1.28.130–131, 1.30.140–150, 1.30.153–159, 1.33.171, 1.36.184–185, 1.38.192–1.39.193, 1.49.242–1.50.247, 1.50.253, 2.4.15–2.5.18, 2.14.66–2.16.85, 2.21.108–111, 2.25.128–2.27.133, 2.28.136–2.29.151, 3.3.20, 3.3.22, 3.9.58, 3.9.63–64. Noted by Gryson, *Le prêtre selon Saint Ambroise*, 244; Becker, *Die Kardinaltugenden bei Cicero und Ambrosius*, 70–114.

account. In private, they will have to resist the temptation to shun the duty of hospitality. They will also need to avoid the preferential treatment of children by parents. But, for the male members of his neophyte audience, Ambrose regards monogamy and marital chastity as the major challenge they will have to overcome, given what Roman law and social custom permit to men in this area of life. As with his priests, practicing responsible poor relief rather than using diocesan funds to grease the wheels of patronage, his male *competentes* will have to adhere to a higher standard than what Roman practice accepts as normal. In both cases, a radical counter-socialization is going to be required. At the same time, Ambrose sees positive elements that they can carry over from their Roman inheritance. As with the virgins, widows, and priests, there is much in the classical tradition that will continue to serve his *competentes* well as they proceed to the font and beyond it, into the Christian life.

This brief comparison of the message of Ambrose's patriarch treatises with the messages he conveys in hortatory works destined for other ears indicates that, as a skilled rhetorician, he was sensitive to the importance of highlighting the specific needs, sensibilities, and potential roadblocks facing the audiences at which he aimed his ethical teachings. He does so effectively, with a different positive and negative *paideia,* a different emphasis, and an appeal to different models in each case. In the patriarch treatises alone, however, he also proposes a distinctive Ambrosian anthropology as the basis for his moral advice. For this reason as well as for their actual ethical content, the patriarch treatises deserve to be foregrounded more than they have been, in considerations of Ambrose as an ethicist. For it is in these treatises, uniquely, that he delineates the theory of human nature and the ethics that he thinks will be profitable for the vast majority of Christians in his Milanese congregation.

Ambrose's ethics for the common man in the patriarch treatises constitutes a first, in patristic literature. It is also an ethics that speaks to a particular historical time, place, and culture, one in which most people entering the Christian church were adult converts from Roman paganism. In succeeding centuries the adult converts who entered the church were more likely to be the leaders of the Germanic tribes who established successor states in Western Europe in the wake of Rome's fall. Won to orthodoxy from Arianism or to Christianity as such, they were not likely to recognize or to respond to Ambrose's references to classical philosophy and literature or to Roman law in these works. In the stage of church history after that, there was a major demographic shift away from adult conversion, with infant baptism becoming the norm.

The declining relevance of the instruction conveyed in Ambrose's patriarch treatises to the then-current Christian neophytes can be seen in the fortunes of these works in the medieval manuscript tradition. As Karl Schenkl has found, in the census of manuscripts that precedes his critical edition, while the patriarch treatises were often preserved and transmitted together as a corpus in the early manuscripts, their appearance together—or even at all—falls off in the later medieval centuries.[14] Given the disappearance of their original audience, the reasons for that outcome are understandable. Nonetheless, if we wish to gain a true understanding of Ambrose the ethicist in his own time and place, the patriarch treatises deserve a wider hearing and a more accurate appreciation than they have tended to receive. They clearly show that Ambrose was a scribe instructed in the kingdom of heaven, a householder who knew how to bring from his treasury things both old and new. They also reveal him, as the proponent of the first and only patristic ethics for the common man, as a teacher of moderation for the many, and not merely as a teacher of asceticism for the few.

14. Schenkl, intro. to his ed. of Ambrose, *Opera*, CSEL 32:1, lxxxv–viii.

Primary Sources

Ambrose. *De Abraham*. Ed. and trans. Franco Gori. Sancti Ambrosii episcopi mediolanensis opera, 2:2. Milano: Biblioteca Ambrosiana, 1984.

———. *De apologia prophetae David ad Theodosium augustum. Apologia David altera.* Ed. Karl Schenkl. Trans. Filippo Lucidi. Sancti Ambrosii episcopi mediolanensis opera, 5. Milano: Biblioteca Ambrosiana, 1981.

———. *De bono mortis*. Ed. and trans. William Theodore Wiesner. Catholic University of America Patristic Series, 100. Washington, DC: Catholic University of America Press, 1970.

———. *De Helia et ieiunio. De Nabuthae. De Tobia.* Ed. and trans. Franco Gori. Sancti Ambrosii episcopi mediolanensis opera, 6. Milano: Biblioteca Ambrosiana, 1985.

———. *De institutione uirginis. De uiduis. De uirginibus.* Ed. Egnatius Cazzaniga. Trans. Franco Gori. Sancti Ambrosii episcopi mediolanensis opera, 14:1. Milano: Biblioteca Ambrosiana, 1989.

———. *De Isaac uel anima. De bono mortis. De Iacob et uita beata. De Ioseph.* Ed. Karl Schenkl. Trans. Claudio Moreschini and Roberto Palla. Sancti Ambrosii episcopi mediolanensis opera, 3. Milano: Biblioteca Ambrosiana, 1982.

———. *De officiis.* 2 vols. Ed. and trans. Ivor J. Davidson. Oxford: Oxford University Press, 2001.

———. *De officiis.* 2 vols. Ed. and trans. Maurice Testard. Paris: Société d'Édition "Les Belles Lettres," 1984–92.

———. *De patriarchis. De fuga saeculi. De interpellatione Iob et David.* Ed. Karl Schenkl. Trans. Gabriele Banterle. Sancti Ambrosii episcopi mediolanensis opera, 4. Milano: Biblioteca Ambrosiana, 1980.

———. *De uirginibus libri tres.* Ed. Egnatius Cazzaniga. Corpus scriptorum latinorum paravianum. Torino: G. B. Paravia & Co., 1948.

———. *De uirginitate liber unus.* Ed. Egnatius Cazzaniga. Corpus scriptorum latinorum paravianum. Torino: G. B. Paravia & Co., 1952.

———. *De uirginitate. Exhortatio uirginitatis.* Ed. Egnatius Cazzaniga. Trans. Franco Gori. Sancti Ambrosii episcopi mediolanensis opera, 14:2. Milano: Biblioteca Ambrosiana, 1989.

———. *Epistularum liber decimus.* Ed. Michaela Zelzer. Corpus scriptorum ecclesiasticorum latinorum, 82:3. Wien: Hoelder-Pichler-Tempsky, 1982.

———. *On Abraham.* Trans. Theodosia Tomkinson. Etna, CA: Center for Traditional Orthodox Studies, 2000.

———. *Opera.* Ed. Karl Schenkl. Corpus scriptorum ecclesiasticorum latinorum, 32:1. Wien: Hoelder-Pichler-Tempsky, 1897.

———. *Principal Works.* Trans. H. De Romestin with E. De Romestin and H. T. F. Duckworth in *A Select Library of Nicene and Post-Nicene Fathers of the Christian Church.* Ed. Philip Schaff and Henry Wace. 2nd ser., vol. 10. New York: Christian Literature Company, 1896.

———. *Isaac, or the Soul. Jacob and the Happy Life. Death as a Good. Joseph. The Patriarchs* in *Seven Exegetical Works.* Trans. Michael P. McHugh. Fathers of the Church, 65. Washington, DC: Catholic University of America Press, 1972.

———. *The Mysteries. The Sacraments.* Trans. Roy J. Deferrari. Fathers of the Church, 44. Washington, DC: Catholic University of America Press, 1963.

Cassiodorus. *An Introduction to Divine and Human Readings.* Trans. Leslie Webber Jones. Records of Civilization, Sources, and Studies, 40. New York: Columbia University Press, 1946.

Coogan, Michael D., et al., eds. *The New Oxford Annotated Bible.* 3rd ed. Oxford: Oxford University Press, 2001.

Meeks, Wayne, et al., eds. *HarperCollins Study Bible.* New Revised Standard Version. New York: HarperCollins, 1993.

Metzger, Bruce, ed. *The Oxford Annotated Apocrypha of the Old Testament.* Revised Standard Version. New York: Oxford University Press, 1977.

Origen. *An Exhortation to Martyrdom, Prayer, and Selected Works.* Trans. Rowan A. Greer. New York: Paulist Press, 1979.

———. *Homilies on Genesis and Exodus.* Trans. Ronald E. Heine. Fathers of the Church, 71. Washington, DC: Catholic University of America Press, 1982.

———. *On First Principles.* Trans. G. W. Butterworth. Gloucester, MA: Peter Smith, 1973 [repr. of New York, 1966 ed.].

———. *The Song of Songs: Commentary and Homilies.* Trans. R. P. Lawson. Ancient Christian Writers, 26. Westminster, MD: Newman Press, 1957.

Philo. *On Abraham. On Joseph.* Trans. F. H. Colson. Loeb Classical Library. Cambridge, MA: Harvard University Press, 1935.

————. *On the Migration of Abraham.* Trans. F. H. Colson and G. H. Whitaker. Loeb Classical Library. Cambridge, MA: Harvard University Press, 1932.

————. *Questions and Answers on Genesis.* Trans. Ralph Marcus. Loeb Classical Library. Cambridge, MA: Harvard University Press, 1953.

Secondary Sources

Altaner, Berthold. *Patrology.* Trans. Hilda C. Graef. Freiburg: Herder, 1960.

Amir, Yehoshua. "Die Begegnung des biblischen und des philosophischen Monotheismus als Grundthema des jüdischen Hellenismus." *Evangelische Theologie* 38 (1978): 2–19.

Argal Echarri, Miguel Angel. "El Patriarca José: Tipología Cristológica y Ecclesiológica en el commento de San Ambrosio." *Miscélanea José Zunzunegui (1911–1974).* Vitoria: Editorial Eset, 1975, 3:61–85.

————. "Isaac y Rebeca, figuras de la Iglesia según San Ambrogio." *Scriptorium Victoriense* 20 (1973): 132–70.

————. "Las bendiciones del Patriarca Jacob en el commentario de San Ambrogio." *Scriptorium Victoriense* 18 (1971): 295–325; 19 (1972): 63–83.

Argyle, A. W. "Joseph the Patriarch in Patristic Teaching." *Expository Times* 67 (1955–56): 199–201.

Assmann, Jan. *Moses the Egyptian: The Memory of Egypt in Western Monotheism.* Cambridge, MA: Harvard University Press, 1997.

Badura, Methodius. *Die leitenden Grundsätze der Morallehre der hl. Ambrosius.* Prague: Cyrillo-Method'schen Buchdruckerei, 1921.

Bardy, G. "L'Entrée de la philosophie dans le dogme au IVe siècle." *L'Année théologique* 9 (1948): 44–53.

Baskin, J. R. "Job as Moral Exemplar in Ambrose." *Vigiliae Christianae* 35 (1981): 222–31.

Baus, Karl. "Das Nachwirken des Origines in der Christusfrömmigkeit des heiligen Ambrosius." *Römische Quartalschrift* 49 (1954): 21–54.

Becker, Maria. *Die Kardinaltugenden bei Cicero und Ambrosius: De officiis.* Chrêsis: Die Methode der Kirchenväter in Umgang der antiken Kultur, 4. Basel: Schwabe & Co. AG, 1994.

Berger, Adolf. *Encyclopedic Dictionary of Roman Law.* Transactions of the American Philosophical Society, n.s. 43:2. Philadelphia: American Philosophical Society, 1953.

Bernet, Anne. *Saint Ambroise.* Étampes: Clovis, 1999.

Berton, Ramond. "Abraham dans le *De officiis ministrorum* d'Ambroise." *Revue des sciences religieuses* 54 (1980): 311–22.

————. "Abraham est-il un modèle? L'opinion des Pères dans les premiers siècles de l'Église." *Bulletin de littérature ecclésiastique* 97 (1996): 349–73.

Bickel, Ernst. *Das asketische Ideal bei Ambrosius, Hieronymus und Augustin: Eine kulturgeschichtliche Studie.* Leipzig: B. G. Teubner, 1916.

Bonato, Antonio. "Il ruolo universale del sacerdozio di Cristo nell'allegoria delle città-rifugio (*Fug. Saec.* 2, 5–13; 3, 14–16): Una rilettura dell'esegesi filoniana da parte di Ambrogio." *Studia Patavina* 36 (1989): 57–87.

Brown, Peter. *Power and Persuasion in Late Antiquity: Towards a Christian Empire.* Madison: University of Wisconsin Press, 1992.

———. *The Body and Society: Men, Women, and Sexual Renunciation in Early Christianity.* New York: Columbia University Press, 1988.

Cameron, Averil. *Christianity and the Rhetoric of Empire: The Development of Christian Discourse.* Berkeley: University of California Press, 1991.

Campenhausen, Hans von. *The Fathers of the Latin Church.* Trans. Manfred Hoffmann. Stanford, CA: Stanford University Press, 1972.

Capelle, B. "Notes de théologie ambrosienne." *Recherches de théologie ancienne et médiévale* 3 (1931): 183–90.

Cataneo, Enrico. *La religione a Milano nell'età di Sant'Ambrogio.* Milano: Archivio Ambrosiano, 1974.

———. "Storia del rito ambrosiano." *Storia di Milano.* Milano: Fondazione Treccani degli Alfieri per la Storia di Milano, 1954, 3:763–837.

Cavadini, John C. "Exegetical Transformations: The Sacrifice of Isaac in Philo, Origen, and Ambrose." *In Dominico Eloquio. In Lordly Eloquence: Essays on Patristic Exegesis in Honor of Robert Louis Wilken.* Ed. Paul Blowers et al. Grand Rapids, MI: Eerdmans, 2002, 35–49.

Chadwick, Henry. *Early Christian Thought and the Classical Tradition: Studies in Justin, Clement, and Origen.* New York: Oxford University Press, 1966.

———. *The Church in Ancient Society from Galilee to Gregory the Great.* Oxford: Oxford University Press, 2001.

Christman, Angela Russell. "Ambrose of Milan on Ezekiel 1 and the Virtuous Soul's Ascent to God." *L'esegesi dei padri latini dalle origini a Gregorio Magno.* Studia Ephemerides "Augustinanum." Roma: Institutum Patristicum Augustinianum, 2000, 2:547–59.

Citterio, B. "Spiritualità sacerdotale nel 'De officiis' di S. Ambrogio." *Ambrosius* 32 (1956): 157–65.

Clark, Elizabeth A. *Reading Renunciation: Asceticism and Scripture in Early Christianity.* Princeton, NJ: Princeton University Press, 1999.

———. "The Uses of the Song of Songs: Origen and the Later Latin Fathers." *Ascetic Piety and Women's Faith: Essays on Late Ancient Christianity.* Lewiston, NY: Edwin Mellen Press, 1986, 386–427.

Claussen, Martin A. "Pagan Rebellion and Christian Apologetics in Fourth-Century Rome: The *Consultationes Zacchaei et Apollonii.*" *Journal of Ecclesiastical History* 46 (1995): 589–614.

Colish, Marcia L. "Cosmetic Theology: The Transformation of a Stoic Theme." *Assays* 1 (1981): 3–14.

———. *The Stoic Tradition from Antiquity to the Early Middle Ages*. Vol. 2: *Stoicism in Christian Latin Thought through the Sixth Century*. Rev. ed. Leiden: E. J. Brill, 1990.

———. "Why the Portiana? Reflections on the Milanese Basilica Crisis of 386." *Journal of Early Christian Studies* 10 (2002): 361–72.

Colpe, Carsten. "Mysterienkult und Liturgie: Zum Vergleich heidnischer Rituale und christlicher Sakramente." *Spätantike und Christentum: Beiträge zur Religions- und Geistesgeschichte des griechish-römischen Kultur und Zivilisation der Kaiserzeit*. Ed. Carsten Colpe, Ludger Honnefelder, and Matthias Lutz-Bachmann. Berlin: Akademie Verlag, 1992, 203–28.

Courcelle, Pierre. "Ambroise de Milan, 'professeur de philosophie.'" *Revue de l'histoire des religions* 181 (1972): 147–55.

———. "Anti-Christian Arguments and Christian Platonism." *The Conflict between Paganism and Christianity in the Fourth Century*. Ed. Arnaldo Momigliano. Oxford: Clarendon Press, 1963, 151–92.

———. *Connais-toi toi-même de Socrate à Saint Bernard*. Vol. 1. Paris: Études Augustiniennes, 1974.

———. "De Platon à saint Ambroise par Apulée." *Revue de philologie* 35 (1961): 15–28.

———. "L'Âme en cage." *Parusia: Studien zur Philosophie Platons und zur Problemgeschichte des Platonismus. Festgabe J. Hirschberger*. Frankfurt am Main: Minerva, 1965, 103–16.

———. *Late Latin Writers and Their Greek Sources*. Trans. Harry E. Wedek. Cambridge, MA: Harvard University Press, 1969.

———. "Le corps-tombeau (Platon, *Gorgias* 493a; *Cratyl* 400c; *Phèdre* 250c)." *Revue des études augustiniennes* 68 (1966): 101–22.

———. "L'humanisme chrétien de saint Ambroise." *Orpheus* 9 (1962): 21–34.

———. "Nouvelle aspects du platonisme chez saint Ambroise." *Revue des études latines* 34 (1956): 220–39.

———. "Plotin et saint Ambroise." *Revue de philologie, de littérature, et d'histoire anciennes* 76 (1950): 29–56.

———. *Recherches sur les Confessions de Saint Augustin*. 2nd ed. Paris: E. De Boccard, 1968.

———. *Recherches sur Saint Ambroise: "Vies" anciennes, culture, iconographie*. Paris: Études Augustiniennes, 1973.

———. "Saint Ambroise devant le précepte delphique." *Forma futuri: Studi in onore del cardinale Michele Pellegrino*. Torino: Bottega d'Erasmo, 1975, 178–88.

———. "Tradition platonicienne et traditions chrétiennes du corps-prison." *Revue des études latines* 43 (1965): 406–43.

Cramer, Peter. *Baptism and Change in the Early Middle Ages, c. 200–c.1150*. Cambridge: Cambridge University Press, 1993.

Cribiore, Raffaela. *Gymnastics of the Mind: Greek Education in Hellenistic and Roman Egypt.* Princeton, NJ: Princeton University Press, 2001.

Daniélou, Jean. "Abraham dans la tradition chrétienne." *Abraham, père des croyants.* Ed. Eugene Cardinal Tisserant. Paris: Éditions du Cerf, 1952, 68–87.

———. *From Shadows to Reality: Studies in the Biblical Typology of the Fathers.* Trans. Wulstan Hibberd. London: Burns & Oates, 1960.

———. "La typologie d'Isaac dans le christianisme primitif." *Biblica* 28 (1947): 363–93.

———. "L'Unité des deux testaments dans l'oeuvre d'Origène." *Revue des sciences religieuses* 22 (1948): 27–56.

Dassmann, Ernst. "Ambrosius und die Märtyrer." *Jahrbuch für Antike und Christentum* 18 (1975): 49–68.

———. *Die Frömmigkeit des Kirchenvaters Ambrosius von Mailand: Quellen und Entfaltung.* Münsterische Beiträge zur Theologie, 29. Münster: Aschendorff, 1965.

———. "Die Kirche und ihre Gleider in der Hoheliedklärung bei Hippolyt, Origenes, und Ambrosius von Mailand." *Römische Quartalschrift* 61 (1966): 121–44.

Davidson, Ivor J. "Ambrose's *De officiis* and the Intellectual Climate of the Late Fourth Century." *Vigiliae Chrisitanae* 49 (1995): 313–33.

De Lubac, Henri. *Medieval Exegesis: The Four Senses of Scripture.* Vol. 1. Trans. Mark Sebanc. Grand Rapids, MI: Eerdmans, 1998.

De Vivo, Arturo. "Nota ad Ambrogio, *De Abraham* I 2, 4." *Ambrosius Episcopus.* Atti del Congresso internazionale di studi ambrosiani nel XVI centenario della elevazione di sant'Ambrogio alla catedra episcopale, Milano, 2–7 dicembre 1974. Ed. Giuseppe Lazzati. Milano: Vita e Pensiero, 1976, 2:233–42.

Di Lorenzo, Raymond D. "Ciceronianism and Augustine's Conception of Philosophy." *Augustinian Studies* 13 (1982): 171–76.

Dörrie, Heinrich. "Das fünffach gestufte Mysterium: Der Aufstieg der Seele bei Porphyrios und Ambrosius." *Mullus: Festschrift Theodor Klauser.* Ed. Alfred Stuiber and Alfred Hermann. Münster: Aschendorff, 1964, 79–92.

Drecoll, Volker Henning. "Neuplatonismus und Christentum bei Ambrosius, De Isaac et anima." *Zeitschrift für antikes Christentum* 5 (2001): 104–30.

Droge, Arthur J. *Homer or Moses? Early Christian Interpretations of the History of Culture.* Tübingen: J. C. B. Mohr, 1989.

Dudden, F. Homes. *The Life and Times of St. Ambrose.* 2 vols. Oxford: Clarendon Press, 1935.

Dulaey, Martine. "Joseph le Patriarche, figure de Christ." *Figures de l'Ancien Testament chez les pères.* Cahiers de Biblia Patristica, 2. Strasbourg: Centre d'Analyse et de Documentation Patristiques, 1989, 83–105.

———. "La figure de Jacob dans l'exégèse paléochrétienne (Gn 27–33)." *Recherches augustiniennes* 32 (2001): 75–168.

Duval, Yves-Marie. "Ambroise, de son élection à son consécration." *Ambrosius Episcopus.* Atti del Congresso internazionale di studi ambrosiani nel XVI centenario della elevazione di sant'Ambrogio alla catedra episcopale. Milano, 2–7 dicembre 1974. Ed. Giuseppe Lazzati. Milano: Vita e Pensiero, 1976, 2: 243–83.

Feldman, Louis H. "Abraham the Greek Philosopher in Josephus." *Transactions of the American Philological Association* 99 (1968): 143–56.

———. "Josephus' Portrait of Joseph." *Revue biblique* 99 (1992): 379–417.

Felici, Lea. "Il *De Iacob et vita beata* di S. Ambrogio e il *De vita beata* di Seneca: Rapporti di contenuto e forma." *"Humanitas" classica e "sapientia" cristiana: Scritti offerti a Roberto Iacoangeli.* Ed. Sergio Felici. Roma: Libreria Ateneo Salesiano, 1992, 163–73.

Fernández Marcos, Natalio. *The Septuagint in Context: Introduction to the Greek Version of the Bible.* Trans. Wilfred G. E. Watson. Leiden: E. J. Brill, 2000.

Figueroa, Gregory. *The Church and the Synagogue in St. Ambrose.* Washington, DC: Catholic University of America Press, 1949.

Finn, Thomas M. *Early Christian Baptism and the Catechumenate: Italy, North Africa, and Egypt.* Collegeville, MN: Liturgical Press, 1992.

———. *From Death to Life: Ritual and Conversion in Antiquity.* New York: Paulist Press, 1997.

Fitzgerald, Alan. "Ambrose at the Well: *De Isaac et anima.*" *Revue des études augustiniennes* 48 (2002): 79–99.

Francesconi, Giampietro. *Storia e simbolo: "Mysterium in figura." La simbolica storico-sacramentale nel linguaggio e nella teologia di Ambrogio di Milano.* Pubblicazioni del Pontificio seminario lombardo in Roma, Ricerche di scienze teologiche, 18. Brescia: Editrice Morcelliana, 1981.

Freyburger, Gérard. "De l'*amicitia* païenne aux vertus chrétiennes: Damon et Phintias." *Du héros païen au saint chrétien.* Actes du colloque organisé par le Centre d'Analyse des Rhétoriques Religieuses de l'Antiquité (C.A.R.R.A.), Strasbourg, 1–2 décembre 1995. Ed. Gérard Freyburger and Laurent Pernot. Paris: Institut d'Études Augustiniennes, 1997, 87–93.

Fuhrmann, Manfred. "Obscuritas (Das Problem der Dunkelheit in der rhetorischen und literarästhetischen Theorie der Antike)." *Immanente Ästhetik, ästhetische Reflexion: Lyrik als Paradigma der Moderne.* Ed. W. Iser. München: Wilhelm Fink Verlag, 1966, 47–72.

Gager, John G. *Moses in Greco-Roman Paganism.* Nashville, TN: Abingdon Press, 1972.

Gaudemet, Jean. "Droit séculier et droit de l'église chez Ambroise." *Ambrosius Episcopus.* Atti del Congresso internazionale di studi ambrosiani nel XVI centenario della elevazione di sant'Ambrogio alla catedra episcopale, Milano, 2–7 dicembre 1974. Ed. Giuseppe Lazzati. Milano: Vita e Pensiero, 1976, 1: 286–315.

———. *Le droit romain dans la littérature occidentale du IIIe au Ve siècle.* Milano: Giuffrè, 1978.

Gori, Franco. Introduction to his edition and translation of Ambrose, *De Abraham.* Sancti Ambrosii episcopi mediolanensis opera, 2:2. Milano: Biblioteca Ambrosiana, 1984.

Gregg, Robert C. "Joseph with Potiphar's Wife: Early Christian Commentary Seen against the Backdrop of Jewish and Muslim Interpretations." *Studia Patristica* 34 (2001): 326–46.

Gryson, Roger. "La médiation d'Aaron d'après saint Ambroise." *Recherches de théologie ancienne et médiévale* 47 (1980): 5–15.

———. *Le prêtre selon Saint Ambrose.* Louvain: Édition Orientaliste, 1968.

———. "Les Lévites, figure du sacerdoce véritable, selon saint Ambroise." *Ephemerides Theologicae Lovanienses* 56 (1980): 89–112.

Hadot, Pierre. "Explication du 'De Isaac' d'Ambroise." *Annuaire de l'École pratique des hautes études,* Section des sciences religieuses, 73 (1965–66): 150–52.

———. "Platon et Plotin dans trois sermons de saint Ambroise." *Revue des études latines* 34 (1956): 202–20.

Hagendahl, Harald. *Latin Fathers and the Classics: A Study of the Apologists, Jerome and Other Christian Writers.* Studia graeca et latina Gothoburgensia, 6. Göteborg: Almquist & Wiksell, 1958.

Hahn, Viktor. *Das wahre Gesetz: Eine Untersuchung der Auffassung des Ambrosius von Mailand vom Verhältnis der beiden Testamente.* Münsterische Beiträge zur Theologie, 33. Münster: Aschendorff, 1969.

Harrington, Daniel J. "Joseph in the Testament of Joseph, Pseudo-Philo, and Philo." *Studies on the Testament of Joseph.* Ed. George W. E. Nicklesburg. Missoula, MT: Scholars Press, 1975, 127–31.

Hebein, Richard John. "St. Ambrose and Roman Law." PhD diss., St. Louis University, 1970.

Heim, François. "Les figures du prince idéal au IVe siècle: Du type au modèle." *Figures de l'Ancien Testament chez les pères.* Cahiers de Biblia Patristica, 2. Strasbourg: Centre d'Analyse et de Documentation Patristiques, 1989, 277–301.

Hill, Carole. "Classical and Christian Tradition in Some Writings of Saint Ambrose of Milan." PhD diss., Oxford University, 1980.

Hollander, Haim W. *Joseph as an Ethical Model in the Testaments of the Twelve Patriarchs.* Leiden: E. J. Brill, 1981.

———. "The Portrayal of Joseph in Hellenistic Jewish and Early Christian Literature." *Biblical Figures outside the Bible.* Ed. Michael E. Stone and Theodore A. Bergren. Harrisburg, PA: Trinity Press International, 1998, 237–63.

———. and De Jonge, M. *The Testaments of the Twelve Patriarchs: A Commentary.* Leiden: E. J. Brill, 1985.

Huhn, Josef. "Bewertung und Gebrauch der Heiligen Schrift durch den Kirchenvater Ambrosius." *Historisches Jahrbuch der Görres-Gesellschaft* 77 (1958): 387–96.

Humphries, Mark. *Communities of the Blessed: Social Environment and Religious Change in Northern Italy, AD 200–400*. Oxford: Oxford University Press, 1999.

Iacoangeli, Roberto. "Anima ed eternità nel *De Isaac* di Sant'Ambrogio." *Morte e immortalità nella catechesi dei Padri del III–IV secolo*. Ed. Sergio Felici. Roma: Libreria Ateneo Salesiano, 1985, 103–37.

———. "'Humanitas' classica e 'sapientia' cristiana in S. Ambrogio." *Crescita dell'uomo nella catechesi dei padri (età postnicena)*. Ed. Sergio Felici. Roma: Libreria Ateneo Salesiano, 1988, 129–63.

Ihm, Max. "Philon und Ambrosius." *Jahrbücher für Philologie und Pädegogik* 141 (1890): 282–88.

Jackson, Pamela. "Ambrose of Milan as Mystagogue." *Augustinian Studies* 20 (1989): 93–107.

Jacob, Christoph. *"Arkandisziplin," Allegorese, Mystagogie: Ein neuer Zugang zur Theologie des Ambrosius von Mailand*. Theophaneia, 32. Frankfurt: Anton Hain, 1990.

———. "The Reception of the Origenist Tradition in Latin Exegesis." *Hebrew Bible/ Old Testament: The History of Its Interpretation*. Ed. Magne Saebø with Chris Brekelmans and Menahem Haran. Göttingen: Vandenhoeck & Ruprecht, 1996, 1:682–700.

Kellner, Johann Baptist. *Der heilige Ambrosius, Bischof von Mailand, als Erklärer des Alten Testamentes: Ein Beitrag zur Geschichte zur biblischen Exegese*. Regensburg: G. J. Manz, 1893.

Kelly, J. N. D. *Early Christian Creeds*. 3rd ed. London: Longmans, 1972.

Labriolle, Pierre de. *The Life and Times of St. Ambrose*. Trans. Herbert Wilson. St. Louis: Herder, 1928.

Layton, Richard A. "Plagiarism and Lay Patronage of Ascetic Scholarship: Jerome, Ambrose, and Rufinus." *Journal of Early Christian Studies* 10 (2002): 489–522.

Lazzati, Giuseppe. *Il valore letterario della esegesi ambrosiano*. Milano: Archivio Ambrosiano, 1960.

Lenox-Conyngham, Andrew. "Ambrose and Philosophy." *Christian Faith and Greek Philosophy in Late Antiquity: Essays in Tribute to George Christopher Stead*. Ed. Lionel R. Wickham and Caroline P. Bammer. Leiden: E. J. Brill, 1993, 112–28.

———. "Law in St. Ambrose." *Studia Patristica* 23 (1989): 149–52.

———. "Sin in St. Ambrose." *Studia Patristica* 18:4 (1985): 173–77.

Lewy, Hans. *Sobria ebrietas: Untersuchungen zur Geschichte der antiken Mystik*. Zeitschrift für die neutestamentliche Wissenschaft und die Kunde der alteren Kirche, Beiheft 9. Giessen: A. Topelmann, 1929.

Lizzi, Rita. "Ambrose's Contemporaries and the Christianization of Northern Italy." *Journal of Roman Studies* 80 (1990): 157–73.

Loiselle, André. "'Nature' de l'homme et histoire de la salut: Étude sur l'anthropologie d'Ambroise de Milan." PhD diss., Université de Lyon, 1970.

Lucchesi, Enzo. *L'Usage de Philon dans l'oeuvre exégétique de saint Ambroise.* Leiden: E. J. Brill, 1977.

———. "Note sur un lieu de Cassiodore faisant allusion aux sept livres d'Ambroise sur les patriarches." *Vigiliae Christianae* 30 (1976): 307–9.

Lutz-Bachmann, Matthias. "Hellenisierung des Christentums?" *Spätantike und Christentum: Beiträge zur Religions- und Geistesgeschichte der griechisch-römischen Kultur und Zivilisation der Kaiserzeit.* Ed. Carsten Colpe, Ludger Honnefelder, and Matthias Lutz-Bachmann. Berlin: Akademie Verlag, 1992, 77–98.

MacMullen, Ramsay. *Christianizing the Roman Empire (A.D. 100–400).* New Haven, CT: Yale University Press, 1984.

Madec, Goulven. "Le milieu milanaise: Philosophie et christianisme." *Bulletin de littérature ecclésiastique* 88 (1987): 194–205.

———. "Le 'platonisme' des pères." *Connaissance des pères de l'église* 86 (2002): 34–53.

———. "L'Homme intérieure selon saint Ambroise." *Ambroise de Milan: XVIe centenaire de son élection épiscopale.* Ed. Yves-Marie Duval. Paris: Études Augustiniennes, 1974, 283–308.

———. *Saint Ambroise et la philosophie.* Paris: Études Augustiniennes, 1974.

———. "*Verus philosophus est amator dei*: S. Ambroise, S. Augustin, et la philosophie." *Revue des sciences philosophiques et théologiques* 61 (1977): 549–66.

Maes, Baziel. *La loi naturelle selon Ambroise de Milan.* Analecta Gregoriana, 162, Facultas theologicae, B52. Roma: Presses de l'Université Grégorienne, 1967.

Maldon, R. H. "St. Ambrose as an Interpreter of Holy Scripture." *Journal of Theological Studies* 16 (1915): 509–22.

Malherbe, Abraham J. *Moral Exhortation: A Greco-Roman Sourcebook.* Philadelphia: Westminster Press, 1986.

Malone, Edward. *The Monk and the Martyr: The Monk as the Successor of the Martyr.* Studies in Christian Antiquity, 12. Washington, DC: Catholic University of America Press, 1950.

Mara, Maria Grazia. "Ambrose of Milan, Ambrosiaster, and Nicetas." *Patrology.* Ed. Angelo de Berardino. Trans. Placid Solari. Westminster, MD: Christian Classics, 1986, 4:144–94.

Markschies, Christoph. "Ambrosius und Origenes: Bemerkungen zur exegetischen Hermeneutik zweier Kirchenväter." *Originiana Septima: Origines in den Auseinandersetzungen des 4. Jahrhunderts.* Ed. W. A. Bienert and U. Kühnweg. Leuven: Leuven University Press, 1999, 545–70.

———. *Ambrosius von Mailand und die Trinitätstheologie: Kirchen- und theologiegeschichtliche Studien zu Antiarianismus und Neunizänimus bei Ambrosius und im lateinischen Westen (364–381 n. Chr.).* Beiträge zur historischen Theologie, 90. Tübingen: J. C. B. Mohr, 1995.

Markus, Robert A. *The End of Ancient Christianity.* Cambridge: Cambridge University Press, 1990.

Matter, E. Ann. *The Voice of My Beloved: The Song of Songs in Western Medieval Christianity*. Philadelphia: University of Pennsylvania Press, 1990.

Mazza, Enrico. *Mystagogy: A Theology of Liturgy in the Patristic Age*. Trans. Matthew J. O'Connell. New York: Pueblo, 1989.

McLynn, Neil B. *Ambrose of Milan: Church and Court in a Christian Capital*. Berkeley: University of California Press, 1994.

Medeiros, Humberto S. "The *De Mysteriis* and *De Sacramentis* of St. Ambrose." PhD diss., Catholic University of America, 1952.

Meeks, Wayne A. *The Origins of Christian Morality*. New Haven, CT: Yale University Press, 1993.

Michel, Alain. "Du *De officiis* de Cicéron à saint Ambroise: La théorie des devoirs." *L'Etica cristiana nei secoli III e IV: Eredità e confronti*. Studia Ephemerides "Augustinianum," 53. Roma: Institutum Patristicum Augustinianum, 1996, 39–46.

Mirri, Luciana. *Il monachismo femminile secondo sant'Ambrogio di Milano*. Vicenza: Edizioni LIEF, 1991.

Mitchell, L. L. "Ambrosian Baptismal Rites." *Studia Liturgica* 1 (1962): 241–53.

Mohrmann, Christine. "Observations sur le *De Sacramentis* et le *De Mysteriis* de saint Ambroise." *Ambrosius Episcopus*. Atti del Congresso internazionale de studi ambrosiani nel XVI centenario della elevazione di sant'Ambrogio alla catedra episcopale, Milano, 2–7 dicembre 1974. Ed. Giuseppe Lazzati. Milano: Vita e Pensiero, 1976, 1:103–23.

Mohrmann, Margaret Elizabeth. "Wisdom and the Moral Life: The Teachings of Ambrose of Milan." PhD diss., University of Virginia, 1995.

Monachino, Vincenzo. *S. Ambrogio e la cura pastorale a Milano nel secolo IV*. Milano: Centro Ambrosiano di Documentazione e Studi Religiosi, 1973.

Moorhead, John. *Ambrose: Church and Society in the Late Roman World*. London: Longman, 1999.

———. "The Greeks, Pupils of the Hebrews." *Prudentia* 15 (1983): 3–12.

Moos, Peter von. *Geschichte als Topik: Das rhetorische Exemplum von der Antike zur Neuzeit und die historiae im "Policraticus" Johanns von Salisbury*. Hildesheim: Georg Olms Verlag, 1988.

Moreschini, Claudio. Introduction to translation of Ambrose, *De Isaac uel anima*. Sancti Ambrosii episcopi mediolanensis opera, 3. Milano, 1982.

Moretus, Henri. "Les bénédictions des patriarches dans la littérature du IVe au VIIIe siècle." *Bulletin de littérature ecclésiastique* 11 (1909): 398–411; 12 (1910): 28–40, 83–100.

Nauroy, Gérard. "Du combat de la piété à la confession du sang: Ambroise de Milan, lecteur et critique du *IVe Livre des Maccabées*." *Revue d'histoire et de philosophie religieuses* 70 (1990–91): 49–68.

———. "Jérôme, lecteur et censeur de l'exégèse d'Ambroise." *Jérôme entre l'occident et l'orient*. XVIe centenaire du départ de saint Jérôme de Rome et de son installation à Bethlehem. Ed. Yves-Marie Duval. Paris: Études Augustiniennes, 1988, 173–203.

————. "La méthode de la composition et la structure du *De Iacob et vita beata.*" *Ambroise de Milan: XVIe centenaire de son élection épiscopale.* Ed. Yves-Marie Duval. Paris: Études Augustiniennes, 1974, 115–53.

————. "La structure du *De Isaac vel anima* et la cohérence de l'allegorèse d'Ambroise de Milan." *Revue des études latines* 63 (1985): 210–36.

————. "L'Écriture dans la pastorale d'Ambroise de Milan."*Le monde latin antique et la Bible.* Ed. Jacques Fontaine and Charles Pietri. Paris: Beauchesne, 1985, 371–408.

————. "Les frères Maccabés dans l'exégèse d'Ambroise de Milan ou la conversion de la sagesse judéo-hellénique aux valeurs du martyre chrétien." *Figures de l'Ancien Testament chez les pères.* Cahiers de Biblia Patristica, 2. Strasbourg: Centre d'Analyse et Documentation Patristiques, 1989, 215–45.

Navoni, Marco. "Notizia sulla liturgia ambrosiana." *La città e la sua memoria: Milano e la tradizione di sant'Ambrogio.* Ed. Marco Rizzi. Milano: Electa, 1977, 229–38.

Nawrocka, Anna. "L'état d'études concernant l'influence de l'éthique de Cicéron sur l'éthique de Saint Ambroise." *Helikon* 28 (1988): 315–24.

Newton, Benjamin Wills. *The Old Testament Saints Not to Be Excluded from the Church of Glory, with Some Remarks on the Heresy of Marcion.* London: Houlston and Sons, 1887.

Niehoff, Maren. *The Figure of Joseph in Post-Biblical Jewish Literature.* Leiden: E. J. Brill, 1992.

Nikiprowetzky, Valentin. "Saint Ambroise et Philon." *Revue des études grecques* 94 (1981): 193–99.

North, Helen. *Sophrosyne: Self-Knowledge and Self-Restraint in Greek Literature.* Cornell Studies in Classical Philology, 35. Ithaca, NY: Cornell University Press, 1966.

Oberhelman, Steven M. *Rhetoric and Homiletics in Fourth-Century Christian Literature: Prose Rhythm, Oratorical Style, and Preaching in the Works of Ambrose, Jerome, and Augustine.* American Classical Studies, 26. Atlanta, GA: Scholars Press, 1991.

Oberti Sobrero, Margherita. *L'Etica sociale in Ambrogio di Milano: Ricostruzione delle fonti ambrosiani nel "De iustitia" di san Tommaso, II II. qq. 57–122.* Torino: Edizioni Astera, 1970.

Otten, R. H. "Caritas and the Ascent Motif in the Exegetical Works of St. Ambrose." *Studia Patristica* 8:2 (1966): 442–48.

Palanque, Jean-Rémy. *Saint Ambroise et l'empire romain: Contribution à l'histoire des rapports de l'église et de l'état à la fin du quatrième siècle.* Paris: E. De Boccard, 1933.

Palla, Roberto. Introduction to translation of Ambrose, *De Iacob et uita beata.* Sancti Ambrosii episcopi mediolanensis opera, 3. Milano, 1982.

————. "Temi del *Commento* origeniano al *Cantico dei Cantici* nel *De Isaac* di Ambrogio." *Annali della Scuola normale superiore di Pisa,* Classe di lettere e filosofia, ser. 3, 9:2 (1979): 563–72.

Paredi, Angelo. *Saint Ambrose: His Life and Times.* Trans. M. Joseph Costelloe. Notre Dame, IN: University of Notre Dame Press, 1964.

Parodi, Bonaventura. *La catechesi di sant'Ambrogio: Studio di pedagogia pastorale.* Genova: Scuola Tipografia Opera SS. Vergine di Pompei, 1957.

Pasini, Cesare. *Ambrogio di Milano: Azione e pensiero di un vescovo.* 2nd ed. Cinisello Balsamo: Edizioni San Paolo, 1997.

Passetti, Emilio Ermote. "I temi di Abramo 'peregrinus' e 'adventa' (Gen. XII. 1–3; 9–10): A la ricerca di una tradizione esegetica antica." *Studi e ricerche sull'oriente cristiano,* 5 (1982): 13–46, 103–24, 141–55.

Pelikan, Jaroslav. *The Christian Tradition: A History of the Development of Doctrine.* Vol. 1. Chicago: University of Chicago Press, 1971.

Pellegrino, Michele. "'Mutus . . . loquar Christum': Pensieri de sant'Ambrogio su parola e silenzio." *Paradoxos politeia: Studi patristici in onore de Giuseppe Lazzati.* Ed. R. Cantalamessa and L. F. Pizzolato. Milano: Vita e Pensiero, 1979, 447–57.

Petit, Hervé. "Sur les catéchèses post-baptismales de saint Ambroise: À propos de *De sacramentis* IV, 29." *Revue bénédictine* 68 (1958): 256–65.

Piccolo, Giuseppe. "Per lo studio della spiritualità ambrosiana: I sermoni *De Isaac vel anima.*" *La Scuola cattolica* 98 (1970): 32–74.

Piredda, Anna Maria. "La tipologia sacerdotale del patriarca Giuseppe in Ambrogio." *Sandalion* 10–11 (1987–88): 153–63.

Pizzolato, Luigi F. *La dottrina esegetica di Sant'Ambrogio.* Milano: Vita e Pensiero, 1978.

———. "La Sacra Scrittura fondamento del metodo esegetico di sant'Ambrogio." *Ambrosius Episcopus.* Atti del Congresso internazionale di studi ambrosiani nel XVI centenario della elevazione di sant'Ambrogio alla catedra episcopale, Milano, 2–7 dicembre, 1974. Ed. Giuseppe Lazzati. Milano: Vita e Pensiero, 1976, 1:393–426.

———. "Una società cristiana alle prese con un testo radicale: L'esegesi della pericope nella Chiesa latina post-costantiniana." *Per foramen acus: Il cristianesimo di fronte alla pericope evangelica del 'giovane ricco'.* Milano: Vita e Pensiero, 1986, 264–328.

Quasten, Johannes. "'Sobria ebrietas' in Ambrosius *De sacramentis.*" *Miscellanea liturgica in honorem L. Cuniberti Mohlberg.* Bibliotheca "Ephemerides Liturgicae," 22. Roma: Edizioni Liturgiche, 1948, 1:117–25.

Ramsay, Boniface. *Ambrose.* London: Routledge, 1998.

Rajak, Tessa. "Dying for the Law: The Martyr's Portrait in Jewish-Greek Literature." *Portraits: Biographical Representation in the Greek and Latin Literature of the Roman Empire.* Ed. M. J. Edwards and Simon Swain. Oxford: Clarendon Press, 1997, 39–67.

Rand, Edward Kennard. *Founders of the Middle Ages.* New York: Dover Books, 1957 [repr. of Cambridge, MA, 1928 ed.].

Riley, Hugh M. *Christian Initiation: A Comparative Study of the Interpretation of the Baptismal Liturgy in the Mystagogical Writings of Cyril of Jerusalem, John Chrysostom, Theodore of Mopsuestia, and Ambrose of Milan.* Studies in Christian Antiquity, 17. Washington, DC: Catholic University of America Press, 1974.

Rivière, Jean. "'Trois cent dix-huit': Un cas de symbolisme arithmétique chez saint Ambroise." *Recherches de théologie ancienne et médiévale* 6 (1934): 349–67.

Rossi, Custode. "Il *De officiis* di Cicerone e il *De officiis* di Ambrogio: Rapporti di contenuto e forma." *"Humanitas" classica e "sapientia" cristiana: Scritti offerti a Roberto Iacoangeli.* Ed. Sergio Felici. Roma: Libreria Ateneo Salesiano, 1992, 145–62.

Rowe, William V. "Adolf von Harnack and the Concept of Hellenization." *Hellenization Revisited: Shaping a Christian Response in the Greco-Roman World.* Ed. Wendy E. Halleman. Lanham, MD: University Press of America, 1994, 69–98.

Runia, David. "L'exégèse philosophique et l'influence de la pensée philonienne dans la tradition patristique." *Philon d'Alexandrie et le langage de la philosophie.* Ed. Carlos Lévy. Turnhout: Brepols, 1998, 327–48.

———. *Philo in Early Christian Literature: A Survey.* Assen: Van Gorcum, 1993.

Russell, A. D. "*De imitatione*." *Creative Imitation and Latin Literature.* Ed. David West and Tony Woodman. Cambridge: Cambridge University Press, 1979, 1–16.

Sagot, Solange. "La triple sagesse dans le *De Isaac vel anima*: Essai sur les procédés de composition de saint Ambroise." *Ambroise de Milan: XVI centenaire de son élection épiscopale.* Ed. Yves-Marie Duval. Paris: Études Augustiniennes, 1974, 67–114.

———. "Le 'Cantique des Cantiques' dans le 'De Isaac' d'Ambroise de Milan: Étude textuelle et recherche sur les anciennes versions latines." *Recherches augustiniennes* 16 (1981): 3–57.

Salzman, Michele Renee. *The Making of a Christian Aristocracy: Social and Religious Change in the Western Roman Empire.* Cambridge, MA: Harvard University Press, 2002.

Sanders, Mechthild. *"Fons vitae Christus": Der Heilsweg des Menschen nach der Schrift De Isaac et anima des Ambrosius von Mailand.* Münsteraner theologische Abhandlungen, 42. Altenberg: Oros Verlag, 1996.

Sargenti, Manlio and Bruno Siola, R. B., ed. *Normativa imperiale e diritto romano negli scritti di S. Ambrogio: Epistulae, De officiis, Orationes funebres.* Milano: A. Giuffrè, 1991.

Satterlee, Craig Alan. *Ambrose of Milan's Method of Mystagogical Preaching.* Collegeville, MN: Pueblo, 2002.

Savon, Hervé. *Ambroise de Milan.* Paris: Desclée, 1997.

———. "Ambroise lecteur d'Origène." *Nec timeo mori.* Atti del Congresso internazionale di studi ambrosiani nel XVI centenario della morte di sant'Ambrogio. Ed. Luigi F. Pizzolato and Marco Rizzi. Milano: Vita e Pensiero, 1998, 221–34.

———. "Les intentions de Saint Ambroise dans la Préface du *De officiis*." *Valeurs dans le Stoïcisme du Portique à nos jours: Textes rassemblés en hommage à Michel Spanneut.* Ed. Michel Soetard. Lille: Presses Universitaires de Lille, 1993, 155–69.

———. "Quelques remarques sur la chronologie des oeuvres de Saint Ambroise." *Studia Patristica* 10 (1970): 156–60.

————. *Saint Ambroise devant l'exégèse de Philon le Juif.* 2 vols. Paris: Études Augustini-ennnes, 1977.

Schenkl, Karl. Introduction to Ambrose, *Opera.* Ed. Karl Schenkl. Corpus scriptorum ecclesiasticorum latinorum, 32:1. Wien: Hoelder-Pichler-Tempsky, 1897.

Schmitz, Josef. *Gottesdienst im altchristlichen Mailand: Eine liturgiewissenschaftliche Untersuchung über Initiation und Messfeier während des Jahres zur Zeit des Bischofs Ambrosius (d. 397).* Theophaneia, 25. Köln: Peter Hansten Verlag GMBH, 1975.

Seibel, Wolfgang. *Fleisch und Geist beim heiligen Ambrosius.* Münchener theologische Studien, 2:14. München: Karl Zink, 1958.

Solignac, Aimé. "Il circolo neoplatonico milanese al tempo della conversione di Ago-stino." *Agostino a Milano: Il battesimo.* Agostino nella terra di Ambrogio (22–24 aprile 1987). Palermo: Edizioni Augustinus, 1988, 43–56.

————. "Nouveaux parallèles entre saint Ambroise et Plotin: Le *De Jacob et vita beata* et le Περὶ εὐδαιμονίαζ *(Ennéade* I, IV)." *Archives de philosophie,* n.s. 19 (1956): 148–56.

Spanneut, Michel. "Le Stoïcisme dans l'histoire de la patience chrétienne." *Mélanges de science religieuse* 39 (1982): 101–30.

Steidle, Wolf. "Beobachtung zu des Ambrosius Schrift *De officiis.*" *Vigiliae Christianae* 38 (1984): 18–66. Repr. in idem, *Ausgewählte Aufsätze.* Amsterdam: Hakkert, 1987, 507–55.

————. "Beobachtung zum Gedankengang in 2. Buch von Ambrosius, *De officiis.*" *Vigiliae Christianae* 39 (1985): 280–98. Repr. in idem, *Ausgewählte Aufsätze.* Amsterdam: Hakkert, 1987, 649–67.

Stenger, Silvester. "Das Frömmigkeitsbild des hl. Ambrosius nach seinen Schriften *De Abraham, De Isaac,* und *De bono mortis.*" Inaugural-diss., Universität Tübingen, 1947.

Studer, Basil. "Ambrogio di Milano teologo mistagogico." *Vescovi e pastori in epoca teo-dosiana.* XXV incontro di studiosi dell'antichità cristiana, Roma, 8–10 maggio 1996. Studia Ephemerides "Augustinianum," 58. Roma: Institutum Patristicum Augustinianum, 1997, 2: 569–86.

Swain, Simon. "Biography and the Biographic in the Literature of the Roman Em-pire." *Portraits: Biographical Representation in the Greek and Latin Literature of the Roman Empire.* Ed. M. J. Edwards and Simon Swain. Oxford: Clarendon Press, 1997, 1–37.

Szydzik, Stanis-Edmund. *"Ad imaginem dei*: Die Lehre von der Gottebenbildlichkeit des Menschen bei Ambrosius von Mailand." Inaugural-diss., Freie Universität Berlin, 1961.

————. "Die geistigen Ursprünge der Imago-Dei-Lehre bei Ambrosius von Mailand." *Theologie und Glaube* 53 (1963): 161–76.

Taormina, Lorenzo. "Sant'Ambrogio e Plotino." *Miscellanea di studi di letteratura cris-tiana antica.* Catania, 1954, 41–85.

Testard, Maurice. "Le *De officiis* de saint Ambroise: Observations philologiques et historiques sur le sens et contexte du traité." *Recherches augustiniennes* 28 (1995), 3–35.

———. "Observations sur le thème de la *conscientia* dans le *De officiis ministrorum* de saint Ambroise." *Revue des études latines* 51 (1973): 219–61.

———. "Recherches sur quelques méthodes de travail de saint Ambroise dans le *De officiis*." *Recherches augustiniennnes* 24 (1989): 65–122.

———. "Saint Ambroise de Milan." *Bulletin de l'Association Guillaume Budé* 69 (1992): 367–94.

Thamin, Raymond. *Saint Ambroise et la morale chrétienne au IVe siècle: Étude comparée des traités 'Des devoirs' de Cicéron et de saint Ambroise.* Paris: G. Masson, 1895.

Tolomio, Ilario. "'Corpus carcer' nell'Alto Medioevo: Metamorfosi di un concetto." *Anima e corpo nella cultura medievale.* Atti del V Convegno di studi della Società italiana per lo studio del pensiero medievale, Venezia, 25–28 settembre 1995. Ed. Carla Casagrande and Silvana Vecchio. Firenze: SISMEL-Edizioni Galluzzo, 1999, 3–19.

Treggiari, Susan. *Roman Marriage: Iusti Coniuges from the Time of Cicero to the Time of Ulpian.* Oxford: Clarendon Press, 1991.

Trigg, Joseph William. *Origen: The Bible and Philosophy in the Third-Century Church.* Atlanta, GA: John Knox Press, 1983.

Van der Lof, Laurens J. "The 'Prophet' Abraham in the Writings of Irenaeus, Tertullian, Ambrose, and Augustine." *Augustiniana* 44 (1994): 17–29.

Vasey, Vincent R. *The Social Ideas in the Works of St. Ambrose: A Study of De Nabuthae.* Studia Ephemerides "Augustinianum," 17. Roma: Institutum Patristicum Augustinianum, 1982.

Völker, Walther. "Das Abraham-Bild bei Philo, Origenes, and Ambrosius." *Theologische Studien und Kritiken* 103 (1931): 199–207.

Welter, J.-Th. *L'Exemplum dans la littérature religieuse et didactique du moyen âge.* Paris: Occitania, 1927.

Wiesner, William Theodore. Introduction to his translation of Ambrose, *De bono mortis.* Catholic University of America Patristic Series, 100. Washington, DC: Catholic University of America Press, 1970.

Wilbrand, W. "Ambrosius und Plato." *Römische Quartalschrift* 25 (1911): *42–*49.

Wilken, Robert L. "The Christianizing of Abraham: The Interpretation of Abraham in Early Christianity." *Concordia Theological Monthly* 43 (1972): 723–31.

Williams, Daniel H. *Ambrose of Milan and the End of the Nicene-Arian Conflicts.* Oxford Early Christian Studies. New York: Oxford University Press, 1995.

Yarnold, Edward. "Baptism and the Pagan Mysteries in the Fourth Century." *Heythrop Journal* 13 (1972): 247–67.

———. "The Ceremonies of Initiation in the *De sacramentis* and *De mysteriis* of S. Ambrose." *Studia Patristica* 10 (1970): 453–63.

Young, Robert, ed. *Analytical Concordance to the Bible.* 22nd ed. New York: Funk & Wagnalls, 1955.

Zelzer, Klaus. "L'Etica di sant'Ambrogio e la tradizione stoica delle virtù." *L'Etica cristiana nei secoli III e IV: Eredità e confronti.* Studia Ephemerides "Augustinianum," 53. Roma: Institutum Patristicum Augustinianum, 1996, 47–56.

———. "Randbemerkungen zu Absicht und Arbeitsweise des Ambrosius in 'De officiis'." *Wiener Studien* 107–108 (1994–95): 481–93.

———. "Zur Beurteilung der Cicero-Imitatio bei Ambrosius, *De officiis*." *Wiener Studien* 90 (1977): 168–91.

Zelzer, Michaela. "Ambrosius von Mailand und das Erbe der klassischen Tradition." *Wiener Studien* 100 (1987): 201–26.

———. "Symmachus, Ambrosius, Hieronymus und das römische Erbe." *Studia Patristica* 20 (1993): 146–57.

———. "Zur Chronologie der Werke des Ambrosius: Überblick über die Forschung von 1974 bis 1997." *Nec timeo mori.* Atti del Congresso internazionale di studi ambrosiani nel XVI centenario della morte di sant'Ambrogio. Ed. Luigi F. Pizzolato and Marco Rizzi. Milano: Vita e Pensiero, 1988, 73–92.

MARCIA L. COLISH
is Frederick B. Artz Professor of History, emerita, at Oberlin College
and visiting fellow in history at Yale University.